WHITE FEVER

White Fever

A Journey to the
Frozen Heart of Siberia

JACEK HUGO-BADER

Translated from the Polish
by Antonia Lloyd-Jones

Portobello
BOOKS

Published by Portobello Books 2011

Portobello Books
12 Addison Avenue
London
W11 4QR
United Kingdom

Copyright © Jacek Hugo-Bader 2009

English translation copyright © Antonia Lloyd-Jones 2011

First published in Polish in 2009 as *Biała gorączka*
by Wydawnictwo Czarne, Sękowa, Poland.

This publication has been funded by the Book Institute
– the © POLAND Translation programme

The rights of Jacek Hugo-Bader to be identified as the
author of this work and of Antonia Lloyd-Jones to be identified
as the translator of this work have been asserted by them in
accordance with the Copyright, Designs and Patents Act 1988.

Photograph on page 130 by Vladimir Vyatkin © AP/Press
Association Images. Reproduced by kind permission.

All other photographs by the author © Jacek Hugo-Bader 2009

Map on pp. 2–3 copyright © Vera Brice and Leslie Robinson 2011

WHITE FEVER

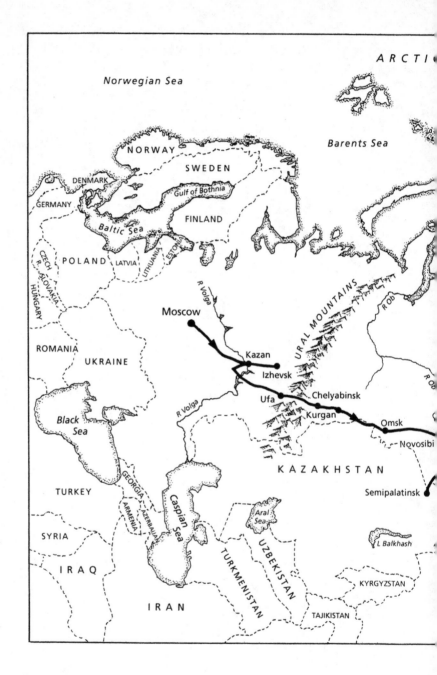

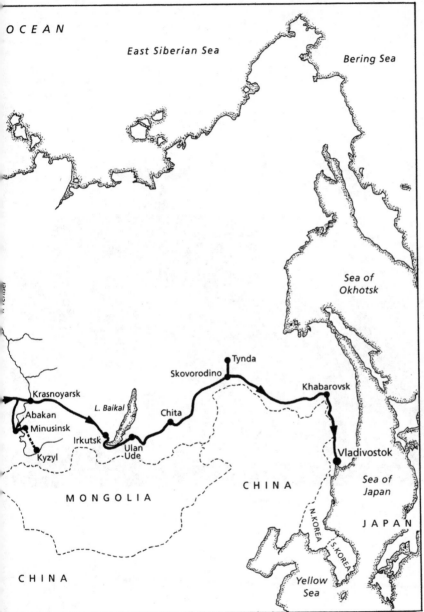

OCEAN

East Siberian Sea

Bering Sea

Sea of
Okhotsk

Tynda

Skovorodino

Krasnoyarsk
L. Baikal
Chita
Khabarovsk

Abakan
Minusinsk
Irkutsk
Ulan
Ude
Vladivostok

Kyzyl
Sea of
Japan

CHINA

MONGOLIA

N. KOREA

S. KOREA

JAPAN

Yellow
Sea

CHINA

Chin Li, the wandering Chinese man somewhere near Novosibirsk.

Bonnet into the wind

My only prayers were not to break down in the taiga at night, and not to run into any bandits. I was ready for the first of these misfortunes, but not for the second. I must have been the only madman to travel across that terrible ocean of land without a weapon, and on my own into the bargain.

The locals' favourite sport is shooting. They drive normally, on the right-hand side of the road, but they've got the steering wheel on the right too, because the cars are imported from Japan. They hold it in their left hand, so they can easily stick the right one out of the window and blast away, while on the move, with whatever weapon they have, at road signs, adverts and notice boards.

In eastern Siberia I didn't see a single road sign that wasn't as full of holes as a colander. Large and small bores, single shots and whole bursts, and even some huge holes made by a heavy shotgun.

And every few dozen metres there's the wreck of a burned-out car. They must have broken down in the winter, at night too, and their desperate owners set them alight to keep warm.

There's little chance this would have helped them to survive.

What idiots. Before leaving they should have found out how to survive a winter's night in the taiga.

I always stop the car with the bonnet facing into the wind, just in case. If it's blowing from another direction, it can pump poisonous exhaust fumes inside.

I keep the engine idling to warm the car up. It won't run out of fuel, because it only uses about a litre an hour, and the tank is always at least half full.

This is the most sacred principle of travelling by car across Siberia in winter – keep filling up, so you've always got at least half a tank of petrol. However, before lying down to sleep I always switch off the engine – there's too big a risk of the wind changing direction during the night, in which case I'll never wake up again. But I set the alarm in my phone to wake me every two hours, then I get up and start the car, leaving it running for ten to fifteen minutes. It's not even to warm up the cab, but to keep the engine and the oil sump from freezing, and to charge up the battery. At minus thirty degrees you've no chance of the car starting in the morning without these manoeuvres, because the engine oil goes as dense as plasticine. I once tried adding it to the engine at that sort of temperature, and while I was about it, I tried to top up the brake fluid and the power steering fluid too. They were all so thick they refused to come out of the bottles.

But suppose the phone battery ran down and I didn't wake up until morning? Then I'd have to light a bonfire. Of course no-one in their right mind travels across Siberia without an axe. You chop some firewood and pile it up, but you can't even light it with petrol because it's terribly cold and windy, and everything's covered in snow. I took a jar with me containing a special mixture of petrol and engine oil in proportions of one to one. Even wet wood will catch light if you pour that on it.

However, suppose I got stuck in the steppes beyond Baikal, not in the taiga? There's no kindling there. But I've brought some with me. I'm actually carrying a box of wood from Europe all the way across Siberia, not for warming my hands, of course. You have to put the bonfire on a shovel (which is just as vital as the axe) and stick it under the car to heat up the engine, and above all the oil sump. I can just as well do it with a petrol burner – it's a very simple device, a bit like a small flame-thrower, which I bought at a scrap-metal shop for 600 roubles (£12).

But suppose the frost is so awful and you've slept so long that the battery has gone dead? Easy – I've got a second one, in the cab, where it's much warmer. I don't even have to shift it, because it's joined to the first one by cables. I only have to flick a switch.

But suppose the engine that's keeping you warm has broken down? You've got to survive at least until morning. In fact the Siberians have a saying that in their country you don't even leave an enemy alone in the taiga, but that doesn't apply to the road situation or night-time. The traffic volume is much lower, though it doesn't stop entirely, but there is no force strong enough to make the Russian driver stop after sunset. They're afraid of bandits.

The best solution is a *vebasto*, an independent heater driven by a small combustion engine, which heats separately from the workings of the car. It costs 1000 Euros, so I didn't indulge myself by getting one, but instead I have a small portable camping stove that I light in the cabin, and before going to sleep I turn it off, to save gas. At night I'm warmed by one or two candles that I stand on the floor. On the coldest night I spent in the car, the temperature at dawn fell to minus thirty-six degrees, but in the cab it was only minus fifteen.

Of course I've got a wonderful down sleeping bag and a down jacket, and I always keep enough food and drink for several days.

DREAM

In March 1957, possibly on the 9th at one in the afternoon, because Saturdays were when the science department of *Komsomolskaya Pravda* newspaper held its weekly meetings, two reporters were given an unusual assignment by the editor-in-chief. (On that day and at that time, on the polished wooden floorboards between the kitchen and the bedroom in my grandmother's flat at 62 Warszawska Street in Sochaczewo, rather unexpectedly, I made my entrance into the world.)

'We must tell our readers about the future', said the editor-in-chief. 'Describe what life in the Soviet Union will be like fifty years from now, let's say at the time of the ninetieth anniversary of the Great Socialist October Revolution.'

That meant in 2007.

The book written by Mikhail Hvastunov and Sergei Gushchev, the journalists working for *Komsomolskaya Pravda*, is called *Report from the Twenty-First Century*. The authors wrote that we would use electronic brains on a daily basis (nowadays we call them computers), miniature transmitting and receiving stations (mobile phones) and 'biblio-transmission' (i.e. the Internet), open cars from a distance (with remote control), take photographs with an electric camera (digital) and watch satellite television on flat screens.

They wrote about it at a time when in the house where I was born there was not even a black-and-white television set, a toilet or a phone to call the doctor.

Hvastunov and Gushchev spent most of their time in the Moscow laboratories of the Soviet Academy of Sciences, and from there they made a mental journey into the future, setting off for Siberia in the year 2007 in a wonderful jet plane.

I decided to give myself a fiftieth birthday present, which was to travel with this book right across Russia, from Moscow to Vladivostok. But I wouldn't take the plane like Hvastunov and Gushchev. I'd already been there several times by train.

Good God!, I thought – here was my one chance to repeat the exploits of Kowalski, American warrior on wheels, demigod and lone traveller, the last heroic soul on this planet, for whom speed meant freedom. That's how he seemed in *Vanishing Point*, the famous American road movie that in the 1970s was the rebel manifesto of my generation. Finally here was a chance to make a dream of my youth come true, and, just like him, drive alone across an entire continent, except that my one was two-and-a-half times bigger than America, there was no road beyond Chita, and I was insisting on going in winter. I absolutely had to get a taste of the winter in Siberia.

'In *winter*? If you're not home for Christmas, don't bother coming home at all', said my wife, and I know she wasn't joking.

Damn! That meant I'd have to hurry up. Just like Kowalski! Except I was hurrying for Christmas, while he had made a bet for a fix of speed. And he had a Dodge Challenger 1970 with a 4.4-litre engine that did 250 kilometres an hour.

SPONSOR

All travellers have had problems with them, not excluding Columbus, Amundsen, Livingstone and Nansen.

The head of the features department said there was no way he'd send me abroad for several months, because I'd eat up the travel budget for the entire department.

So I personally called and sent written proposals for a joint project to the marketing directors of all the Polish firms representing car corporations that I could find in the phone book. I told them I needed money and a car, arguing that it would be the best advertisement they could possibly have if it survived the journey to the other end of Europe and Asia with me, across the whole of Russia, from Warsaw to Vladivostok.

Toyota, Nissan, Honda, Hyundai, Suzuki, Subaru, Mitsubishi, KIA, all the Asian makes, and also Volvo never replied to my invitation at all. I didn't call the French firms, Fiat or Ford, because my brother, who knows about cars, said he wouldn't let me go in a car starting with an 'F'. BMW, Mercedes and Land Rover had no 'free vehicle capacity'. Jeep was prepared to give me a car, but without any money. The only company to agree to all my conditions was Kulczyk Tradex, importer of Audis, VWs and Porsches.

They were offering a powerful, luxury SUV, the Audi Q7. Four-wheel drive, a 4.2-litre petrol engine, 350 horsepower, from nought to a hundred in seven seconds, maximum speed 240 kilometres per hour – two-and-a-half tons of bourgeois excess for 350,000 zlotys (£70,000). In my mind's eye I imagined driving up to the shop at the run-down 'Ilyich's Dream' collective farm for some beer and chatting about life with the locals.

Winter was approaching, but I kept putting off signing a contract with the sponsor. I can sum up the entire philosophy of my work as a journalist in two words: blend in. Merge into the background, don't stand out, don't attract attention, slip through unnoticed, but with my Audi at the 'Ilyich's Dream' collective farm I'd be about as inconspicuous as a Martian. Besides, my way of working is very safe, because it doesn't attract the attention of baddies.

I called the sponsor and told him I'd take the money, but I wouldn't need the car.

And so we parted ways.

In desperation I went to see my editors-in-chief. I tossed a map on the desk, told them about my dreams, and that I had just got divorced from Dr Kulczyk (who owns Kulczyk Tradex), and said that if they wouldn't give me the money, I'd have to get it off my wife (because she holds the purse strings), but wasn't it a shame for a poor woman to have to sponsor a successful newspaper like *Gazeta Wyborcza*? And they gave me some cash. However, it wasn't enough for a car, so my wife did have to fork out 25,000 zlotys (£5000).

I decided to buy a Russian car with local number plates in Moscow, because then I could quietly make my way to the Pacific Ocean without sticking out like a sore thumb. The only Russian vehicles with four-wheel drive are the Lada Niva – which the local experts say can't be fixed properly beyond the Urals – and the 'Lazhik' jeep, which even the tractor driver at any collective farm would be able to repair for me with a hammer, because apparently it's the least complicated car on earth.

KRUZAK

The UAZ-469 (UAZ is the Ulyanovsk Automobile Factory) that I was looking for is known as the Soviet jeep or the Russki *kruzak*, because that's what they call all off-road cars, after the Japanese Land Cruiser. But the most common names for it are *Ulaz* or *Lazhik*, meaning a tramp, because it goes everywhere. This model has been produced the same way without change since 1972, but they also keep churning out an off-road microbus, known because of its shape as the *bukhanka* – the loaf of bread. Beyond the Urals they call it the *tabletka* – the tablet, or pill. It hasn't changed an iota since 1958. Both models weigh two-and-a-half tons each, they have petrol engines of 2.4-litre capacity, four-speed transmission and almost 72 horsepower.

Lazhiks were sold to eighty countries, mainly in the Third World. To this day there are 70,000 of them registered in Poland that remember the Council for Mutual Economic Aid and the Warsaw Pact. In the 1970s the Russians conquered the Sahara in these vehicles and climbed a glacier up Mount Elbrus to a height of 4200 metres. There are two million Lazhiks on Russia's roads.

'Do you like fiddling with engines?' asked Grisha, when I asked him to help me buy one.

'No, I hate it', I replied sincerely.

'Then you'll get to like it.'

I found Grisha on the Internet. He's a member of the Ulaz fan club. Four of his friends have paid for their passion with their lives, because they tried sleeping in them with the engines on. Grisha runs a small garage for club members on the outskirts of Moscow.

It's very hard to find a decent Lazhik in Moscow, because they're only for the army, for working in the forest or for agriculture. Luckily during my search it turned out that one of the club members wanted to sell his car. To my mind it wasn't cheap – 170,000 roubles (£3400), but Grisha knew it was in good condition. It was a 1995 vehicle on old-fashioned springs like a horse-drawn chaise, but three years earlier Grisha had changed its entire chassis and body for a brand new one, given it bigger wheels, a steering wheel from a smart Volga, put in new disk brakes and added a rare luxury in these cars, which are about as nimble as wheelbarrows – power steering.

The main thing was that Andrei, the owner of the Lazhik, agreed to sell it to me on notarized power of attorney, which means that for three years I'd be able to drive it on his number plates. If I wanted to reregister the car in my own name, I'd have to spend at least two weeks standing in queues at various offices.

I beat Andrei down another 10,000 roubles, we each drank a glass of vodka to seal the deal, and I drove the car round to Grisha's workshop so he could get it ready for arctic conditions. The notary, MOT and new insurance cost me 8000 roubles (£160). I gave Grisha 24,000 (£480) for spare parts and necessary materials.

My Ulaz had no safety belts, so I had them installed. In the

European part of Russia no-one, including the militia, obeys the law about wearing seat belts, or the one about driving with your lights on at all times.

I also wanted to have a radio with a CD player, as I was going to spend several weeks behind the wheel, and a place to sleep instead of a back seat. I had to have the second battery installed together with an extra heater (which we took from a Volga), and have the metal floor lined with warm foam, the bonnet insulated and the cold air vent from underneath the engine covered. Grisha also used a gadget from a Lada, thanks to which the engine in my car was to inhale warm air, and fitted a new starter motor, because they're extremely good at breaking down. I took the old one in case it did go wrong, and a spare fuel pump.

I was supposed to collect the car on a Wednesday, but they hadn't even started to work on it by then, and when I went to the garage on Friday a giant man the size of a bridge support with a thug-like face clambered out of a small red sports car and chased me out of the yard. So I call Grisha, and he cries down the phone that it's a tragedy and he can't talk to me now. He explains that he's behind with the protection money he owes the gangsters, and now he's running about town, trying to borrow some cash.

I picked up the car on Sunday night. Grisha took 9000 roubles for his work (£180), so, ready to go, the car had cost me 201,000 roubles (£4020).

Finally he gave me instructions on how to service the Lazhik. Every day I start by checking the oil level, the brake fluid and the coolant. Each day I drive on a different battery, so they take it in turns to charge up, and I ignore the fact that I can't switch off the heating ('It's winter, isn't it?'), that the fuel gauge doesn't work ('You'll have to shine a torch into the tank'), that the spare wheel is much smaller than the others ('You'll make it to a tyre repair shop somehow'), that the third gear works very badly when coming down from fourth, and that the horn doesn't work, without which I feel disabled.

Do you know what a micro-second is?

It's the fraction of time between the appearance of a yellow light and a horn sounding behind you. That's a joke foreigners make about Russian drivers, who honk like crazy.

SKATES

Nor do they ever switch on their lights as long as something is visible, and they never dip their headlights, not even when you do. The bigger car has priority. And when they change a wheel, they like to burn the ripped tyre – they have a stinking bonfire instead of a warning triangle. Most of them never undress in the car, but drive all day long in their overcoats and fur caps.

Russians die on the roads like flies. In 2007 more than 32,000 people lost their lives, as many as in the entire European Union, which has three-and-a-half times more citizens and six times as many cars. Every couple of kilometres there's a symbolic grave on the hard shoulder. It's usually a small metal plinth with a star on top, or an open-work pedestal made of welded reinforcing wire, like a stand for flowers from the 1960s. According to the Russian custom, there's a bench and a small table with a vase bolted on to it next to many of the graves, with artificial flowers in it. Sometimes a driver stops there and leaves a lighted cigarette for his pal, two or three spares, and sometimes a small bottle with a drop of vodka left in it, which is sure to be what killed the guy.

I set off from Moscow on 24 November 2007. On the very first day the CD player broke. It couldn't withstand the dreadful bumps, because the further east, the worse the road. Then came Kazan, and Ufa; Asia began at the Urals and the climate changed radically. The temperature fell by more than ten degrees. I drove around Chelyabinsk, crossed Omsk and Novosibirsk, and stopped in Krasnoyarsk. I turned directly south to Khakassia and Tuva. Two weeks later I came back along the same road to Krasnoyarsk and sped south-east to Irkutsk.

I had already driven 1700 kilometres. It was a few days to Christmas, so I left the Lazhik at a parking lot, the batteries with Losha, my friend in Irkutsk, and flew to Poland.

I came back a month later. Ahead of me was the hardest, iciest stretch of road, or rather roadless wasteland. And February – the coldest month.

Circling around Lake Baikal I reached Ulan Ude. I wanted to cross this sacred sea of Siberia, which contains more water than the Baltic, by hopping over the ice, but it only starts to freeze solid in mid-January. I got there on 2 February. The locals categorically advised against crossing the lake, but I did put on the skates I had brought halfway round the world, and played ice hockey with the lads from Sludianka. And out on the ice I saw the most unusual Lazhik in the world. It had a hole cut in the floor for ice fishing, and there was a smoking pipe sticking out of the roof from a coal-fired stove. A Siberian *vebasto* heater, you could say.

From Ulan Ude I drove to Chita, beyond which the normal road ends, the tarmac, human habitations and civilization. For over 2000 kilometres to Khabarovsk there's nothing but mountains, marshes, snow and taiga.

In 2007, on the 'Dark Roasted Blend' blog, Internet users from all over the world selected their choice of the most dangerous roads on Earth that have claimed the most lives. Of the six roads on their short-list, three were in Russia. One of these is on the Caucasian border between Georgia and Russia; meanwhile I had the opportunity to get a taste of the other two. First of all in Moscow, because one of them is the 4.5-kilometre Lefortovo tunnel, which runs under the river and leaks, and when the temperature drops below freezing it gets as slippery as the ice hockey rink at the Luzhniki Olympic stadium.

The other road of death that I drove along branches off from my route beyond Chita but is no less charming. This is the highway running north to Yakutsk. 'Highway' is definitely an overstatement. It is a narrow, winding track, muddy in summer and snow-bound in winter, which runs along an eternal stretch of icy ground without a scrap of tarmac. I travelled it as far as the city of Tynda, then made my way on from there, across the taiga, to visit some friendly reindeer herders.

In the spring of 2006, on the middle section of the road to Yakutsk, thawing snow trapped several hundred cars. Even the caterpillar-tracked vehicles sent to rescue them got bogged down in the terrible mud. After several weeks desperate people were pointing guns at each other and fighting over food.

I reached Khabarovsk towards the end of February, from where I had only 770 kilometres of fairly good road to go to Vladivostok, where I finished my journey.

SNOW

You can eat on the road at a bar or a cafeteria, but that doesn't mean they have cakes, liqueurs, coffee and tea there – more like chops, borscht, herrings and vodka. The word *blinnaya* on a sign doesn't mean they serve blini there, *bulochnaya* doesn't mean *bulki*, bread rolls, and *shashlichnaya* doesn't mean they have shashlik, though it's possible.

In a *zakusochnaya* you might have a problem getting *zakuski* – snacks or appetizers, but they will serve soup and main courses.

They're usually shabby huts, barracks, or oversized kiosks. The further east, the nastier they are. Dirty plastic tablecloths, greasy forks, nowhere to wash your hands, and to relieve yourself you have to go outside.

Take for example the *zakusochnaya* near the small town of Yerofey Pavlovich in Siberia. Behind the building there's a huge, seething rubbish heap and a barrel cut in half. There's rubbish smouldering non-stop in both halves of it. Next to it there's a bog that no-one ever uses. Of the two evils they prefer to go near the rubbish heap.

Who has not stood here! This one didn't drink much today, because he left a very yellow hole in the snow. Surely a *peregonshchik* – literally a 'race-across-man' – who bought a Japanese used car in Vladivostok and is now racing west to get home in it. They're always in a great hurry, they rarely stop for something to eat and drink, and they sleep in their cars. Meanwhile this guy over here had been driving for ages and hadn't pissed in a long while, because his hole is big and deep. Sure to be a *dalnoboyshchik* – a 'distant-battle-man' on a long route – what we'd call a long-distance lorry driver. They're professionals, they eat and drink on the move and they don't like stopping either.

This one was here when the wind was blowing – or else he's an artist, because he likes making patterns. But he was definitely well tanked up, rather unsteady on his feet. Almost every driver likes to have a drink with his dinner here. In the wilds between Chita and Khabarovsk there's a 100 per cent chance they won't meet a militiaman on duty. There might be one driving privately. Here's the mark he leaves – straight, disciplined, and if it has a bend in it, it's at right angles.

No-one travels alone across Siberia. The *peregonshchiki* drive in groups of several cars to help each other in case of a breakdown. Often, if one of them has a soldier or militiaman friend, they pay him to travel with them, armed and in uniform. He protects them from the bandits and the militia, because as everyone knows, guys in uniform always have a common language.

And over here a woman must have squatted down, because the hole's been made at a large angle. A woman is a rarity here. Sometimes she's keeping her husband company so he won't fall asleep on the way. The *peregonshchiki*, especially the professional ones who buy cars for resale, are mostly young, unmarried men. Here's the mark he leaves – he has made his hole two-and-a-half metres away from where he was standing.

And this one's the opposite. He's got a prostate problem and has pissed on his own boots. He must have a sitting job, or else he's not a young man any more. Maybe a professional driver, or a reporter.

Everyone on the road takes some emergency 'iron rations' with them. For years I've been using hunter's sausage, but dried to an extreme state. It's as hard as wood, so you can't just bite it, but you can chew it slowly. The Russians are fond of dried fish, which remains edible for several years. In Siberia I saw lorry drivers who carried a supply of calories and protein in the form of so-called *struganina*. They keep it in their tool chest or with the spare wheel, because it's a big, raw, frozen fish; depending on need, they carve bits off it with a large knife like a piece of wood, then dip these shavings in salt and pepper and eat them quickly. Defrosted *struganina* is impossible to swallow, and only a dog would devour it without vodka.

BED

I tried to end each day in a sizeable town where I could find a hotel. If night came upon me in the middle of nowhere, I slept in the car or drove to the nearest village, looked for a house with flowers in the window and asked to stay the night. Russians love helping if you ask them to. They hardly ever do it of their own accord.

East of the Urals there are no decent roadside motels. I slept at three. They rent beds in two or four-person rooms by the hour. It's forty roubles (80p) for one hour, but you have to pay in advance for at least six. If you sleep for longer, you pay the rest afterwards. You stow your luggage and the car battery in the sofa bed you're lying on, so you're not worried about getting robbed while you sleep.

Meanwhile the Lazhik stays in the parking lot. It was on the road for three months, and it only spent one night outside without protection, not counting the few when I slept in it. There was always someone guarding it.

Just like most of the cars in Russia. What an army of people is needed to guard everyone, everything and everywhere! Because it's not just cars. They guard houses, people, gardens, crops, forests, woodland and farm animals . . . Tens, hundreds of thousands, millions of men do nothing but keep an eye out, stay on alert, guard, watch over and mind to make sure other men don't steal whatever it is they're guarding. Millions of security guards, caretakers, watchmen, sentries, minders – born, trained and educated just in order to guard objects.

If I ask five Russian men what they do for a living, one of them is almost sure to reply that he's a driver, and two that they work in security.

Not counting the militiamen.

MIENTY

The militia is an army of one-and-a-half million people. Statistically for every hundred citizens of the Russian Federation there is one militiaman – four times as many as in Poland.

And the *gaishniki* (GAI is the State Automobile Inspectorate), or traffic police, are a more hated, despised profession than the tax collectors from the Bible.

The Prosecutor General has calculated that the earnings of state officials from corruption are equal to one third of Russia's budget. This means they drain about 125 billion dollars out of the public in the course of a single year. A vast amount of it goes to the militia, especially the traffic section. Their staggering impunity, rapacity and corruption are legendary.

In a city or beyond it, at a crossroads, a roundabout or on a straight bit of road you might very often encounter a lone militiaman who has driven there in a private car, quite often outside of working hours, to check drivers' documents. He's often a gentleman of advanced age, an officer, a colonel even, but he's marrying off his daughter, changing his car or buying a flat, so he's in urgent need of money.

There's no power in the world strong enough to get out of his clutches. If the *mient* decides you're going to pay through the nose, you haven't a chance. (A *mient* is a cop, and in Russian that term is more or less as contemptuous as 'cop'). You may be sober, your car may be roadworthy, your documents may be in order and you may not have committed a violation, but in that case you'll pay because your car looks shabby, or you've got a dirty number plate.

If you've just come out of the carwash, the militiaman takes your documents, tells you to wait in the car and goes off to inspect other cars. After fifteen minutes you're seething with rage, so you intervene, to which he replies that you were meant to wait in the car. There are already several others like you waiting on the hard shoulder. After another fifteen minutes you take 500 roubles out of your wallet and put it in his paw 'to say goodbye'.

More refined methods have to be set up in advance. Outside the police station there's a STOP sign, where you have to stop for your documents to be checked. The militiaman doing the checking stands ten metres further on. So you obediently stop next to him.

'Why have you committed a violation?' they always ask.

22

'God forbid! I haven't committed anything', you explain.

'You didn't stop at the STOP sign.'

'But I have stopped.'

'The sign was back there', he says, pointing.

A bribe for this sort of violation costs 1000 roubles (£20). I don't know how much an official fine costs, but no-one in Russia ever pays them. When I express surprise, even the drivers, the victims of the militiamen, say that it has to be like that because they earn very little. It's true. The authorities keep their pay at the lowest level, because they know they can manage for themselves.

Between Chelyabinsk and Omsk I met Marat, a Kazakh from Petropavlovsk. He was drinking tap water at a roadside bar. He was dead tired, desperate and hungry, because he hadn't eaten for two days. He had bought a car in Hamburg and was driving home on German licence plates, and with every kilometre his supply of money for the journey was melting away. He had been economizing on food, until finally he had stopped eating altogether. Before Chelyabinsk he had tanked up the car for the very last time.

'And outside Kurgan I kneeled before a militiaman and begged him to show mercy', the tearful Kazakh told me. 'I've got nothing left. I showed him my wallet, my empty pockets . . . There was no mercy. He took my jacket and the empty wallet. At the next few police stations I gave away the spare wheel, the jack and my personal belongings, and at the last checkpoint I unscrewed the side mirrors so they'd let me through.'

I fed Marat and topped up his petrol, but personally I can't complain about the Russian militiamen. They always helped me, showed me the way and gave me good advice. Four times they caught me on violations, for example turning around on a bridge, but each time I managed to wriggle out of it. I just had to tell them exactly who I was, why I was alone, what sort of car it was, where I had come from and where I was going. This made such a dazzling impression that they let me spend the night in the car at their post, in other words at one of their permanent traffic checkpoints, set up at toll gates and crossroads. Another time they escorted me like a guard of honour to a hotel in town and drove my car to a warm covered parking lot for me.

Just like the lorry drivers, I liked stopping near their posts for the night, because it was safe there. These checkpoints are very often like miniature roadside fortresses with wire entanglements, road spikes, concrete barriers, sandbags and machine guns poking out of little firing slits. Sometimes they're in the middle of a roundabout, which the cars are obliged to drive across in single file at a speed of five kilometres an hour, keeping a distance of twenty metres apart. Of course the militiamen are in bullet-proof vests and have machine guns.

In Kuzbas, a large industrial zone known for atrocious banditry, there are armoured cars at most of the traffic police checkpoints.

I only had to pay up once, though I had made a vow to myself that I would never give a bribe to a policeman or a militiaman. I'd rather pay the fines.

It was on the busy M7 road, on the great, flat steppes between Kazan and Ufa. If there is an uphill stretch, it's not steep, but it might go on for two or three kilometres, and there's always a solid line the entire length of it, so you're not allowed to overtake. On this sort of stretch there were two lorries, one pulling the other on a tow rope. Their wheels were hardly turning. They were definitely going more slowly than an old man on crutches.

Along with all the other cars I overtook this convoy, and then a few hundred metres further on I saw a militiaman with binoculars.

His colleague was stopping everyone who had done the same as I had. There were several dozen cars on the hard shoulder. Everyone was handing over a bribe of 1000 roubles each without protest, because in Russia for overtaking on a solid line you can lose your licence for six months.

I paid up and drove off. But a few hundred metres later I stopped and looked back. The convoy with the broken-down lorry had just lumbered up to the highest point. There it quickly turned around, drove back down, turned around and, occasionally overtaken by other cars, started its laborious climb up the hill again.

HORSE

Battledress, a jacket underneath, and big boots that hardly fit in the stirrups. Behind him, on either side there are bicycle panniers, on his back he has a sleeping bag and a rucksack, and at the front of the saddle there's a sleeping mat. His face is almost black, dirty and suntanned, dry and haggard. He has a sparse but long beard and moustache. He looks like a Mongol warrior, except the uniform and direction aren't right for that. He's going east.

He has already begun to stink with poverty, dirt and hunger. The horse doesn't look any better. Whenever they stop, it lunges for the dry stalks sticking out of the snow as if they were lush grass. And the rider even more voraciously consumes the dry stalks of sausage from my 'iron rations'. They've been on the road for two months. They've travelled almost 3000 kilometres, they're getting close to Novosibirsk and they're barely able to stay upright.

The rider is called Chin Li. He's Chinese, a librarian who has lived in Moscow for twenty-seven years, but in September he left his job, used all his savings to buy the horse in Bashkiria, near Ufa, and set off for China. He paid 1000 dollars, as much as I spent on spare parts for the car. Chin is forty-five, and he has a wife and nine-year-old son.

'And you've left them on their own for all this time?'

'Yes', he says in a resolute tone. 'It's tough, but between the fortieth and fiftieth years of life is the last chance to achieve something unusual. I want my son to be proud of me, to follow my example. And not just beer, vodka and cigarettes like the Russian boys.'

'Why did you set off in winter?'

'What's the difference? I'll be on the road for almost a year, so I'll catch the winter one way or another. I want to reach Beijing for the opening of the Olympics, then go on to my home town of Wuhan on the Yangtze.'

Chin is travelling without money. He sleeps under the open sky, eats when the locals invite him in for the night and offer him something. The horse digs out stalks from under the snow, and sometimes gets a slice of bread from his master or a handful of barley from the collective-farm workers. At the start they did as much as sixty kilometres a day, but lately only twenty at most.

It was stuck into her head.

I had about 100 kilometres to go to reach Khabarovsk. Alexander's car was lying in a ditch, and his wife was inside it with the spanner. A spanner for changing the wheel. A heavy, solid object, about forty centimetres of iron.

Alexander wanted me to take him to Smidovich, the nearest town, where we'd be sure to find a militia post. We couldn't phone because we were out of range.

Alexander's car was a 'Japonka' – i.e. a Japanese one, with the steering wheel on the right. A white Honda Accord, on which the man had left lots of bloody hand prints.

The woman was not wearing her seatbelt, but she hadn't slumped torpidly off the seat. She was stuck, as if nailed, to the headrest. Her husband covered her with a jacket, locked the car and we drove off.

He found a roll of toilet paper underfoot, tore off a piece and spent the whole journey wiping his hands.

He's from Irkutsk. He and his wife had gone to Vladivostok, because any car is roughly 1000 dollars cheaper there than in their city. On the way back they reached Khabarovsk safely, but once they left it, they realized there was another Honda driving after them. It had no licence plates. They started trying to get away, but the other car overtook them and stopped across the road. Alexander drove around it and raced on like mad.

The attackers overtook them once again, turned around, and drove straight at them with tyres squealing. As they passed each other,

Alexander heard a crash. Like in a slow-motion film he saw a huge spanner come flying through the windscreen of his Honda with the force of an anti-tank missile. He braked, went into a skid and flew into the ditch.

'It was a bit of road with quite good tarmac', he says. 'I was going at about 140. They must have been too. I tried to pull that thing out of Larissa, but it was impossible. The other end had come out at the back of her head and stuck into the headrest. She was called Larissa.'

'Haven't you got a gun?' I asked.

'Yes, I have', he said, taking a pistol from under his belt, and holding it the entire way. 'It's legal, because I work in security.'

'Why didn't you shoot?'

'Because I couldn't see them well. And they never shoot.'

'Then why the hell do you all drive with guns?'

'How should I know?'

Criminals will always attack *peregonshchiki* who have bought cars in Vladivostok and are driving on transit licence plates along my route, but going west, homewards. It's worst of all to the south of Khabarovsk. The bandits overtake anyone who doesn't stop on demand and smash his windscreen with a rock. The point is for everyone to know it's worth paying up, because a windscreen costs 300 or 400 dollars, but they only take 100 from a passenger car. Or 150, if the driver is going a long way, to Irkutsk for example, which means he has more money on him. Sometimes they check his documents.

No-one ever has to pay twice. The criminals pass on information to each other by phone to say who has paid protection money, and sometimes they even issue a sort of receipt.

The professionals who buy cars for resale drive home in big groups, and won't let them get split up for anything in the world, even if they have to run the red lights in Khabarovsk. The bandits are a little afraid of them because they know that at least one of them is armed, so some groups manage to get through without paying.

STATION

I drove 13,000 kilometres across Russia and I used 2119 litres of petrol, because my Lazhik guzzled (as the Russians say too) an average 16 litres of fuel per 100 kilometres. Whenever I switched to four-wheel drive, it burned two litres more, and in the mountains it doubled again. It was shamelessly greedy, but luckily in Russia petrol is half the price it is in Poland. On my entire route it was most expensive in Tyumen province. That's the Russian Kuwait, where most of the fuel in the country comes from.

Russian petrol stations are usually tiny but solid buildings, where a single employee sits barricaded behind bullet-proof glass and metal bars, as if locked inside a safe. To hand him the money, you have to pull out a drawer in the wall, bellow into a hole or a speaker to say how much you want to pay for your petrol, toss the money in the drawer and push it shut. The employee switches on the right pump, which gives out only as much petrol as you have paid for.

I always filled right up, so I usually left lots of extra money with the cashier, and then collected the change, depending how much fuel I had room for. It was a very complicated operation, all the more since my Lazhik had two fuel tanks and two petrol intakes, one on each side. After filling up one of them, I had to put down the nozzle, turn the car around and fill it up again.

I kept putting forty litres in a single tank, though each held 37.5 litres. But they wouldn't close, so several times I had petrol siphoned off at parking lots (the guarded ones), and as the fuel gauge didn't work I had to count the kilometres as I drove to work out how much petrol I'd used, and when I ran the tanks dry I had to fetch the emergency canister out of the boot.

Fifty kilometres before Shimanovsk, between Chita and Khabarovsk, there were some roadworks. The road was covered in large stones. There wasn't much snow, but there was dreadful dust, and not a breath of wind, typical for Siberia when there's a hard frost. I could only find my way thanks to the lights coming towards me. Even full headlights were hardly visible. My eyes were stinging terribly, so I put on skiing goggles, sealed them with a paper tissue, and tied a bandana over my mouth. I had a bundle of rags round my neck which was a talisman from the most powerful shaman in Tuva (it was supposed to protect me from large metal objects), and on my left foot I had a big felt boot, which for comfort I'd shortened by half with a knife. I had thrown the right one away, because it didn't fit on the gas pedal, and in any case only my left foot kept freezing.

'You, who are you?' I was asked at the petrol station.

There were three of them, and the question contained boundless amazement and disapproval – downright menace.

It did not sound pleasant.

'Just a bloke,' I replied curtly, so they couldn't tell from my accent that I was foreign, and slid the goggles onto my brow.

'Who are you', he said, seizing me by the sleeve, 'to pour all that petrol into a Lazhik?'

In a country that is one of the biggest producers of crude oil in the world, in the provinces they usually fill up for 100 roubles – about five litres of the cheapest, 76-octane petrol. I was pouring 92-octane petrol into the worst Russki car, right to the top.

They hated me, as if I were feeding asparagus to a pig or sirloin steak to a dog.

A superb machine, the 2007 model. We're approaching a silver car the shape of a falling water drop. Its tapering rear end is like the tail of a jet plane. On its perfectly smooth surface there are no handles, bumpers or sunken windows – in short, nothing to protrude above the streamlined hull of this horizontally positioned droplet.

Report from the Twenty-First Century, 1957.

Til at his flat in Moscow.

The loony's exam, or a small and impractical Russian–English dictionary of hippy slang . . .

. . . that I collected in November 2007 while waiting for the chance to buy my Lazhik on the cheap in Moscow and then having it adapted for the Siberian winter. Taking advantage of the opportunity, I decided to seek out my contemporaries, people aged about fifty, who must have been hippies in the 1970s, just like me.

A IS FOR . . .

Askat' – to beg, to con, to wheedle. From the English 'ask'. The main source of income for most hippies.

This is not ordinary begging, but creative deception by means of a tall story, an artistic way of taking in a sucker. For more than thirty years one of the most effective methods has been 'the Estonian way'.

You accost an old person in the street, and in a fake Estonian accent you say you are from Tallinn and that you are well aware the Russians can't stand the Estonians. Anyone brought up in the USSR will vehemently deny it. You only have to do a little arguing about it, then finally ask for a few roubles because you haven't enough for the ticket home. You'll always get something, just so it won't look as if Soviet people are nationalists.

Б (B) IS FOR . . .

Bitnitsy – rock 'n' rollers, the golden Soviet youth of the late 1960s. In the USSR it was a very offensive word. They were the children of diplomats, senior officials and the Party *nomenklatura*. In Moscow they used to gather on Pushkin Square, in the little park around the poet's statue. They didn't do anything, they just sat on the benches and drank very cheap, sweet but strong plonk – Russian port wine.

Volodya 'John-the-Baptist', known as 'Bep' for short, joined them in 1971. He was twenty-three years old.

'Two or three years later we started calling ourselves hippies', he says. 'The militia never touched us because they were afraid of our parents. My father was an air force general. Only we had foreign books and newspapers at home, from which we found out all about hippies.'

The situation changed at the end of the 1970s with the advent of another, larger, generation of flower children. These were young people from normal educated families.

'And without even knowing it, the hippies became a protest movement', says Bep. 'A not very active, passive movement refusing to take part rather than to fight.'

These people did not inspire the militiamen's fear.

Volosaty – the shaggies. That was what Russian hippies most often called themselves.

The shaggies' slang is based on a mixture of four elements. Most of it comes from English and youth jargon, with an injection of words from the southern USSR, to where the hippies used to hitchhike every summer on holiday for poppy straw and marijuana. The fourth element is prison jargon, because lots of shaggies have done time for drug offences.

Vint – a screw, and in hippy language a militia round-up, custody, and the verb *vintit'* means to nab, to bang up, to put in jail.

The passengers in the Moscow metro are a terribly gloomy sight. I don't know how they do it, but the ones who manage to get a seat fall asleep in seconds. The rest of them read or play with their phones. Like all Russians they are dressed in grey or beige, with some in dark blue, and to a man they all have desperately sad, tired faces. Even the young people are cheerless and joyless with no sparkle in their eyes.

Until one day I heard a lively, clownish tune played on a flute. By the carriage door stood a shaggy little man with a wild beard. He was wearing a great big hat with a pompom, enormous boots and a sweater down to his knees. He had a red clown's nose on a piece of elastic, a scarf several metres long wound around his neck and a big bag, from which he had fetched out the flute.

And it was a miracle – the passengers looked up and their faces brightened. Several people even smiled, because the little man went on and on playing, and amazingly didn't want any money.

That was how I met Til, also known as Vitya Morozov, a forty-one-year-old hippy and professional clown, an itinerant, folk jester. The militia have nabbed him several dozen times, and once he even got a sentence.

In 1989 he decided to try for a job as a night watchman at the military rocket-engine plant. He was planning to obstruct weapons production, but they took one look at him and it was clear he would never get the job. On his way out, he happened to notice a phone booth in the entry-pass office. He went into the booth, ripped the phone off the wall and hid it under his clothes.

'I have no idea why I did it', says Til, laughing fit to burst. 'The sirens went off and they caught me. They said the phone had been connected to an alarm because it had been stolen five times already.'

He got a year in prison, but he was escorted from the court room by a paramedic in a white coat. He ended up in a psychiatric institution for criminals, and on top of that 'indefinitely', which meant he would spend at least a year there, but maybe two, five, or even ten years.

Daniil Kaminsky, known as Dan, was banged up in 1980. Before the Olympic Games the authorities purged Moscow of its superfluous elements. Hippies, prostitutes and tramps were packed into buses and deported far from the city. They found some marijuana on Dan, so he got eighteen months in prison, and after serving the entire sentence they transferred him to a mental hospital for another eighteen months.

Dan is fifty years old. He's the sort of hippy who gives you a pair of slippers when you come to see him. He is a ceramicist. He has dragged an enormous kiln into his flat to fire his pots, and every time he does it he has a row with the upstairs neighbour who complains that the floor is burning his feet.

Г (G) IS FOR . . .

Gerla – girl, from the English.

Dan has had three wives. He was divorced from the first one after a month, and the third a month ago. He has three daughters with her.

'It was me that got my second wife into shooting up', he says. 'I gave her the first injection myself.'

'Was she a hippy?'

'No. She was a civilian, but she went hippy and really got into the drugs. I don't even know if she's still alive.'

Til spent a year at the mental institution. Then he spent six years looking for his own kingdom of heaven on earth. He lived like a tramp, sleeping in stairwells, in cellars and on park benches. For the next four years after that he lived in a hippy commune, and in 2001 he married Irina. She gave birth to Anna and Ilya, he spent the whole of 2005 in a mental hospital again, and when he came out he and his family moved in with his mother.

Bep, the patriarch, who at sixty is the oldest living Russian hippy, has five children with his first wife and two with his second. Both women were hippies.

'The first one', he tells me, 'was a great, seventeen-year love, which was destroyed by capitalism after the collapse of the USSR. Everyone thought it was the beginning of history and that a time of plenty was coming, prosperity and wealth. Like all Russian women, my wife fell into the trap of materialism and said I had to start a business, and that hippieness was nonsense and passé. She threw me out of the house.'

'Because you weren't earning?'

'It was enough for food.'

He married for the second time in 2001. He was fifty-three, and his new bride was his student at the University of Hippy Culture that the shaggies had founded.

'What's it like having a hippy for a father?'

'Shameful. The Russians despise us. To them we are victims of fate who are incapable of earning a living. For the children a father like that is a source of shame.'

Д (D) IS FOR . . .

Durka – short for *durdom*, 'house of fools', a lunatic asylum or psychiatric hospital.

In the USSR from 1967 to 1987 for political reasons more than two million people were regarded as mentally ill and were subjected to treatment.

The career of most hippies began with the *durka*. Bep was there five times.

'For us they were sanctuaries', he says, 'sacred places where along with the patients they locked up the dissidents, die-hard intellectuals, hippies and whole crowds of unusual people whom Soviet psychiatry regarded as lunatics. I was in there with the folk singer Volodya

Vysotsky, with a guy who hijacked a steamroller and swanned around Moscow in it, and there was another guy who broke into a kiosk selling beer and spent all night carrying the beer home in buckets. He had filled the bath and the fish tank by the time they caught him next morning. In 1989 I met a completely normal artist in the *durka* who had made a banner saying 'Communists Out of Afghanistan!' and hung it from the balcony.'

'Whose balcony?'

'His own.'

'Then he was a loony! Are you surprised they hauled him off to the funny farm?'

'But he'd been there for ten years by then. When I left, they were still keeping him there. Thanks to people like that there was an unusual artistic spirit in there, more genuine than at liberty. There was no duplicity, hypocrisy or conformism, because inside the *durka* there was nothing to be afraid of. It was the only place where I could be myself – that's where our movement was born.'

Ж (ZH) IS FOR . . .

Zholty dom – the yellow house.

'That's another hippy name for the loony bin', says Bep. 'But lately the craziest place was Bulgakov's house on the Sadovoye Koltso road.'

At the end of the century a quasi-documentary film was made in Moscow about the hippy communes, for which the film-makers rented a large, burned-out flat in the writer's house. The actors were real hippies, and their task was to live there in their usual style for a year. But once the filming was finished they showed absolutely no desire to move out. Every few days the militia evicted them by force, but they kept coming back and carrying on as before, drinking, getting stoned, listening to music, scrawling on the walls, dying, making love . . .

'It's scary to think what was going on in there', says Bep. 'It was vital to give them something to do, so Til, who had been living there with a hundred other shaggies for almost four years, decided to found the University of Hippy Culture. He found twelve tutors who gave classes on theatre, literature, history of art, religion . . . I lectured on the aesthetics of poverty and the philosophy of hippyism with elements of psychology.'

They soon had an audience flocking in through the doors and windows: scholars, students, militiamen, tramps, film-makers and literary folk – the flower of the Moscow intelligentsia, and journalists from all over the world.

Til gave lectures on the theory of madness and workshops on going out of your mind. He taught how to go mad on a given topic, and how to go crazy without being sick or feeling ill.

I'm sure Til is exactly that sort of lunatic. He doesn't suffer because of it – instead he cultivates his madness as a source of happiness.

'At the lectures, I used to change my state of awareness in full view of everyone', he tells me. 'I used to tear my shirt, and people saw a real madman.'

'You can swig booze or do drugs and you'll change your state of awareness too', I said cleverly.

'I do not indulge in those practices', he replied, looking disgusted.

40

'That's easy, primitive and uninteresting. Of course, like any hippy I've tried drugs, but I don't need them.'

The militia broke up the university after two years of activity.

3 (Z) IS FOR . . .

Zabivat' – to roll a joint, make a spliff with marijuana.

In the Soviet era the militia itself very often planted drugs on the hippies. Just a single gram of marijuana could get you two years in prison.

И (I) IS FOR . . .

Ishnyaga – home-made heroin prepared from an extract of poppy straw to drink or inject.

K IS FOR . . .

Klikukha – from the general slang word *klichka*, meaning a nickname or tag.

'Til', or properly 'Till', is the German folk figure Till Eulenspiegel, prankster, trickster and clown. The character was created in Germany in the early sixteenth century, and in the nineteenth his adventures were described by a Belgian writer called Charles De Coster. Til got this nickname from the old hippies twenty-four years ago, just after school, when he was eighteen and they accepted him into their circle. They could not have known that in another ten years or so the lad

would become a *skomorokh*, or folk clown. Troupes of these professional clowns used to wander about Russian before the October
Revolution.

In the first few years after his marriage Til supported his family on
appearances in the suburban railway. Day by day, in his clown's costume
he played the flute for the passengers, sang, performed tricks, impro-
vised sketches and involved the public in his show. He is even Til for
his own small children. Whenever he travels on the metro he plays his
flute just for pleasure. He is never parted from it.

The nickname Bep, or John the Baptist, came from his endless religious quest. Finally he chose paganism.

Kaif – something wonderful. A mysterious Russian concept. A strange
state of mind, a sense of happiness, fulfilment and equilibrium . . . The
word comes from Turkish, into which it passed from Arabic. It was
probably brought to Russia by the Crimean Tatars. For the Russians,
kaif is often provided by a distant journey: the infinite yonder, a snow-
storm, a mouth organ and vodka, which preserves and prolongs this
state. For hippies *kaif* is quite simply drugs.

Anyone who didn't do *kaif* was not 'one of us'. He was shady,
suspect, maybe a secret police plant.

In the USSR drugs began with ephedrine, a psychostimulant
obtained from cough mixture on sale at the pharmacy for seven
kopecks without a prescription. In the oral form the drug was called
mulka and the intravenous version was *dzhez* ('jazz').

To this day, every summer the hippies go south for marijuana and
hashish. The best in the world is in the Chuy Valley on the borders of

Kyrgyzstan and Kazakhstan. In that one valley alone 138,000 hectares of Indian hemp grows to the height of a man.

Until 1978 morphine could be bought in Russia on ordinary prescriptions, which the hippies used to steal from doctors and write out for themselves. In 1980 the drug addicts discovered a way of concocting home-made heroin out of poppy seed.

'Terrible, merciless, treacherous filth,' says Dan, the ceramicist, who injected his second wife with it. 'Because if I drink vodka when I have pain in my soul, it just makes me feel worse, the suffering's even greater, but after heroin all problems really do disappear. One shot and it's all right. That's how I got hooked. For many years.'

Л (L) IS FOR . . .

Lomka – breaking, smashing, and for drug addicts it means going cold turkey, withdrawal syndrome.

There are four million drug addicts in Russia. Like most of the heroin users, Dan has black, terribly damaged teeth.

'But I gave it up when I married for the third time. She knew she was marrying an addict. I did it for her, and out of fear, because my friends were dying one after another.'

'How did you come off it? In the loony bin?'

'No, just with my wife. I shut myself up at a dacha out of town and spent a month on the spot in agonies. I didn't sleep, I didn't eat, I didn't think, I just swayed, howled and shat myself like an animal. I hit the bottom. I know I won't get caught again – for fear of coming off it. But there's a problem with alcohol.'

'Now you drink?'

'Now if I go on a bender, I shoot up once and stop drinking. Then I shoot up again, and I'm off the drink.'

'You're mad!' I clapped my hand to my forehead. 'You're using heroin to help you fight vodka! Whichever of them wins, you'll be the loser.'

'That's what my wife said too. She took my daughters and left a month ago. We were together for eighteen years. I've lost everything.'

M IS FOR . . .

Mient – a cop. General slang word for a militiaman.

According to Til, the militia is worse nowadays than in the Soviet era. In those days they lived in fear of the top brass, so they preferred not to beat up even hippies without permission. Broken arms, legs, ribs, cracked skull and knocked-out teeth – most of these things happened to Til after the collapse of the USSR.

'I kept getting beaten up all the time, so I learned how to avoid it. Very often a plain old joke, a bit of humour will work on a furious cop. I'm a past master at it. You have to tear the universal hatred from his heart and see the human being in him.'

In the 1980s a book called *Til and the Militiamen*, about his unusual adventures with the police officers, started to be compiled. Each incident was described by a different author who witnessed it. It was never published or finished, because new stories were always being added, but you could read it on the Internet.

'Lately the militiamen often mistake me for a Caucasian Mujahidin. It's the long beard and hair, and when it's cold I tie my long scarf around my waist . . .'

'Why do you wrap your scarf around your stomach, Til?' I asked, and I got what I deserved, because he talked about it for an hour and a half, but I couldn't understand a word of it. Then he continued: 'I can't have a peaceful kip on a park bench because immediately someone prods me, and I see militia caps above me. They ask what I've got on my stomach. I reply that it's a scarf, and they say: what's under the scarf? So I slowly take it off, and they jump on me, slap handcuffs on me, summon the bomb squad and evacuate the citizens from the park.'

In Til's district all the militiamen know him, and the new ones are warned not to argue with the strange man who plays chess against himself on an invisible board, with invisible pieces.

H (N) IS FOR . . .

Nakolka – in dictionary terms it's a fastener, a clip or clasp, and in hippy language it's a bed for the night, an address where you can stay in a foreign city.

Once the weather warmed up, the hippies would set off on the road. The shaggies from Moscow went to Leningrad, and the Leningrad ones went to Moscow. From 1978 illegal hippy festivals were organized in Latvia or Estonia in the summer, so you had to show up there too. After that you had to go south. Best of all to Crimea, where you could sleep on the beach, and the wine was cheap as chips. And better yet to Central Asia, to stock up on hemp and poppy seed.

They also travelled aimlessly. On a map of the vast Land of Soviets they would choose the remotest city they could find and set off towards it.

Before leaving they would collect addresses from their friends of places where they could stay the night on the way. There was a great big hippy accommodation system. In any of the larger cities there was either a shaggy or a commune, and if you didn't have an address, it was enough to accost the first hairy guy you ran into. In the cities the hippies never had to sleep out in the open.

O IS FOR . . .

Oldovy – an old hippy, from the English word *old*.

All the heroes of this chapter are *oldovy*, but not because of their age. An *oldovy* hippy may be twenty-two, but he is an authority, a leader in the very feebly hierarchical hippy community, which is based on freedom.

The most *oldovy* of all was Yura 'The Sun' Burakov, whom the girls called 'Sunshine' and who was regarded as the first Soviet hippy. He is the author of the saying that 'by killing yourself you're destroying the Soviet Union'. He took drugs and drank a terrific amount, and all the hippies believed that really was the way to have a revolution.

The Sun died in 1989 of cirrhosis of the liver. He was forty-six.

Π (P) IS FOR . . .

Perenta – parents, from the English word of the same meaning.

Most hippies left home and ended up on the streets straight after coming of age, in other words after finishing the compulsory tenth year at school.

'I left home without saying goodbye and only got in touch with them seven years later', Dan tells me. 'That is, I called. I didn't even take anything with me. What would I take? Everything my parents ever bought me was embarrassing. What the hell did I need a suit for?'

'Didn't you love your parents?'

'I did, but I had to get free. They spent a very long time looking for me, until they found out from the militia where I was and what I was doing. They were terribly upset. Most of all about my time in prison and the loony bin.'

Masha Remizova, known as 'Mata Hari', and Sasha Dialtsev, known as 'Pessimist', are a hippy married couple who have been together for twenty-five years. In this respect they are unique, and uniquely, rather than using their nicknames people say 'Masha and Sasha' in a single breath, because they're always together.

Sasha moved out of home after the third year of studies at the Architecture Institute, when to his parents' dismay he married Masha, who was also a hippy.

'Sasha's mum said she'd rather her son were an alcoholic', Masha tells me. 'For us a drunk is a normal thing, but she was terribly ashamed of a hairy hippy. What she found shameful was his appearance, the militia calling at the house and letters sent to her workplace, saying that her son took part in illegal, hooligan gatherings. They sent something like that when the Moscow shaggies got together after the murder of John Lennon to commemorate him, and the cops nicked us.'

Prikid – clothes.

'Did you have a pair of jeans?' I ask Sasha.

'Yes, I did. Mum brought me some in 1979 from a business trip to Poland. I can't remember the brand name.'

'Not many people could afford to buy jeans in this country because you could only get them from the profiteers and they cost a fortune. Two hundred roubles! That was a teacher's whole monthly salary. But they were the height of elegance, especially when they were covered in patches after years of wear.'

'I never wore jeans', Masha puts in.

'The hippies didn't have enough money for Western trousers, so we used to make them ourselves out of tarpaulin', says Sasha. 'Flared, of course, bell-bottoms. I've still got a pair. Worn with a flowery shirt, a shoulder bag, sandals, and a headscarf or a *hairatnik* – that's what we used to call an Indian headband, from the English word "hair". But real hippieness relies on making everything by hand. Even more important is not to be a tramp, in spite of being poor. Never to be dirty or stinky.'

They called this 'the aesthetics of poverty'.

To be a real, 100 per cent hippy you only had to meet three conditions – to travel, take drugs and wear *fenechki*, bracelets made of beads or bits of coloured string. This was the identification badge and ornament of all Soviet hippies. Even more important than a peace symbol, which they called a *patsifik*.

None of the characters in this chapter wears *fenechki* nowadays.

P (R) IS FOR . . .

Rassekat' – to cut precisely, break or chop, and in hippy language it means to roam, wander, or drift aimlessly, just to kill time.

It was a wise man who named Sasha 'Pessimist'. For a hippy, he's bloody serious and principled. On principle he never took money from his parents, although he and Masha hadn't enough to eat, on principle he never cheated money out of people in the street because he was ashamed to, and his pride wouldn't let him, and on principle a year before finishing his studies he blatantly withdrew from the Komsomol – the Communist youth organization.

'It was clear I'd be kicked out of college', he says, 'so to make sure they didn't put me straight in the army I spent two weeks in the mental hospital and got my lunatic's papers.'

Also on principle he never wasted time on a bench under the statue of Pushkin. He says hippies like that are common, but he's genuine and went to college, and when he was thrown out in 1983, he got a job.

The only jobs the shaggies found acceptable were as janitors and night watchmen. Sasha preferred the latter, because there was nothing to do but sit and read books. And Sasha even wrote too.

He earned seventy roubles a month. That was what a dealer charged for a single Pink Floyd record. He and Masha rented their flat for forty roubles a month. She was a student, so they only ate bread and margarine, pasta and buckwheat. So did their child. They made their own clothes.

In 1991 when the Soviet Union collapsed, Sasha went back to college and finished his degree. He was thirty years old. He was tired of idleness, poverty, killing time and the whole hippy lifestyle.

'We didn't want to be on the margins of society any more. We had grown up and were feeling the need for self-fulfilment. We wanted to do something.'

'A career!' came a revealing shout from Vanya, Sasha and Masha's younger son.

'Some career!' replied his father irritably. 'Go to your room and shut the door. We wanted to fulfil ourselves professionally. We felt there was a lot we could do. We have strength, energy, taste, talent, and at last there was the long-desired freedom.'

They had their own bookshop and got work at *Niezavisimaya Gazeta* ('The Independent Newspaper'). Sasha is a sought-after architect, literary critic and writer. He has published five excellent novels.

New friends appeared – literary people, journalists and artists – and the old ones no longer sufficed. They had abandoned the hippy world.

'We left the system.'

C (S) IS FOR . . .

Sistema – the system. That's what they call themselves as a whole. The hippy community, the shaggy nation.

'A few years ago they showed a documentary on television about a detox centre for drug addicts', Masha tells me. 'There was a long scene showing group therapy, and I recognized several of my friends among the patients. I hadn't seen them for ten years. They were sitting in a circle in a large room. Shaggy, sad and motionless. And I had left them. I felt like the Indian girl who abandoned her tribe and went to join the white man's society. She has a normal, comfortable life, she has a home, a car and a job, and suddenly she notices that her tribe is dying out. I cried like anything. The tribe has truly died out now.'

T IS FOR . . .

Telega – the hippies' main, legendary form of creativity. Literally it means a cart, a wagon, but for the shaggies it is a wonderful, sophisticated creative act. They talk of 'driving the cart' (*gnat' telegu*), in other words being crazy, pretending to be mad.

The psychiatric hospital saved you from military service. You only had to be in there once to avoid ending up in army boots, so the hippies were eager to go there voluntarily. Just that once. An even safer method was to pull a minor but bizarre hooligan stunt, so you were arrested and then taken to the mental hospital.

'There you took the state loony's exam', says sixty-year-old Bep, who was in the *durka* five times. 'You had to pretend to be mad. You only had to say straight out what you thought about the Soviet regime, or demonstrate your religious belief. And if you were shaggy and ragged, like the antithesis of Soviet man, after just two weeks in hospital they wrote the desired phrase in your army registration booklet: "Unfit for military service even in time of war." And if you made a really good loony, you got a pension. I managed to do it. They paid eighty-five roubles a month, which was enough to be free of poverty, be creative, do some reading and travelling. It was important not to be too good at it, or they might slap an indefinite sentence on you and lock you up in the hospital for years.'

Tusovka – a place where hippies gather, and also the group ascribed to it.

The first and biggest was in the centre of Moscow, on Pushkin Square, under the poet's statue. The second was in the Moscow University park, but the most famous, magnetic place was the one just off Arbat Street, near the 'Aromat' cafe. This legendary, no longer extant *tusovka* was called 'Babylon'. Altogether there may have been only about a thousand hippies living in the city, but even so they represented the largest group to be independent of Communist authority.

Y (U) IS FOR . . .

Urlak or *urka* – a word from criminal slang meaning a hooligan or street thug. Short for *ugolovny element*, meaning 'criminal element'. This is the hippy's eternal enemy.

They would come down to the city centre from the peripheral estates and neighbouring towns to 'fuck up the shaggies'. They were tolerated, even encouraged by the militia and Communist youth organizations, who for twenty years had been incapable of eliminating the hippy plague.

'That's why the second generation of hippies was no longer as laid-back and peace-loving', says Dan. 'It's hard to be a pacifist when you see them dragging off your girlfriend by the hair, kicking her and getting ready to rape her. We had to learn to fight.'

'There were the *druzhinnitsy* too', I say, meaning the volunteer militia helpers organized by the Komsomol.

'They at least didn't beat to kill. At the *tusovka* on Pushkin Square the "Beryozka" squad was in operation. There was no hippy who didn't fall into their clutches. They had a huge card index with photos. Their headquarters was on a neighbouring street. Once they caught my friend, Jimmy. They booked him, and used some manual hair clippers to give him a buzz cut. So he picked up the hair, stuck it onto a hat and paraded about in that head gear for the rest of his life. One morning we begged a lot of money, so we bought several bottles of plonk each and drank it in the courtyard next to their headquarters.'

'You must have gone mad!'

'You may be right. And we decided to break into their place. We borrowed a saw from their neighbours to cut off the padlock. We made a terrible mess of the place, but we couldn't get into the archive, because it was in a safe, so we made a big pile of all the papers and furniture, poured floor polish onto it and set it alight. There was an awful big fire. They were moved to another district.'

'Did they catch you?'

'No. But not long after that Jimmy jumped off a tower block', says the old hippy, his voice faltering. 'He drank a terrible lot. The freedom we were so eager to have can kill. A man who doesn't do anything, but lives at the cost of others, debases himself. You have to give, not just take. I buried dozens of friends before I really understood that. I am one of the last survivors.'

Φ (F) IS FOR . . .

Fakatsya – to do something unpleasant. Put simply, to work. From the English word 'fuck'.

So in order not to live at the cost of others, Dan models and fires vases, and Bep founded and has for some years been running a museum of Old Slavonic culture. He earns 12,000 roubles a month (£240) and has his lunatic's monthly pension of 3500 roubles (£70).

Til handed me a small card that passes as his business card. Under his name it says: 'Manager of the Ladybird Arts Theatre, poet, teacher, director, actor, artiste, playwright and musician.'

The Ladybird is a children's theatre based at a cultural centre run by Til and his wife Irina.

Sasha and Masha have so many occupations they don't know what to turn their hand to next.

Flet – a flat or apartment, from the English. Viktor Fedotov from Saint Petersburg, known in his youth as *Molodozheniets* ('Young Husband'), because at the age of eighteen he had a wife and child, is a building contractor and is the only person featured in this chapter who doesn't have long hair. He is a friend of Father Sergei, a hippy turned priest, whose new church he is building. Years ago, when Father Sergei used to go to Leningrad, like many of the Moscow hippies he used to stay at Viktor's flat, because it was a famous, highly populated commune.

'I had two anarchist friends', Viktor begins his story. 'In 1980 they were arrested for posting bills. The KGB also interrogated a girlfriend of theirs, who warned me that the boys had been caught. So I told everyone at our commune that we'd have to clean out the flat. They could put you inside just for having Solzhenitsyn, and we also had anarchist newsletters, foreign newspapers, banned Black Sabbath records and Pink Floyd's *The Wall*. We finished cleaning up, and an hour later the secret police came thundering up to our flat.'

'Did they find anything?' I ask.

'No. But my friends started asking me how I knew they'd arrested the lads and that there was going to be a search.'

'That girl had told you.'

'But I had sworn I wouldn't tell anyone about her', says Viktor, nervously looking for a cigarette. 'She was making an academic career for herself at the university, and if it came out that she had warned me about the raid, the KGB would have destroyed her. She took a risk just to save us. Everyone believed I must have been a traitor and that those two were in prison because of me. It was all a very clever psychological operation by the secret police. By undermining my honesty, they smashed up the whole group, they smashed up our commune. All the hippies moved out to get away from me, and the ones from other cities stopped coming to stay. So I was left all on my own in a flat where a crowd of seventeen hippies had been living. Not even my wife believed me. She took our four-year-old son and left. She refused to live with a traitor.'

After three years in prison both anarchists came out and explained that Viktor couldn't have betrayed them because he hadn't known anything about their activities. At this point his wife wanted to come back to him, but Viktor couldn't get over the fact that she hadn't believed him.

'Do you know who was in charge of that operation?' he asks me.

'Well?'

'Vladimir Putin.'

'You're joking!'

'He was a young lieutenant, and in the Leningrad KGB he was responsible for informal youth groups', says Viktor. 'He called us in, and he conducted the interrogations in person.'

'Did he ever hit you?'

'Not once. There were others who beat us like devils – they broke my fingers, injured me and punched out my teeth, but he never even used swear words or threats. He has nothing to be ashamed of . . .'

'You don't say!' I interrupt. 'He ruined your life!'

'My wife never got hers back in shape either. She's alone, and our son grew up without a normal family. He's thirty-one and he's a drug addict. My one and only child. That man wrecked all our lives.'

X (H) IS FOR . . .

Haik – hitchhiking, and a *haiker* is a hitchhiker, from the English.

This was the only way the hippies ever travelled. Sometimes they used the electric railway, the suburban trains that ran on short routes. In small jumps like that you could get right to the far end of the country, all the way to Vladivostok. It took about a month, because the hippies never had any money and didn't buy tickets, so the conductor would throw them out at the next station, where they'd wait for the next train.

Ч (CH) IS FOR . . .

Chornaya – black, because it is as black as death. This is another name for the home-made heroin concocted from boiled poppy straw. The hippies used to hitchhike to Kyrgyzstan for the best poppy seed, but the collective-farm fields were protected by armed guards, and a lot of young people died at their hands.

Ш (SH) IS FOR . . .

Shiz – schizophrenia or a schizophrenic.

Viktor, Dan, Bep, Til and almost all the hippies who ended up in psychiatric hospitals were given the dissident's diagnosis, which was 'asymptomatic schizophrenia'. Only a psychiatrist could tell the person was sick.

After the collapse of the USSR the authorities admitted that the Soviet lunatic asylums were the site of political repression.

'They said I was a victim of the regime, and they wanted to invalidate all the diagnoses', says the indignant Bep, patriarch of the Russian hippies. 'I went to hospital twice to make sure they wouldn't change anything. That pension of mine may be small, but it is something. I have never worked in my life, because they wouldn't give jobs to lunatics in those days, so who would employ me now? I told the doctors I don't want to be rehabilitated, so I'm the last person to be suffering from an illness that doesn't exist.'

'Maybe you'd get some compensation', I reply.

'What do you mean? The authorities didn't do it for the people's sake – they only did it to pay out less pension money. The state is the worst evil of all. Both the old Soviet one and the one we have now.'

Sasha, Masha's husband, was one of the few hippies in whom the Soviet psychiatrists identified a case of manic depressive psychosis, because he said that if they cut off his hair he would hang himself.

'So just in case they never even took the cross off my neck', says Sasha. 'And they took them away from everyone else.'

'Why did they take away their crosses?' his son Vanya calls out from his room.

'So the hippies wouldn't hang themselves on the leather thongs.'

Sasha and Masha abandoned the world of the shaggies and began a new, free and affluent life in 1991, when the Soviet Union collapsed.

'We left the hippy system', says Sasha, 'but ten years later we felt it was the best, most beautiful part of our lives. And those were the best friends we had. I wrote a book about it. On 1 June we went to a place outside Moscow where the hippies get together, because we have our special holiday then, on Children's Day. We rediscovered Dan and some other old friends. We publish a cheap hippy journal, and every year we go to our festival in Ukraine.'

'Do you hitchhike?'

'We take the car', says Sasha, embarrassed.

'I'll show you our *oldovy* car, so you won't get the wrong impression!' cries Masha, and drags me onto the balcony.

Down below, covered in snow, there's a purple 1989 Zhiguli (the Russian name for a Lada), on which Masha has painted huge flowers.

'And I've bought a Lazhik – the day after tomorrow I'm off to Vladivostok', I boast, and my hosts' eyes light up.

'Oh, how I'd love to come with you!' says the delighted Sasha. 'I never got further than the Altai Mountains, and this is such an opportunity . . . What a *haik* . . .'

'So then go. I'll take care of everything at home', says Masha, and for an hour she badgers him until he breaks.

'I promised to get this project finished . . .'

'Sod that', says Masha, not giving up. 'You can be on the road again.'

'Do you want me to get thrown out of my job?' Sasha shouts, causing Vanya to come running from his room.

For a long time no-one says a word.

Finally Masha breaks the silence.

'Another hippy's dead.'

Of course in the first stage supplies for people who settle on the Moon will be brought from the Earth. But it will be a very expensive pleasure. The value of a loaf of bread supplied to the Moon from the Earth will be as much as the same loaf would cost on Earth if it were made of gold. And so one of the first tasks will be to adapt the Moon to self-sufficiency. I think that by the twenty-first century this task will have been successfully realized.

Report from the Twenty-First Century, 1957.

Mani drinking outside his block in the Marino area.

Rabid dogs

I was still in Moscow, waiting for my Lazhik jeep to be kitted out for my trip. The frost had made the vodka so thick it could barely trickle out of the bottle. In fact by now, according to the *Report*, an artificial sun with the power of a million kilowatts was supposed to be casting light and warmth over Moscow. There should have been only five million citizens, and no-one was meant to be hungry, no-one suffering from tuberculosis or cancer, no-one even tired, so there should have been hardly any need to sleep. There weren't supposed to be any cars, snow on the streets or stinking rubbish chutes in the flats.

Only the final dream on this list has actually come true, and that only partially, because now it stinks in the stairwells.

DIRTY RAP — THE PERFUME FACTORY

Right now the first solid frost of the autumn is making me shiver.

We're drinking in the bushes under a block that stretches 700 metres in a sleepy district of Moscow called Marino. We're sitting on old tyres, and for a table we have a large wooden spool that once held electrical cable. This is a morning booze-up round the bonfire to celebrate Russian Militiaman's Day. It's Saturday, 10 November 2007, and one of us is a cop.

He's a mate of Misha Naumov, otherwise known as Mani, a thirty-two-year-old rapper from the hip-hop band DOB, whom I have arranged to meet here. DOB is at the very bottom of the Moscow musical underground, so-called dirty rap (close to 'gangsta rap'), which in this city is affectionately known as *griazny riapchik*.

Although he plays the scumbag and the slob, Mani is extremely likeable. He's the only person I know whose fingernails are black and bitten all at once. On top of that, his stubbly, battered face is blue from the vodka and the cold weather, he has some teeth missing and a skull and crossbones on his hat. Like any self-respecting rapper, he writes his own songs.

'About the lads from the block, about my job replacing windows with plastic ones, about my wife and my little girl', he says, and spits through the hole where a tooth has gone. 'And I also sing about how Brindik from our band drugged himself to death, and about drinking with my mates on Militiaman's Day.'

> *And along came this guy – he looked like a wuss,*
> *But he had a bottle – so he was one of us.*
> *He's the first Polak – I ever seen*
> *The guy is a writer – I slip him some skin.*

As the rapper improvises, his friends tap out the rhythm on their bottles. Mani records his whole life on disk. He caused the biggest furore in the district with a rap story about some guests he had. One day Mani's wife brought these two men home from work with her. One of them was English, the other a Czech.

'That one spoke a bit of Russian', says the rapper, 'but the English guy didn't know a single word. They ended up with us by accident, because my wife was chosen by lottery to host them. They lived with us for a week.'

'And so?' I enquire.

'I treated them royally. To vodka and beer. They *loooved* it! They were planning to open a perfume factory in Moscow, and they wanted to see how the average Russian family lives and how their workers would relax.'

'And so?' I ask again.

'They decided not to go ahead with it.'

'Why not?'

'Because in a single evening the workers drink their way through more than they were prepared to pay.'

Today's Moscow is a gigantic metropolis of fifteen million people, where the cars are stuck in jams even at night. Mani has a twenty-two-year-old cream-coloured Volga, and he can't get over the fact that in his city there are more S-Class Mercedes cars, the most luxurious ones, than in Germany, a country with eighty million inhabitants, where they are produced.

But what's strange about that, when there are about ten thousand dollar-millionaires in Moscow? What is strange is that for almost every millionaire there is one homeless child and ten homeless dogs.

To get to the metro from outside Mani's block I have to take a trolleybus.

Blondie jumped on board through the exit door, to be the first to jump off at the next stop. As I was buying my metro ticket at the window, she was there too. She was behind a newspaper stand, scratching under her foreleg as she watched five helmeted militiamen armed with machine guns. The officers lined up in the narrow passage leading to the escalator, and sifted the human stream passing through it.

Finally they stopped a bearded man with a dark complexion, pinned him to the wall and started plunging their paws into his large bag. That's what she'd been waiting for. In two quick bounds she was on the escalator, with me right behind her.

On the platform she walked indifferently past the girls positioned every few dozen metres with cards saying: 'Help! My four-year-old son is dying', 'My mum's dying. Please help with her treatment', 'Help me to get home', 'Help a pregnant woman to survive'.

She stood under an advert for 'Putinka' vodka ('Tough character, gentle soul') and yawned noisily. When the train came, she boarded the first carriage.

With great curiosity we both observed a very young bill sticker, who in just a few minutes between stations plastered our entire carriage in dozens of small, colourful advertising cards. Most of them were aimed at the immigrants who come here looking for work and a livelihood. The adverts offered them help arranging a flat, a work permit, a health-care booklet, a diploma from their chosen college, various professional permits, a driving licence, school certificates and an income certificate, which is necessary for getting credit. But there was also one that said: 'We give cash to all residents of the Russian Federation in thirty minutes without documents or guarantors.'

Most of the cards were about getting a residency document, without which, if you are not of Slavonic appearance, it is impossible to live in this city. Shady legal firms arrange shady residency documents in shady hotels and college dorms. Every time I stay in Moscow I myself buy residency for fifty roubles (£1) from one of these firms. It has an office on the main street.

Posting advertisements in the metro is not illegal either.

Blondie changed trains twice. At the Prazhskaya station she had a long rest. She removed a sandwich from a waste bin, carefully unwrapped the paper, ate it and dozed off. Then she went up the stairs.

There, howling with joy, Blondie and another dog completely blocked the way as they tumbled about in the underground passage. They chased each other, tugging with their teeth, and then Blondie rolled onto her back, spread her paws and showed her sister her belly.

I can't think of a single Moscow metro station where there isn't a pack of stray dogs living near the entrance. They stick to these places, because in winter warm air, and in summer cool air belches out from underground. There are often at least ten of them, always very big, strong mongrels. Almost every courtyard, hospital, nursery school and university has its own pack of them too.

From generation to generation, the Russian capital's stray dogs teach each other the art of riding the metro without a ticket. Usually they travel for some purpose, not like homeless people, whose aim is to sleep in a train that's going in a circle.

In 2001 the city authorities recognized that Moscow is a humane city and put a ban on catching the homeless dogs and putting them down. Instead they had to be caught, sterilized and 'released at the place of acquisition', in other words, where they were found. Since then the number of stray dogs has increased five times over, and a trip to the limits of the city, where the packs are bigger and more aggressive, is a gamble with fate. Three years ago one of these packs almost entirely devoured their own carer, but Professor Poyarkov of the Academy of Sciences' Ecology Institute announced that only thanks to the dogs does Moscow have no problems with rabies, because the mongrels do not let carriers into the city.

'That's the silliest thing I've ever heard in my life', says Yevgeny Ilinsky, who is head of what is probably the world's only organization for the defence of animal rights that is fighting for dogs to be put down.

PUNK ROCK — COLD-WAR STYLE

The energy of the artificial sun over Moscow would be a mere spark compared with the fire the Land of Soviets once succeeded in kindling off Novaya Zemlya in the Arctic Ocean. In 1961 the biggest nuclear bomb in history was tested off this archipelago. It had a power of fifty megatons, equivalent to fifty million tons of TNT, and during its launch it released energy equal to six hundredths of the thermal power of our Sun.

In those days Moscow was ready for an attack even of that kind – as long as you didn't emerge from underground, from the metro tunnel, because from the Taganskaya station, for example, you could walk through to the Taganka ZPD, in other words the Transport Police Emergency Command Point, hidden sixty metres underground, which is also protected by twenty-metre-thick concrete walls and a three-ton iron door.

These are four two-storey underground blocks, in which about a thousand Soviet dignitaries and military people could have survived for three months without contact with the outside world – on condition they observed the internal regulations that are displayed on the wall. Point Eight says: 'Do not panic.'

I came here for the birthday party of the daughter of a Moscow oligarch. The Russians contemptuously call these young people *mazhory*, from a contraction of the words *maladoy burzhui* meaning 'young bourgeois'. The birthday girl's father hired the musicians and the venue for the party.

I was invited by Sid, aka thirty-two-year-old Dima Spirin, leader of an extremely abrasive punk rock band called Tarakany, meaning 'The Cockroaches'. Sid is polite, mild mannered and highly knowledgeable, as well as being festooned in earrings and pockmarked with tattoos. He also has skulls and crossbones on his signet ring, hat and shirt, and a fiancée who looks the same. They are the leading Russian punk rock band, but they're not seeking a major career.

'I like life to be easy, without too much work', he says. 'And it has been, ever since I dropped out of school in March 1991 and founded Tarakany. The Soviet regime was still in power, but it had lost its teeth by then. Everyone was doing what they wanted, so the boys from my class and I grabbed a cellar on Arbat Street in the city centre, fitted some padlocks, lugged in our gear and started to play. It was fab. A new life was born in that cellar.'

Life was also being born in cellars in the small towns outside Moscow. There the boys were pumping iron, sculpting their physiques, sweating buckets, and then finally shaving their heads and going onto the streets.

They were known as *gopniki*, from a term for street mugging. They had an allergic reaction to hippies, punks and all shaggies, as well as tramps and the non-Slavonic immigrants, who after the collapse of the USSR started pouring into Moscow in droves.

Once again things became very bad. Common bandits swelled the ranks of the *gopniki* and thus, to put it briefly, the famous Russian mafia was born.

Any enterprise that brought in even the smallest profit, be it a vegetable stall or a rock band, had to have a so-called *krysha*, meaning a 'roof' or 'lid', i.e. protection, for which they had to pay the bandits.

Only Alyosha Puliakov, guitarist with the anarcho-punk band Pochta Mongolska – 'Mongolian Post' – stood up to them, the man who in 1992 founded Russia's first rock club, Atrishka. The next year Alyosha was shot and the club folded.

'Nowadays it's easier', says Sid. 'The crime element have gone into the coal and gas business, steel and the arms industry, so we don't have any contact with them, but the owners of the clubs where we play still pay for protection to this day.'

There are lots of bunkers like the Taganka ZPD under Moscow, but only this one was put up for auction and sold in 2006. The authorities could no longer afford the repairs.

CHANSON − BANDIT MUSIC

Not only rock went underground during perestroika. So did *blatna* music, in other words criminal, bandit, jail or prison camp music. The communists hated it, because it wiped its feet on Soviet democracy. They only allowed the first festival to take place a few months before the death throes of the USSR, in December 1991, once its name had been changed to the 'Festival of Russian Chanson'.

Every Russian taxi or lorry cab has nothing but chanson belting out. The rock stars featured in this chapter sell three thousand records each, the Russian musical elite sell thirty thousand each, and the chanson performers sell three hundred, a million, or three million each.

The word *blatny* probably comes from Yiddish, into which it passed either from the German word 'Blut', meaning blood, or 'Blatt' meaning a page, a sheet of paper, because whenever the bandits in Odessa came to rob the stores of an old Jew or a German, they stuck a revolver barrel in his face and said it was their 'Blatt', in other words their receipt or goods delivery document. Thus bandits came to be called *blatniye* in Russian.

ANARCHO-PUNK − BATTLEFIELD SYNDROME

'Russia is dying', says Pit gloomily at the café, as I set before him an

Americano and an extremely bourgeois 'Brabant' cake with almond flakes on top.

Then he tells me at length how seventeen years ago they opened the first McDonald's in Russia on Tverskaya Street. He had stared through the window in horror, as all night long a crowd of exhausted people had thronged outside the place, who were only there to eat a burger in a bun the next morning. That was the first time he thought Russia was dying. He was five years old.

Pit studied philosophy and theology at Moscow University. He has asked me not to write his name. He and his punk band Ted Kaczynski – named after the US terrorist known as the Unabomber – have gone underground. They only perform at private parties for their fans, and in photos on the Internet they have their faces covered.

He is only just twenty-two, but he is 'racial enemy number one', and for four years he has been living with a death sentence issued by the Moscow fascists. Of course, and not just because his mother is Korean and his father comes from the Caucasus.

Pit is the icon of all the Moscow punks and members of anti-fascist, pacifist, ecological, anti-globalist and anarchist organizations.

Two years ago, his address and photograph appeared next to the death sentence on the Internet. Since then not a month has passed when he hasn't been beaten up in the street by fascists, skinheads, or supporters of the soccer teams Spartak Moscow, CSKA or Dynamo. Nowadays he carries a knife in his pocket.

'In 2001 the Nazis incited war against the punks', he says. 'And the blood is flowing, on the streets and during attacks on our clubs and our bands' concerts. They want to destroy their enemy's symbols. They also persecute immigrants and tramps, and we've been coming to their defence. The punks and all the anti-fascists, who are their allies, have responded in the same way.'

The most radical fascist rock groups are called Korrozya Metalla ('Metal Corrosion') and Kolovrat – the Slavic version of a swastika. The former is closer to the National Bolshevik Party, the latter to the Nazis. They often organize concerts and festivals, for which they have to provide security. Following these events the 'support groups' are not disbanded, and in this way hit squads are formed that operate underground. The fascist right wing has especially powerful ones, because it recruits its soldiers among skinheads and soccer fans.

A recent victim of the war was twenty-six-year-old Ilya Borodayenko, whom on 26 June 2007 the national socialists battered with iron bars during an attack on a camp by the River Angara, where ecologists and anarchists were protesting against the construction of yet another nuclear power plant.

'The fascist organizations were born in the mid-1990s', says Pit, 'when a huge wave of immigrants poured into Russia. And these people are more savage than Russians are abroad. If harm is done to one of them, they all reach for their knives. They intercepted all the trade in Moscow and created various mafias, hellishly brutal of course, typical of savages. What's more, they look different and speak a different language, and when the war in Chechnya began, the television showed them killing Russian soldier boys. In my class all the boys belonged to the Nazis. Except for me. As time went by some strange oddballs started appearing – Nazi punks, Nazi Rastafarians, and even Nazi Negros. Their hero is the football hooligan Eskimo.'

'There used to be an ice cream called Eskimo', I recall.

'Vanilla coated in chocolate. Because he looks black on the outside, but he's white on the inside.'

On the other side of the barricade Pit's friends gained allies in the form of anti-fascist skinheads, red skinheads and apolitical skinheads.

Pit says his anarchist pals obtained a list of the leaders of the Moscow fascist organizations. Half of them do not have Russian surnames. They are young people from Pakistan, Kyrgyzstan, the Caucasus, and even from Chechnya, but from the second generation of immigrants, just like him, who do not know a word of their mother tongue.

'And you should see how many Jewish names there are.'

'Why does that interest you?' I interrupt him.

'Because we can't understand them', he replies. 'If I ask a guy like that, why are you with them when your face is just as dark as mine, he says his ancestors were from Bulgaria, Croatia or Italy. He'd never admit he's from Baku or Dushanbe.'

Pit is a neurotic, terrified intellectual with post-traumatic stress syndrome, as suffered by soldiers returning from war. Out of the goodness of his heart he keeps giving me advice for my journey.

'The main rule is not to trust anyone. Don't talk to anyone on the road, and for God's sake don't drink any vodka. Don't walk about at night, don't stop near a bazaar and don't rent accommodation from the women who stand outside the stations. In Russia the people are savage, very aggressive. If the car breaks down in the middle of no-where and night is coming on, go straight into the depths of the forest and pitch your tent there.'

'Winter's just around the corner.'

'Go into the forest, I say. Go and join the wolves, not the people.'

HEAVY METAL – WHORES, MUSIC AND BOOZING

He's late. An hour later he calls and says he'll be forty minutes late.

'You're already sixty minutes late', I hiss.

'Well, it'll be another forty.'

It was another sixty. Two hours late altogether. He came into the café and didn't say a word of apology. Jeans, green jacket, long fair hair, beard . . . He doesn't look like a fascist. He doesn't even have a strong handshake. But he laughs in a hideous way, and when he does his face (in the manner typical of people with paralysed facial nerves) doesn't change its expression at all.

Sergei Troitsky, known as Pauk – meaning 'Spider' – is the founder and leader of the skinheads' and fascists' favourite heavy metal band, Korrozya Metalla ('Metal Corrosion'). He is forty-one.

He was eighteen in 1984 when he was refused admission to college just because he had long hair. So he founded the band, although it was the worst time for the then underground rock scene, because Yuri Andropov was in power in the USSR, the former head of the KGB, who fortunately died thirteen months after his coronation.

Pauk's mother is a dentist and his father is a professor of philosophy.

'Doesn't it bother them that their son is a fascist?' I ask.

'What might bother them about that?' he replies with a question, and slurps his coffee noisily.

'In the Soviet Union and in Russia "fascist" has always been the worst insult. Twenty million of your compatriots died at their hands.'

'Even more were killed by the communists, and one-and-a-half million Soviets served in Hitler's army.'

But he's not disgusted by the communists either. He even used to be a member of the National Bolshevik Party (the red fascists), and has played at their meetings, rallies and marches.

He and his band have just come back from a concert tour of Siberia.

'Fourteen days and concerts in eleven cities', he tells me excitedly. 'Boozing until dawn after each performance, then a train, another concert, more boozing, then another train ... On tour we do our best to drink no less than half a litre a day each. Vodka and various local potions. To avoid food poisoning and nervous collapse, and as a pick-me-up. Whores, music and boozing are my whole life. Those are the most beautiful things in it.'

In the mining city of Novokuznetsk they were given two tons of coal in sacks by one of their fans. They sold it on the spot for 5000 roubles.

'And after the concert we hired a luxury bathhouse and five whores', Pauk tells me. 'In Moscow a good prostitute costs 10,000, but in the provinces you can get a top model for the whole night for 800 roubles (£16). Three of them came with us for the next bit of the tour and danced naked on stage at the concerts. They were stars, but we threw them out along the way because we like to have new ones in each city.'

Pauk does a lot of concerts in the provinces, because in the capital he has no chance of performing in a large auditorium. His music is not allowed to be played on the radio or television.

'I even spent two weeks in prison', he complains. 'For our songs. For allegedly stirring up national unrest, inciting racial hatred and violence. Bloody hell! Music is pure abstraction – you can't take it so literally.'

'You sing a song saying blacks should have stakes stuck in their chests. What's abstract about that?'

'That's how they staked vampires. Pure abstraction. It's not as if there are any vampires, is it?'

'Your fans take it literally, then go out and beat up or even murder immigrants and African students.'

'It's not my fault if someone understands me wrong.'

PATRIOTIC ROCK – A PRESIDENTIAL REIGN

'It's terrible in Moscow', says Valery Naumov, who also wants to horrify me. 'In my son's class, out of thirty-four kids seventeen are immigrants, foreigners of non-Slavonic origin. Exactly half the class! When I was at school there was only one of them in my class. Here in Moscow land is more expensive than in London, but they're buying it all up. They burn money in the stoves in their palaces. Our country is dying.'

'I know. Every day 1500 people die in Russia. It's a demographic disaster, but Russian women don't want to give birth because children prevent them from working.'

'The television is enemy number one. And drugs, Pepsi-Cola,

McDonalds . . . And all that pro-Western lack of values, the nastiest side of humanity comes dripping from the screens and stops us from producing offspring. They say that if you want to destroy your enemy, educate his children. And television's educating them to think the only goal in life is money.'

He is talking about the generation of people born in the 1980s, which in Russia is scornfully called 'the Pepsi-Cola generation'.

Valery is the leader of a folk rock group called Ivan Tsarevich, which refers in its songs to the traditions of medieval Russia. For eight years they have been unable to make it into the big time. They perform in leather and chains, bash each other with swords on stage, and their biggest hit is a song called 'Russia, Forwards!' Forward march, for the land, for the faith, for the Urals, for Crimea, although Crimea is in another country now, a fact that many Russians cannot accept. On the other hand, it is impossible not to agree with Valery about Russian television. Whenever possible, it apes Western models, but undoubtedly not the ones concerning standards of information. It has outstripped every other country in the world in devising tasks for the stars of reality shows, who for money lick whipped cream off each other's bums, or eat excrement, carrion or live cockroaches . . .

'It was only when Putin came to reign as president and allowed patriotism that things became easier', says the leader of Ivan Tsarevich.

They have become the annual star of the Slava Rossiya ('Long Live Russia') festival organized by Putin's party, United Russia.

'The more young people listen to our music, the less they'll drink Pepsi-Cola. But it's not succeeding, because the whole of show business in Moscow is terrible shit. If you don't pay big money, you've no chance of getting on the radio or television. Two or three people decide what the nation likes. And the Russki lies on the couch, drinks his beer and loafs about – you can give people like that any bullshit you like.'

OLD CHURCH ROCK – SELF-CENSORSHIP

In Russia, since Soviet times there has been a legal requirement for bands to 'hold text consultation with the ideological organs'. Now they have to do it at the FSB (Federal Security Service) – formerly known as the KGB – post on whose terrain the concert is going to take place.

The shaggies have also had a sort of name change. Nowadays they are called *mazerfakery*.

'Before a concert I collect the song texts from the bands and take them where necessary', Pulia tells me. 'But for performances in public places I ask them to choose songs with no nationalism or incitements to violence, and with no swear words.'

'Punks can't talk without swear words', I worry.

'Tough. "Kill the cop" won't get through either.'

'Pulia' means bullet, missile or cartridge. And that's what she's like. Quick and sharp like a bullet from a revolver, energetic, feisty and keen. Slender and agile, but not weedy. A hippy type aged thirty-plus. She is head of the Holy Princess of Petersburg Youth Culture Centre. The centre is a wooden shed on the construction site for the Church of All Muscovite Saints in the Bibirevo district where Father Sergei, the priest who was once a hippy, is the incumbent.

'Father Sergei knows from his own experience', says Pulia, 'that if young people get involved in poetry, painting and music, it's 100 per cent certain there will also be alcohol and drugs. Without God that's how it's bound to end. I sing songs about that. And about how in our cellar there's now a large shop and a common brothel. And I have a criminal case against me saying that while pretending to conduct cultural activities I was running an illegal business.'

The girl is the lead singer of a group called Southern Cross. She says it plays Old Church Slavonic rock.

ANDREI — A MIGHTY BLOW

The Jerry Rubin club in the cellar of number 62 Leninsky Prospekt is a sacred place for all Moscow's *antifa* – the thinking, radical, but anti-fascist youth. For all Moscow's rebels and fighters for a just cause – human rights, but also freedom for laboratory rabbits, rats and mice. On occasion they have broken into poultry farms, abattoirs and scientific institutes, set the animals free and demolished the labs.

This is where Sid and his band, Tarakany, started their underground career, but now the biggest punk hero is young Pit from the band called Ted Kaczynski.

They occupied this cellar in 1992. Its patron saint is Jerry Rubin, the ideologue and leader of the American hippies and anarchists. It is more of a cultural centre, or rather basement, than a club. Moreover, it's alternative, non-commercial culture, with no security guard, cloakroom or entrance tickets.

'We haven't got a bar either', says Andrei Otis Gonda. 'The anti-fascists don't drink or smoke or take drugs, because if you're going to be radical you have to be active, and that means sober.'

Andrei came to Moscow to study to be a vet in the Soviet era, but in 1995, two months before his diploma, he dropped out of college. He explains to me that veterinary science is a branch of the knowledge that serves to breed animals, which are killed and eaten.

So he has been a janitor, a sales assistant at an all-night shop, a teacher of French, English and PT, a manager, a trainer for karate, aikido and tai-chi, a building contractor and a salesman. Every few months each of his businesses in turn came crashing down. But he got married and had children. To save money he got his meals at the Hare Krishna canteen. He worked beyond his strength, but got into more and more debt. Finally he ended up in hospital suffering from physical exhaustion and a nervous breakdown.

Then they were evicted from their flat. The couple and their two small children lived in a cellar, then a garage, in which Andrei installed a small cast-iron stove. And then the worst thing of all happened. His documents were stolen in the metro.

Every second or third day he spent several hours at police stations, repeating the same script a hundred times over ad nauseam, round and round in circles. Who he was, where he came from, what had happened to his documents, where he lived, with whom, how he made his living, what was happening about his residency . . .

'They usually caught me in the metro', he says. 'They stand there so it's impossible to avoid them, and I'm easy to spot.'

'Why?' I ask stupidly.

'Because I've got a black face.'

'You could pull up your hood.'

'They go for those guys even more. They hunt the stream of people for "niggers", meaning Caucasians, but when a real black face comes along, a black person, they're going to check him for sure. Every time I was threatened with deportation, but I haven't even got the money for a bribe. So they told me to open my bag. For many years I was a salesman. They took what they wanted and told me to get lost. That's normal, but there have been disasters too, when they've taken everything.'

'What sort of products did you have?' I ask.

'Cosmetics or music CDs. Once they robbed me when I'd just been to the wholesaler's. Those goods were everything I had. That was a mighty blow. So I go home . . . My wife's at the door asking about medicine for our son. I was supposed to buy it, and something to eat too, because the fridge is empty. It was the worst day of my life. I wanted to do away with myself, but I didn't have the courage. I spent days on end trudging about the city and got myself into some terrible situations.'

'What were you looking for?'

'Death. And I found this club. I'd never heard of Jerry Rubin before, but I went in, because they were letting people in for free. They were showing a film about Che Guevara.'

He fell in love with the place. For several years he has kept order in the club, and runs karate, aikido and tai-chi classes.

In 2002 he was given Russian citizenship.

'And as soon as I had the documents in my hand, the cops immediately stopped checking me.'

They're a very odd couple, a bit like a young version of Laurel and Hardy. The small thin one is twenty-seven and has a very swarthy face, and the big fat one is twenty-nine with size forty-nine feet, and is extremely freckly and ginger-haired. The first is a Georgian from Sukhumi in Abkhazia, and the second is a Jew from Donetsk in Ukraine. Midget – otherwise known as Zurab Sharabidze – is a rapper, and Iceman – real name Sasha Wiseman – is the director (so they say), head of the artist's one-man staff, his manager.

'As a Jew I've got commerce and diplomacy in my blood', he jokes in a booming voice. 'I do a superb job as a creativist . . .'

'A creator', I say, correcting him.

'A creator is for fashion, but I think up strategies, I devise plans and initiate things.'

It was the devil of a job for me to understand the latest strategy he had devised. It was more or less that Stim, a rapper from the rival hip-hop stable of a big star called Seryoga, had not paid him back the money for some bling Iceman had had made for him at a jeweller's. A piece of bling hanging on a thick gold chain is a musician's decoration and trademark, something no rapper can do without. Finally Iceman caught up with Stim and demanded the money, and Stim gave him back the bling. An opportunity like that is too good to miss. Iceman immediately told the whole story in an interview for a very popular online music journal.

'A rapper is a great authority for his fans', he says. 'The kids listen to him and copy him, and I ruined his image. The fact that he did the dirty on me is no big deal – the problem is he gave back the bling! A rapper who loses his bling, it's like he lost his balls, lost his honour. But he didn't feel it like that at all. You know why?'

'Well?'

''Cos he shaves his legs.'

'What?'

'A rapper who shaves his legs! A man! I told them about that on the Internet too.'

'Sasha, I don't get – is that some sort of metaphor?'

'No! He really does shave his legs!' Iceman is bursting with laughter. 'How can a man shave his legs? Especially a rapper. I saw it with my own eyes, because I once worked with Stim and Seryoga. We used to be mates, but now they're threatening me. They said that if I show up at the club now, they'll beat me up. I'm no match for Seryoga. I don't have his sort of fame or money, or even the same physical parameters. He used to be a boxer and he's always pumping iron.'

'You do it for the marketing', I realize.

'Yes, rap thrives on conflict. And everyone will write about a war, some aggro or a fight. Those two can only lose, and I'll gain, even if they kill me. I'll be a hero. They'll write songs about me. Midget will for sure.'

He is wasting his breath, because in any case he knows he's not cut out to be a hero. He could have been one long ago – in Donetsk he fell foul of the local gangsters, but he ran away from the place and left the country.

He had a hundred dollars when he arrived in Moscow in 1999.

When the money ran out, he ended up on the street. He starved. For six months he lived in a stairwell. He was given food by a Georgian guy from the top floor. That was how he met Midget, who dragged him off to his job at a car wash. There they made some money together and got into rap.

'If only for some peace and quiet', says Iceman. 'But with my ginger nut and size it's tricky. Every time I go somewhere, to the cinema with a girlfriend for instance, it always ends in a fight. And they're always from the Caucasus. They insult the girl, they provoke me and shout abuse. They always behave incorrectly. I've had enough of it. I can't stand Caucasians.'

'Sasha, for pity's sake', I respond, 'Midget is from the Caucasus. He's right here with us.'

'But he's different. And the Georgians are the most correct, intelligent people in the Caucasus.'

'I know why that is', puts in Midget. 'In our country all the bandits and people the militia are after end up in Moscow. It's a city with many opportunities. For them too.'

Midget's family had seven dollars when they arrived here. As Georgians they had to escape from the breakaway region of Abkhazia. They chose the country that helped the Abkhazians to drive them out of their own home.

MAZHORY RAP — PASSION AVENUE

Last year Iceman was given Russian citizenship, but as a Georgian Midget has no chance of getting it. Every six months he has to buy a residency certificate on the black market for 10,000 roubles (£200). Other foreigners only pay a thousand.

We drive through the city in Iceman's fabulous old Lincoln, collecting lads for the *strelka* – scrap, row, organized fight or settling of scores. Other cars join us. At midnight we're outside the Zhara club (meaning heat) on Strastnoy Bulvar – 'Passion Avenue'. This is a very expensive, swanky place with a screening policy for hip-hop *mazhory* – the bourgeois youth.

Iceman distributes women's colour magazines to the lads. If they are rolled up very tight, they make an effective, painful blunt weapon with the power of a wooden baton, but without causing bloodshed. This is the Donetsk bandits' favourite inheritance from the Soviet *Spetsnaz* – the special military forces that were subordinate to the KGB.

Iceman and Midget's friends don't look like hooligans from the suburban districts. They are failed clones of New York dudes, plastic *mazhory*, the spoiled little sons of oligarchs in posh hip-hop clothing. Midget's fans.

It's they who set the musical fashions in Moscow, because only they can afford frequent outings to the fiendishly expensive clubs. Tidied-up *mazhory* rap, also known as club rap, is the top favourite now, and its pop, dance variety, R'n'B.

As we wait for Seryoga and Stim's brigade, our teeth chattering with the cold, I tell them how there was supposed to have been an artificial sun shining above Moscow and keeping it warm by the end of the past millennium.

The authors of *Report from the Twenty-First Century*, who died in the 1970s, wrote their book on the basis of conversations with scholars from the USSR Academy of Sciences. There the idea was born of using several enormous mirrors to send electromagnetic waves upwards. Twenty or thirty kilometres above the ground, where the rays crossed, the artificial sun made of heated nitrogen and oxygen molecules would shine forth.

It would have been visible all round the clock, but without harm to the health of Moscow's residents, because by that time medicine was meant to have solved the problem of tiredness pharmacologically. It would be possible to work without resting; Moscow would also be a friendly, affluent metropolis of five million people, with no cars (there would be a ban on driving into the city) and no snow on the electrically heated streets. In the 1950s the scientists estimated that as much fuel was used to clear the snow from Russia's streets as for the entire harvest.

After an hour of waiting, Iceman and Midget's enemies are obviously not going to turn up. The lads invite me into the club, but I have vowed never to go into a place where they have a screening policy (in Russian it's called *fizkontrol*).

'They have to judge if you're suitably dressed and if you can buy something at the bar.'

'If I had a hand missing or were hunchbacked, disabled, they wouldn't let me in', I say angrily. 'Shitbag rappers! Why do you agree to that? That's worse than racism.'

'But what would happen if they let in badly dressed, stinking people or cripples?' Iceman comes to the defence. 'This is a place to be happy. It wouldn't be much fun for me to dance next to a cripple.'

'But they let in midgets', notes Midget.

'Midgets are all right.'

'Cripples look sad, but if they were happy like that, well then ...'

Next day the Internet was buzzing with the news that Seryoga and Stim had chickened out. Two days later, when Iceman and Midget were on their way home at night, five masked men were waiting for them at their door. Four of them beat the lads up badly, while a fifth filmed the incident. In the morning the film was on the Internet.

Three weeks later, before leaving for Siberia, I visited Midget in hospital.

'Moscow is the best city to bounce back, make up for your losses, build a career and make money', whispered the young Georgian from under his bandages. 'It's a beautiful city. I love it. Because it teaches me life, it feeds me and sometimes it punishes me. I love Moscow more than all those nationalists do. I never drop litter in the street in Moscow. I love it so much!'

And now let us move into the distant future and walk across a Moscow street in the twenty-first century. Can you smell how clean the air is, as if scented with the aroma of meadows and forests? The reason for that is not just the large number of parks and squares. We are on the Moscow River embankment. Look, you can count all the stones on the bottom. Small shoals of gold and silver fish weave their way among the water plants. No dirty sewage is channelled into the river any more. Instead it is purified on the spot. Every kind of residue is exploited for a suitable purpose, and only clean water, previously enriched with oxygen, then flows into the river.

Report from the Twenty-First Century, 1957.

Rinat in his front yard in Ufa.

Minefields

In the underpass there's a condom vending machine. 'For people who want to live', says the sign on it. There's also a small card stuck to it reading: 'Out of stock'.

'Here in Russia they say AIDS is a death sentence.' Masha raises her eyebrows as if she were surprised. 'But it saved my life. I even have a child because of it, and a husband. I will never cease to be amazed he wanted an awful drug addict like me with HIV.'

'He just fell in love', I say, as if I'm an expert. 'What's really strange is that you don't use condoms. For him that's an *incredible* risk, which they reduce by 90 per cent.'

'He insists on not using them. I myself have no idea why.'

'Because guys can't stand using condoms. But to that extent?'

'Why can't they stand them?' asks twenty-five-year-old Masha.

'Because it's the same sort of crap as decaffeinated coffee or alcohol-free beer. You're sort of drinking, but it doesn't give you a kick.'

Twenty, thirty and forty-something years old. A Jewish woman, a Tatar, and a Russian. A drug addict, a gay and an alcoholic. Worker, farmer and intellectual backgrounds. Orthodox, Muslim and atheist. False, gold and black teeth. Everything about them is different. Except for the fact that all three live in Ufa, in the Republic of Bashkiria, on the eastern edge of Europe.

And they all have a certain virus, which consumes CD4 lymphocytes. It is weak, so it dies very quickly outside the organism. It cannot even survive a warm shower, but somehow Masha, Rinat and Sergei all contracted it.

LIFE THE FIRST TIME AROUND

Masha's mother was a geography teacher and her father wrote and performed folk songs. So one parent used to take her to the mountains, and the other to festivals – always separately, because they were divorced. She was the best pupil at her school.

I would never have believed Rinat's parents were collective-farm workers. He's very handsome with a dark face, tall, lean and slender. Masculine even, you could say, if not for certain gestures. He drops his hand onto his hip, or props up his chin in a particular way. He has beautiful, long hands, one long fingernail and six rings. And about six gold teeth at the front.

Sergei's parents were workers. When he was in the fifth year, they bought him a guitar.

'Workers in the Soviet Union understood their children's needs', he says with total sincerity. 'They wanted me to be an artist, and the school helped the leading social class with that sort of thing. In the USSR anything was possible. I finished music school and got into the conservatory. I had enormous potential and a fine career ahead of me. But in the evenings I used to listen to rock music with my friends.

Half the performers took drugs, but we loved them and we wanted to be like Jim Morrison or Jimi Hendrix too. We were sure the authorities were cheating us out of drugs. They begrudged us, they were mean, like with everything. Like with jeans, Coca-Cola, trips to the West and music too.'

So they started smoking *anasha* – that's what they call marijuana in Russia. At once they realized that the authorities were refusing to give them a high, but wanted to keep it all for themselves.

'Because drugs give happiness', says Sergei. 'And that's the last thing they wanted to give us.'

In the late 1980s the Soviet Union was already heading for its collapse. Everything was regulated. Even vodka, and happiness most of all.

DEATH THE FIRST TIME AROUND

In a chapter entitled 'The battle for life and well-being' a Soviet professor explains to the authors of the *Report from the Twenty-First Century* that in the new century all illnesses will be conquered for good and all, including cancer, mental illnesses, heart and vascular diseases, just as tuberculosis had been entirely eradicated.

Now we're in the twenty-first century, and Russia's hospitals are bursting at the seams. In Irkutsk, to enter a swimming pool you have to have a certificate proving that you are healthy, or go through a medical consulting room between the changing room and the showers, where the doctor decides who may enter the water.

In 1957 the world had no idea of the existence of human immunodeficiency virus (HIV), although it must already have passed from the grey mangabey monkey to human beings. It never occurred to anyone that the twenty-first century would have its own plague, but of course there were prostitutes and drug addicts then too.

Nowadays in Russia about four million people take drugs as an addiction, the vast majority of them intravenously. At least the same number again are alcoholics. And in Moscow alone paid sexual services are provided by one hundred thousand women.

SERGEI – THE DRAMATIC TENOR

Sergei Yevdokimov studied at the conservatory, while also working at the Opera and Ballet Theatre in Ufa. He was the best dramatic tenor in the company, but he was taking more and more, harder and harder drugs. That ruined him financially, so when he happened to spot a briefcase belonging to the theatre cashier filled with cash to pay the entire company, he took advantage of the opportunity.

'I had lost my mind', he tells me, 'because the cravings made me shake like a paralytic. I went and sat in the theatre restaurant, because for a couple of days I hadn't had the money for a proper meal either, and that was where the manhunt organized by my colleagues from the ballet caught up with me. But I escaped before the militia arrived, and boarded the first train heading for Siberia.'

At Abakan in Krasnoyarsk Krai he started working at the local philharmonic. They were in need of tenors. He did extremely well, because he didn't know where to buy drugs. So he drank himself unconscious for a year, and once he got to know the terrain, he went back to heroin. Of course he knew that AIDS was raging in this city, as in all of Russia, but he didn't worry about that at all. Sometimes at a party a single needle and syringe did the rounds of several dozen people.

Sergei took drugs so intensively that he bungled several concerts and was fired from his job. He went back to Ufa and was immediately arrested. He spent three months in custody, and then got a suspended sentence of several years in prison for theft.

'Did you have a family?' I ask him.

'Yes. A wife and children, but I lost them. More than one family, more than one wife and lots of children. When I was in Abakan I received a document from my first wife saying that she was divorcing me. I started a family there too, but when it all fell apart and I went back to Ufa, there was another woman too.'

'You were extremely amorous.'

'What sort of love is that?' Sergei claps his hand against his brow. 'What room was there in all that for emotions? I only lived for drugs. But to do that you need a victim. To deceive and exploit, in order to have a flat, food, sex, protection and money for drugs. And unfortunately I was an excellent psychologist, added to which there were the superb acting skills I learned at the conservatory. I knew how to start crying, get angry or take offence to order. Neither work, nor love, my wife or children mattered – just taking drugs. I was getting older, but I wasn't growing up. Spiritually I was a teenager in the body of a forty-year-old man.'

'Did your third partner leave you too?'

'Yes. She was an older woman, with grandchildren already, but she had a flat, lots of valuable things and money. I only had to make her fall in love with me, and with older, single women that's not so hard to do. I'm a very good lover. That's how I kept all those women hooked on me, and got myself stuck with another addiction, to sex, to regular intercourse several times a day. Finally, even my older partner threw me out and I ended up on the street. I lived in cellars and stair-wells and on allotments. I became a terrible tramp. I slept on bits of cardboard and fed on garbage, so I got covered in filth and stank like dog shit. I used to rob holiday cottages, cars, the few friends who still let me into their homes, and my parents, because a mother will always take pity and open the door. You can even steal something to sell from a drinking dive.'

RINAT — ONLY WITH STEADY PARTNERS

Rinat Shamilov is a Tatar. He is thirty-five. When he was in the ninth class he discovered he was gay. He was sixteen. He finished school and immediately ran away from the family collective-farm village to Ufa, because in the big city it was easier to find a partner and hide your preferences from the world. The Soviet Union was on the wane, but there was still an article in the penal code that stipulated a prison sentence for homosexual intercourse.

'Did you use condoms?' I ask subtly.

'Yes, usually. I only didn't with steady partners.'

'But you weren't their steady or only partner.'

'I know', he says gloomily. 'Between men sex is the only thing that matters, but I needed more than that. That is definitely why I got married ten years ago. I can't explain how it happened, but I fell in love with her, and she with me. She knew who I was. She is my first and only woman. Our relationship is very strong and we have two children.'

MASHA — SCOT-FREE, SAFE AND RICH

She started taking drugs twelve years ago. She was thirteen, and Larissa, her friend from the same block, was four years older. Larissa's mother was a drug dealer, so the girl used to pinch her wares from a hiding place and hand them out in the yard. The kids used to play at being drug addicts. They weren't able to inject themselves with heroin, so they used to drink it.

'We kept playing that game, and every single one of us got hooked', says Masha Pavlushenko gloomily. 'I was a sweet little rosebud of fourteen, top of the eighth class at an elite school specializing in the performing arts, a young poet and dancer in a folk song-and-dance band, and at the same time I was whacking deadly unpurified heroin into my veins. By then I knew how to shoot up. Before I got to the tenth class I was at the bottom, and had started dealing myself. The only reason they didn't expel me from school was that my mother was a teacher.'

Masha never had any problems with the militia. She paid them, so they gave her protection. In the entire post-Soviet world of legal and illegal business, you pay the mafia for protection, but it's more often the so-called power structures – the militia or one of the state-run special services. A busker or a tramp pays a few hundred roubles to the local beat cop, and Gazprom gives financial support to the election campaigns of candidates from the FSB.

There were even occasions when the militiamen were Masha's suppliers, giving her drugs to sell that they had taken off other dealers. They split the income fifty-fifty.

'Jesus Christ! They were getting cash for drugs from fifteen- or sixteen-year-old kids.'

'Right', says Masha. 'In the late 1990s in a single day I used to earn about five thousand roubles (£100). Two thousand were for them, 2000 for new wares, and there was 1000 left for me. That was an awful lot for a sixteen-year-old girl.'

'And for a cop?'

'For them too. A department head earns 22,000 roubles a month.'

'They don't pay them much. A driver on the Moscow metro gets 30,000 (£600), and a girl at McDonalds gets 12,000.'

'As a teacher my mother earns 7648 roubles a month', says Masha. 'Ordinary operational militiamen get 10,000 more.'

'And they weren't afraid to do business with such a child?'

'What was there to be afraid of? If I'd spilled the beans they'd have locked me up or done me in. After that I no longer did the selling myself. I had a team who worked for me. The militia gave them protection too on my account – I paid for each of them, and if one of them trod on my toes by not paying for the wares, I shopped him to the militia and he ended up in the nick. There were even better tricks with the suppliers. They gave drugs on credit, so sometimes I ran up an enormous debt, as much as a hundred or two hundred thousand roubles (£2000, £4000), so I'd set my cops on them. I wasn't worried about getting supplies because the place of one dealer was immediately taken by another one.'

'Bloody risky', I say. 'They might have slaughtered you.'

'There wasn't much risk. How is a stupid Tajik from the other end of the world going to know who grassed him up when he's got several customers? All the militiamen knew me, but who the hell's he? The cops sometimes have to show a result too, so I used to give them this or that. A Tajik like that, in fact, an Azeri, a black Asian, a foreigner. I was scot-free, safe and rich, and I had as much dope as my heart desired. The only thing that agonized me was my mum's suffering.'

She threw her daughter out of the house. She said: 'Get out!' and wouldn't open the door to her, not even when Masha just came to wash her hair. She reported her daughter dozens of times and tried to hand her over to the militia, but they explained to her that they couldn't do anything because Masha wasn't eighteen and was still going to school.

'That wasn't true of course', the girl weeps. 'But how was my poor mum to know? They made awful fun of her. All her love, respect, home and family lay in ruins . . . I had shat on it all. I ended up all alone, because in a drug addict's life there's no such thing as friends. I couldn't trust the militia an inch either. It's a terrible life. Such terrible emptiness. You stand before the mirror and you see a living corpse. Enormous eyes, sunken cheeks, skin white as paper. On top of that dry, knobbly knees, ribs and collarbone sticking out, sagging breasts. A terrible sight. The worst thing were the eyes. Large, blue eyes with little black dots instead of pupils. But what hurt most was my soul.'

Masha whimpered for mercy outside her mother's door and begged to be rescued. Earlier on, with the help of Masha's grandmother, who is a doctor, her mother had given her detox treatment at home. The girl was terrified of going to a hospital, because there they would have registered her for life on the militia list of drug addicts, and that would mean she could forget her dream of studying law once and for all. So Masha's mother sold her grandfather's garage and paid for her daughter's stay in hospital, because in that case you could be treated anonymously.

DEATH THE SECOND TIME AROUND

The first case of a USSR citizen with acquired immune deficiency syndrome (AIDS) was registered in 1987. He was a homosexual working as a military interpreter in Africa. The first Russian AIDS victim died the next year. The Russian to have carried the HIV virus the longest is sixty-year-old Kola Pinchenko from Saint Petersburg, who was infected in 1981.

The pandemic has been spreading freely and very rapidly, mainly via the shared needles and syringes traditional among Russian drug addicts. Research shows that 83 per cent of drug addicts used to share needles on a daily basis.

The epidemic peaked in 2001, when 87,000 new cases of infection were officially registered. World-wide, Russia is known as the second Africa; some say it will be swept from the face of the earth, and that in the twenty-first century it will die of this plague in the course of a few decades. But since 2006 financing for the fight against AIDS from state and international funds has grown from five million to 150 million dollars, and the situation has stabilized at a level of about 40,000 registered new cases of infection with HIV per year.

Nowadays the situation appears to be worst in the places the virus reached the earliest, before anything was known about it or was done about it. These are Samara, Irkutsk, Orenburg, Saint Petersburg and the Kaliningrad district on the Polish border.

The least serious situation prevails in the poor, neglected regions, because few people can afford drugs there.

Out of poverty people in Russia drink vodka.

SERGEI — MINDLESS WOMEN

The Russian drug addict will do anything to avoid ending up on the militia's list of addicts, because otherwise he can be deprived of parental rights. He almost automatically loses his job too, if he is employed in education, the health service, the state administration, the army or the militia. Professional drivers have their driving licences taken away, and it is a known fact that a huge percentage of taxi drivers take drugs and often deal in them too.

Sergei was not afraid, as Masha was, of ending up on the militia's list, because he had featured on it for years, ever since he stole the case full of money for the opera and ballet artistes. Roughly once a year he would appear at the hospital for detox treatment. They'd patch him up, feed him and let him sleep in fairly clean bedding. There in 2000 he found out he was HIV-positive.

'I wasn't shocked at all', he says, pulling a face. 'Of course I may have caught it through sexual intercourse, but drug addicts get it intravenously, from dirty needles and syringes. From then on I took even more drugs, as if I wanted to bring on my own death faster.'

'Did you want to kill yourself?'

'I thought about suicide, but I didn't have the courage to do it with my own hands. I was afraid. All I had left of my entire humanity was the self-preservation instinct.'

'It actually is an animal's strongest instinct.'

'You can see for yourself. I didn't even have the strength to kill myself, so I was glad an illness had come along that would do it for me. Jesus! How I hated myself! How sick I was of this shitty life. The only way out was to dope myself to death. Or wait until I died of AIDS, hepatitis, cirrhosis of the liver – the booze would kill me, or another junkie whose stash I'd steal. So everything was as before – there were even times when some old woman still fell for me and let me into her home. I didn't hide the fact that I was HIV-positive, but they'd say never mind, infect me, and we'll be together for the rest of our lives. They asked me to infect them! I had several of these mindless women. They just closed their eyes and followed me, like going to their own death, like entering a minefield.'

For two years he rampages about the minefield and ends up in the detoxification ward at a clinic for HIV carriers, but the drug dealers even get in there. There's also plenty of vodka.

The senior registrar closes his eyes to it all, and organizes major booze-ups himself every few days, at which he chats up the female patients and sleeps with them in exchange for vodka and drugs. At one of these parties Sergei overdoes it with a mixture of alcohol and drugs, and ends up in intensive care.

There some people from a Narcotics Anonymous group come to see him. One of them is the head of a gangster outfit, whom Sergei knows from prison.

'I thought I'd go to them, because it couldn't be worse than it already was. I ended up at a rehabilitation centre where former junkies follow the Narcotics Anonymous twelve-step programme.'

From their research it appears that half the Russian addicts who find out they are HIV-positive stop taking drugs. The alcoholics come out not much worse.

RINAT — A NASTY BITCH

'Were you infected by a partner?' I ask Rinat.

'No. By a doctor.'

'Your partner was a doctor?'

'That's a good one! Not by, but at a doctor's.'

'That's what all homosexuals say', I reply, 'to make it sound as if they are not responsible for AIDS along with the drug addicts and prostitutes — it used to be called "the gay plague".'

A few months after his wedding Rinat came down with stomach ulcers. He had to have a gastroscopy, an unpleasant procedure involving sticking a thick tube with a camera at one end down the digestive tract. He had to have an HIV test to be admitted for the procedure.

Six months later he had to have another gastroscopy, but by then he already had the virus.

'Jacek', shouts Rinat, 'I didn't even sleep with my wife in that period! She was pregnant, but she was finding it very hard, so we didn't make love to avoid causing complications. And I was faithful to her. My son was born on 12 February 1998, and the next day they gave me the diagnosis. The doctor at the AIDS clinic said I would live about another three years. She frightened me just for the fun of it.'

'Maybe she doesn't like gays.'

'I didn't tell her I was one.'

'Sorry, Rinat, but it's plain to see.'

'If you have an expert eye. Nasty bitch! She told me to go and find a plot at the cemetery.'

Once he had pulled himself together, he went back to the hospital where they had performed the procedure. He wanted them to check who had had a stomach test before him. That person might not know he was a carrier. The specific feature of AIDS is that people live for years without knowing they have the virus, and in the meantime they infect others.

At the hospital they told Rinat they'd had a computer failure and the data hadn't been saved. Just for that day.

'That's typical of our health service', he says. 'They never admit to making mistakes. In Voronezh, 215 people were given preparations made from infected blood. In my carriers' support group there's a girl who became HIV-positive after a blood transfusion. There are endless cases where they haven't tested the donors' blood, and in our country the main donors are tramps and homeless alcoholics who do it for the money.'

'Why don't they test it?'

'Why on earth spend the money on testing when you can steal it and say it was tested? Before my friend's operation we sought donors ourselves within the family and among friends, and we had them tested at our own cost, because otherwise he'd have been given suspect blood.'

'Don't you have voluntary blood donors?'

'A tiny group of old people brought up in the USSR. In those days to give blood for your neighbour was an honour. In today's Russia people are proud of their money.'

MASHA — DREAM NO. 2

She stopped taking drugs in December 2000, and in the spring it turned out she was sick with hepatitis B, the kind that spreads the same way as AIDS, via blood or sexual intercourse.

At the hospital they took a blood sample, and she turned out to be HIV-positive too. The doctor who filled in her form asked if she was a drug addict, or maybe a prostitute. She realized that ordinary people don't fall sick with this. She was eighteen years old and she had thrown her life away.

For days on end she sat on a bench outside her mother's house and cried. More and more often, a neighbour from the next staircase came and sat with her. He was ten years older. He said it broke his heart to see her crying. She was so small and thin, with very short hair, like a boy. He decided that this child wasn't going to cry any more. He persuaded her to sign up for law studies. If she couldn't be the new Okudzhava — he was a famous singer — why not realize her dream number two to work as a police detective?

He even went fifty-fifty with Masha's mother to pay for her studies, and a year later he asked the girl to marry him.

They were married on 20 December 2002.

'I desperately wanted to live', Masha tells me. 'I wanted to have a son with him, a wonderful, strong Ukrainian boy like him. So we tried, and I spent the whole of Christmas puking into the loo.'

'You were pregnant? After four days . . .'

'The Orthodox Christmas! In January.'

'Is your husband HIV-positive too?' I ask.

'No.'

'Then how did you do it? You have to have artificial insemination! Is he suicidal, or what?'

'I asked him that too, and he said yes, he must be suicidal', she says, laughing nervously. 'He didn't want to do it artificially, into a jar, using tubes . . . He said he wasn't afraid, and then, as we'd done it like that once, why not always? We don't take precautions.'

'Have you infected him?'

'No. The whole time he's had a negative result, and we've been carrying on like that for five years now. Our son is four. Only later did I find out that you have to prepare yourself for pregnancy, because the risk of infecting the child is 30 per cent, but if the level of the virus drops, it falls to 2 per cent. But our son is healthy.'

LIFE THE SECOND TIME AROUND

The risk of being infected with HIV through vaginal sex with a positive partner is one in 2000 for men, and one in 600 for women. Through anal sex the active partner has a one in 125 chance, and the passive partner one in thirty. The risk of being infected by a dirty needle is one in fifteen.

The only opponent of the anti-AIDS campaign in Russia is the Orthodox Church. It protests against programmes to exchange used needles and syringes for clean ones. The Church believes that by telling young people about condoms you increase the danger of an epidemic, because by doing this you are encouraging them to practise un-restrained sex.

In the view of the Orthodox clergy, AIDS is a punishment sent down on homosexuals, drug addicts and prostitutes for their sins.

Nowadays in Russia there are 450,000 registered carriers, but the authorities estimate that there are actually about a million. Three-quarters of them are drug addicts who were infected by a needle or a syringe, but most new cases are people who were infected through sexual intercourse.

UNAIDS, the United Nations anti-AIDS programme, estimates more realistically that the percentage of the population living with HIV in Russia is more than 2 per cent, and thus almost three million people. Russian non-governmental organizations were already talking of four million in 2005. Thirty per cent of them were or are currently in prison. The penal institutions are rife with terrible drug addiction. At the prison camps located in Siberia every third prisoner is HIV-positive.

SERGEI — COME INSIDE!

He hasn't taken drugs for five years now, nor does he drink. He has just stopped having anti-virus therapy to help heal his liver, which has taken a battering from hepatitis, drugs and alcohol. The state of his liver worries him more than the HIV, but one therapy interferes with the other.

He still goes to Narcotics Anonymous and Alcoholics Anonymous group meetings, because he has had both problems. It was at Alcoholics Anonymous that he met the beautiful Larissa, a forty-year-old divorcee whose husband took away their only child because she was drinking. From then on she drank even more, and chose Sergei to save her.

'We have a principle', explains the former junkie, 'that if a friend needs help, you can't refuse. That's our philosophy. She wanted me to stay the night with her, because she only starts drinking at night and goes off on a bender, but I knew that if I stayed over, I simply wouldn't be able to resist. Such a beauty! I didn't want to exploit another woman who'd been ill-treated by fate. So I said no, because she had a nice flat, some income and a rich fiancé. But she preferred a former addict and criminal with HIV, hepatitis and heroin-blackened teeth. The first time we kissed was after a year.'

Sergei works at a non-governmental anti-AIDS organization. His workplace is the street, and his task is to find and stay in touch with active drug addicts.

'Do you hand out needles and syringes?'

'We're not allowed to', he says. 'They hand them out in all the neighbouring provinces, but the authorities in our republic reckon it's an encouragement to take drugs. They even refuse to allow us to exchange used syringes, though that would be a guarantee that an addict is going to shoot up safely, and won't throw the needle into a sandpit where a child will find it.'

'So what do you do with them?'

'I tell them the awful story of my life. I show them that if you stop taking drugs, you get a home, a job, a family, a wife.'

'Did you marry Larissa?' I ask.

'Yes.'

'That's your fourth wife now. Did she have the virus?'

'No. We took precautions. Condoms', says Sergei, ruffling his hair sheepishly. 'For the first year. Then we started using a method without condoms, but I didn't come inside her.'

'You withdrew?'

'Yes, and I ejaculated on her belly.'

'Christ – you must have known the virus isn't just in the semen, but also in the seminal fluid.'

'Sure, but I had this illusion that if I didn't come, then . . .' I can see he's about to explode. 'Fucking hell. Don't torture me! It was she who begged me to come inside her! Get it? I was forty years old and I was in love for the first time in my life. And after two years she was a carrier too. Last year . . .'

'You infected the woman you love!'

'She wanted to have the illness. Because I had it.'

'What sort of crap is that?'

'It's not crap. You completely fail to understand Russian women. For the man they love they'll go to the ends of the earth and even to their death. In our country that's normal. They love being devoted, making a sacrifice of themselves! I've met dozens of women like that!'

Knowing he was the carrier of a fatal illness made Rinat feel power-less against nature. He no longer had the strength to deny his gay side. Now, apart from his wife and two children, he has a regular partner whom he sees once a week.

'Because that's the way I am. Fuck it, that's how I was born! And I don't hide the fact that I'm HIV-positive. And sex is only with condoms. No question.'

He works on the side as a hairdresser. He goes to his clients' homes or receives them at his place. He adores this job, because he can chatter away endlessly. And if that's not enough, he does a shift at the AIDS clinic, where people find out they have the virus. Several people in their city have committed suicide on hearing this news. Rinat explains to the carriers that it is possible to live with it and that it isn't a death sentence.

Like Sergei, he also works on the street, but with the so-called *kaserki*. Russians love new, foreign-sounding words, so they have even invented a more original one for prostitutes. *Kaserki* is an abbreviation of the words *kamercheskiye seks rabotnitsy*, which means 'private-sector sex workers'.

'The street girls', he explains, 'are almost 100 per cent intravenous drug users working to earn the money for their next fix. I'm sure almost all of them are HIV-positive, but they couldn't care less. They never get tested. They say they use the condoms I hand out to them, but I don't know if that's true. Maybe if the client wants to, but everyone prefers to go without. It's a known fact. Their clients are the dregs of society, brainless oafs who can only afford the lowest kind of prostitute for 150, 200 roubles (£3-4). Most of them have wives, and that's how the virus spreads.'

Rinat is apparently the only AIDS-related social worker in Russia to be working in the gay community. He often visits the *pleshka* – the pick-up area where gays too seek opportunities for quick sex with a one-time partner. Here he has had his greatest success, because when he started working with them in spring 2007, hardly anyone used condoms, but now most of them don't forget to, though they refuse to be tested. Men are cowards, they'd rather not know. That is why 75 per cent of the registered carriers in Russia are women. In Europe it is exactly half.

MASHA – THE BIGGEST TURF

In Russia, drug dealers usually set up their sales points in the stairwells near pharmacies. Each one has two or three needles. The customers either get take-aways or shoot up on the spot. Then the dealer wipes the needle on his trousers and hands it to the next one.

Anyone could get a supply of needles at the pharmacy, but that involves serious risk. There are often uniformed militiamen hanging about outside, and inside, worse yet, there might be some of their plain-clothes friends. You have to show your ID, explain yourself, and then pay them to let you go. If you haven't got any money, they'll lock you up for forty-eight hours to establish your personal details, or for being in a state indicating drug-taking.

Masha knows dozens of these places in Ufa, so after her student training at the militia, the heads of the department that fights against drug dealing offered her a permanent job. They needed an expert who knew almost everything about the world of drug addicts and dealers. They weren't at all bothered by the fact that she herself had belonged to it, as they were perfectly aware.

'I wanted to lock up all the dealers who'd made me waste my youth', says Masha, 'but I soon realized there isn't any fight against drugs! Quite the opposite. The militiamen cultivate the drug dealing themselves and milk cash out of it. When I was a dealer I used to pay them too, but only now did I see that it works like a business. For example, in the gypsies' yard, where for years there has been the biggest drug-dealing turf in Ufa, first thing the local cop comes along and takes 500 roubles (£10) from each dealer. Then off he goes and doesn't show up again that day. After him come my colleagues from the anti-drugs unit.'

'And they also get 500 each?'

'A thousand each. And they're gone. You won't see them here again that day either. Finally, along come the guys from Gosnarkokontrol – state drugs control. They're not militiamen, but a major power structure set up within the Ministry of Internal Affairs specially to fight drugs. They take a thousand each too. I've seen it with my own eyes. I held out for a year and a half, then asked the commander to let me go. Of course I didn't tell him what I've told you.'

'Why not?' I ask.

'He knows it all anyway. They all know. It happens quite openly.'

Now Masha is struggling to train as a lawyer and lives like anyone else. No medicines, psychotherapy, support groups or meetings . . . She has a normal sex life, eats whatever she fancies, has the occasional drink and when necessary stays up late. She even takes antibiotics when she falls sick, although they are terribly bad for the immunity.

'And I go hiking in the mountains and to the caves again', she says. 'I go climbing, I ski, ride a motorbike and go parachuting. My husband's the reverse – he loves his home, peace and quiet. He cooks, cleans, and sings lullabies to our son. And a month ago we had the child christened.'

'How come? You're Jewish, aren't you?'

'No, I'm Orthodox. Larissa is the godmother – that's the girl who used to give drugs to the children in our yard. We met up again. Now she's my only female friend. She's given up drugs too and she's HIV-positive too. Possibly she caught it from me. Or I caught it from her.'

By the twenty-first century we shall have conquered most of the illnesses that are still feared today, and we shall have done so radically. In fact the only ones that will not yet have succumbed to a complete cure will be cancer, mental illnesses and cardiovascular diseases . . . But there can be no doubt that in the early twenty-first century they will be no more dangerous that pneumonia is now.

So what will the doctors do then?

I think they will find nothing but preventative medicine, sanitaria and hygiene boring, so they will devise a new, very important task that will never be exhausted: they will take on the perfecting of the healthy human organism.

Report from the Twenty-First Century, 1957.

Sveta and her daughter at her flat in Kazan.

Miss HIV

A CONVERSATION WITH 27-YEAR-OLD
SVETLANA IZAMBAYEVA FROM KAZAN,
RUSSIA'S MISS HIV-POSITIVE

Sveta's mother got drunk and collapsed in the street – it was a fairly typical Soviet birth. Meanwhile in California the worldwide AIDS pandemic was just starting.

Hello, Sveta. I haven't got a cold, sore throat, cough or ear infection, and my teeth are in good shape too.

Thank God, because we have to avoid any kind of infection at all costs. You can get over a cold in a few days, but it takes us two or three weeks. We take a lot of care to keep warm.

Is that why it's so hot in your flat?

No. Getting too hot doesn't do us any good either, but we can't turn down the heating. They were supposed to fit thermostats to the heaters in our block, but they say they can't get them. My husband and I wanted to fit them ourselves, but they said we weren't allowed to put our own ones in.

Then I'll go into the bathroom and take off my long johns, or I'll be too hot. It's way below freezing outside.

And here in the flat it's thirty degrees. We've been longing for them to finally get it done for a whole year now.

So that's Miss Russia's greatest wish?

Not my greatest. What I'd really like to do is to breast-feed my daughter at least once in my life. But I haven't produced any milk for ages. I've dried out my breasts – using medicine. But at the start I had to express it and pour it down the sink. My husband did that, because I couldn't bear to. It broke my heart, and I could see Eva was looking for my breast, grabbing it with her little hands and trying to catch it in her mouth, but I had to dodge and push away my own child to make sure she didn't get a single drop. There's a great deal of HIV in breast milk. I've been bottle-feeding Eva from birth, but I hold her as if she were breast-feeding. Sometimes I undress so she can touch me with her little hands. For me it's very important, necessary and extremely pleasant. Sheer delight. You know what I mean?

I don't, but I envy you like mad. Do you sleep together?

She has her own little bed, but in the morning we hold her between us.

And if her dummy falls out during a walk, can you just lick it and put it back in her mouth?

Better not to.

So it's better not to eat from the same spoon either. Or share an ice cream. But will her father be able to gobble up his daughter's chicken skins?

Not using her fork, just in case, because Ilya is a carrier too. But we have baths together. We have Eva's blood tested frequently, and so far everything's fine. She's seven months old now. In another seven it'll be 100 per cent certain whether or not she has inherited the virus from me. If during pregnancy the woman takes the right precautions according to the recommendations, the risk of infecting the child is about 2 per cent. Without that treatment it rises to 25 per cent, and if at the time of conception or during pregnancy there were drugs, alcohol or nicotine involved, or a generally debauched lifestyle, the risk increases to 50 per cent.

You're very well clued-up on the figures.

It's my job. I have a diploma in economics, but I'm employed as a social worker at our clinic for people with HIV here in Kazan. I run a women's support group. In Tatarstan we have over 8000 registered carriers, three-quarters of whom are women, but a total of twenty come to the meetings, except that never more than six or seven girls meet up at a time. None of them has admitted to being HIV-positive within their own environment. They live in isolation, they have retreated into themselves, or into their families, and the ones who come to the meetings sit there huddled up, with their arms wrapped around their knees. Sex, rape and AIDS are taboo subjects – our women are incapable of talking about them, they are introverted, with-drawn, full of fear. That's why we have separate groups for women and men. To attract them I have employed a professional choreographer. She teaches us to dance and helps us to open our hearts. That gives me a hell of a lot of work to do, and I'm always off on a trip somewhere to teach other people how to set up groups like ours, for men too. I also have a regular programme on the TNT television channel, called 'HIV Emergency Service'.

Is that since 2005 when you were elected Miss HIV-Positive and became the face for the Russian campaign against AIDS?

Yes, that's right. And in my spare time I give people haircuts at their homes.

What for?

To make them look nice. And I love it. A group of people gets together at someone's house, I come along with my little case and I cut their hair. Often it's a whole family, or friends of friends. I get a lot of joy out of seeing how much they like my work. It's a very basic, uncomplicated emotion – instant remuneration for my efforts. And we talk a lot while I'm doing it. I reckon I don't just cut their hair, but also give them psychological help when times are hard. I've been doing it all my life. First in my family village, and when I went away to college, I thrived on all the chat while cutting hair. One day I'll open a hairdressing salon, I'll set it up the right way so it earns money for me, while I spend my time organizing an emergency service for women and children, which will help them to recover their strength after major catastrophes. Rape, violence, emotional exploitation, and what I went through myself. I'll be a coach. I've got the theory already, and right now I'm gaining the practical experience. The misfortune that happened to me has given me a lot of strength. I am very strong.

But the travelling . . .

Awful. I have lots of meetings with women in the zones . . .

Meaning the prison camps, the penal colonies. In Poland people don't know that in Russia prisoners aren't kept in cells, but in wire-fenced camps with huge barracks.

Women too. Thirty per cent of the HIV carriers in our country are former or current prisoners. In the camps almost everyone does drugs. Drugs are several times cheaper in there than on the outside. A single fix costs less than a glass of vodka or a pack of the cheapest cigarettes. It's their only joy, their only pleasure, so they take it, although they all know they might catch the virus, and indeed they do. A huge barrack for a couple of hundred 'zeks' [as Russian prisoners are known], but they have one single needle. I've seen things like that with my own eyes.

How can the guards let something like that happen?

What are you talking about? They're the ones who provide it! Everywhere. They deal in drugs. The administration and the governors know all about it. And they make loads of money out of that business. It's worst of all in Siberia, where one in three prisoners is a carrier. And when he's released, as a parting shot the medical service worker tells him he's got tuberculosis, anaemia and HIV. And that poor, ignorant guy from the Siberian provinces is supposed to get himself cured? How the hell's he going to do that? With honey and herbs?

In Russia there are 450,000 registered HIV carriers, but the authorities estimate that there must be at least twice as many.

In Moscow my husband and I talked to an expert from the federal centre for the fight against AIDS. He admitted that the authorities cover up the true scale of the epidemic.

Why?

Because if they published the real data, there'd be an outburst of panic. According to NGO figures, by 2005 there were already four million carriers. Most of them haven't the faintest idea they are living with HIV.

So how did you find out?

As a competitive athlete I used to have routine tests. I was in training for ballroom dancing and light athletics. I used to run distances of five and ten kilometres.

Let's mention by the way that you have the figure of a long-distance runner, rather than a model or a beauty queen.

I'm 1.67 metres tall and I weight 45 kilos. So I come along for my results, and the doctor tells me straight out I'm HIV-positive and I've got eight or nine years left to live at most.

That's total rubbish.

Quite. He was badly educated, but in 2003 I was twenty-two and I didn't know anything about this illness. I went home, collapsed into bed and didn't get up for six months. I just lay there, howling, and pouring bottle after bottle of valerian drops down my throat. It was grim, nasty, awful, desperate. I wanted to die. My sister Nadyezhda often came by.

Nadyezhda – meaning hope. A good name in this case.

Yes. She sat with me and shared in my suffering. It was very important – otherwise she couldn't have helped me, and here in the provinces there was no-one I could talk to about it. What upset me most was that I would never be a mother. Finally I pulled myself together, went to Moscow and saw that people like me can lead normal lives. They work, make love and have children. Now I know everyone has a very similar reaction to the news that they are infected. Here in Russia it looks as if each person goes through several major stages, just as you have to go through twelve major steps to treat alcoholism. First comes despair, breakdown and resignation. That is the victim stage.

In your case it lasted for six months . . .

Spent lying in bed. We keep wondering: why me and for what sins? Next comes the first steps stage. You get out of bed and look for information. I went all the way to Moscow. Then comes the final stage for most carriers, the acceptance stage. However, some reach a fourth stage – of increasing their potential, when a person realizes that thanks to the virus he has gained a lot. As I have. I have become stronger and I have come to know myself, I have acquired strength and might. That's why I'm such a good coach and people believe me when I tell them how to fight against the stigma, the finger-pointing, rejection and discrimination. Because if a doctor refuses to give a carrier medicine, saying drug addicts aren't entitled to any, we're dealing with discrimination.

At lots of Russian firms infected people are sacked from their jobs. In my view that's discrimination too.

Of course it is. At many private banks and insurance companies the employees have to give blood every six months to be tested for HIV, and those found to be carriers are thrown out on the spot. What's more, that's against the law. The mindset of the arseholes who do that is quite incredible. I spoke to one of these company presidents. Of course he's opposed to discrimination, but he knows that in our country carriers are discriminated against, so he prefers to get rid of them, to be sure no-one will say his bank employs HIV carriers.

Pure schizophrenia.

I have experienced very strong stigmatization in my family village whenever I've been to see my parents. But I've done my best to understand that these are ordinary, simple, ignorant people, and on top of that they're afraid. So I have to explain it all to them, wisely and with strength, tell them Sveta won't infect them, and that I'm the same Sveta as five years ago, who still cuts hair, still helps out and laughs just as before.

So you're a village lass.

Well, from a collective farm. My father is a tractor driver from the village of Shmirsh in the Chuvash Republic. They all know me there, because I used to go round the houses, to the militia station, the little hospital and the local administration cutting people's hair.

Aren't you a Russian?

I'm pure Chuvash. It's a nation that lives west of the Kazan Tatars. I am exactly the same age as the worldwide AIDS epidemic. I was born in 1981, when the first cases of a strange illness were noted in California, and a number of homosexuals died.

That's why the disease was called 'the gay plague'.

And then Acquired Immune Deficiency Syndrome, or AIDS. After my birth, no-one gave me the ghost of a chance of surviving, because I was born three-and-a-half months early. My mother had collapsed.

She was drunk.

How do you know?

What's the usual reason why people keel over in the street in Russia?

Right. There's terrible alcoholism here. I grew up in a world of alcoholics. And in a family of them. My dad drank appallingly. Then there'd be rows, he'd start beating my mum, and I'd get in between them . . . I was the oldest of five siblings. I couldn't deal with the fact that all my male friends, the boys I used to meet, would be just the same – that they were all future alcoholics or drug addicts, because they'd had that sort of childhood too. I even went to see psychologists about it, and straight after school I got out of there. I started college,

had my first great love affair, and then it turned out the boy was . . .
Guess what?

A drunk.

Worse. A drug addict. Only later, thanks to HIV, did I start going out into the world, to Moscow, meeting open-minded people, therapists, former addicts and alcoholics who explained to me what addiction and co-dependency are. I realized that I was a co-dependent alcoholic, and HIV-positive too. I realized that all my relationships were a pathological, frenzied search for the love my drunken family hadn't been able to give me. Because there's no love there, the mothers never hug their children, they don't kiss them or talk to them, they just scream at them and order them about. I realized that in men I had been looking for what I hadn't got from my mother and father as a child. Finally it got through to me that I shouldn't get involved with anyone until I had recovered and become an independent person, free from the searching, free from the sense of emptiness, or of something missing.

Maybe then you'd meet . . .

A good man. In my family both my grandfathers drank, so did my parents . . . There's a sort of drinking tradition that's typical on our collective farms, and in Russia in general. It's a terrible epidemic, a plague of drinking. And after it comes crime and prison. I travel about the camps to visit the girls and I see they are all just like me. From the same sort of families, and they went out looking for love, got into drugs, contracted the virus, and if there are drugs around, sooner or later there'll be prison. Then they fail to give love to their children because they've never experienced it. And it all starts over again.

Do your parents know you're HIV-positive?

My dad never knew. He died in 2003. The worst year of my life. Just after he died I found out I was a carrier. Then my youngest little brother was born. He has infantile paralysis. He can't walk, and as a result of it all my mother drinks even more. My other little brother, aged eight, is still with her too. I brought them to the city, because I fooled myself into thinking that Mum would stop drinking here. She doesn't drink when I go and see them, but as soon as I leave she starts again. The boys have an awful time with her.

How do people live with AIDS?

On pills for the rest of their lives.

I know some people who refuse to take them.

Because they have to let their liver heal, for instance, which that medicine destroys. Lots of infected people have big liver problems because they used to drink or do drugs, or they have hepatitis B. Hepatitis devastates the liver. Three-quarters of Russian carriers were or are drug addicts, and that's why the AIDS and hepatitis epidemics spread so very quickly and freely in this country, via shared use of needles and syringes. The research shows that 83 per cent of drug addicts have done it on a daily basis. Of course thousands of them live for several years, more than ten sometimes without knowing they are carriers, but without medicine the big bad illness is 100 per cent sure to hit them, all the more since anything that weakens the immunity brings that moment closer.

They can fall sick at any moment?

If you drink, do drugs, smoke supposedly innocent marijuana or even cigarettes, then yes. My Ilya smokes, but I only allow him one pack every three days. You have to feed yourself well, get enough sleep, not change your temperature abruptly, avoid stress and people who are sneezing or have runny noses. It's very important. I never sunbathe and I have had to give up sport. I can do some just for fun, gently, but no marathons for sure. I've switched to yoga. And for the rest of my life I'll never be parted from this wretched pill box.

Bloody hell! I thought it was one of Eva's toys, or a Frisbee.

It opens, and inside there are thirty-one compartments for each day of the month. Each one is split into two halves, for morning and evening. I take three pills each morning and one in the evening, but not everyone gets the same.

How long can you live with the virus?

Apparently until your natural death. I know Kola Pinchenko from Saint Petersburg who has lived with it for twenty-seven years now. All my life. He contracted it in 1981 from an infected needle. He was a drug addict, but he gave it up, and he doesn't drink or smoke. He is sixty.

What was the contest for the most beautiful immune deficiency virus carrier, Miss HIV-Positive like?

The contest was advertised by a magazine called *Shaga* ['Step'] and a website for carriers. A few dozen girls sent in their pictures anonymously, and the public voted. Thousands of people voted over the Internet. They chose three winners, but eventually it turned out I was the only one who was prepared to reveal my full identity, first name and surname. I was awarded the 'Miss Positive' title in Moscow on 1 December 2005, World AIDS Day. I thought it would be a quiet, small-scale event attended by no-one but carriers, but they made it as big a ceremony as the Oscars. Lights, cameras, a theatre full of people, and then a press conference. I was terrified. From morning to evening they kept showing me on the news on all the television channels. During a break in the event a man came up to me from the audience and said: 'Such a little thing and so brave.' That was Ilya, who is now my husband.

No more contests have ever been organized since, so you're the only Miss HIV.

Yes. Twelve days later I defended my dissertation for my diploma in economics. I walk in, and I can see they all know me and are treating me like a star. That was nice, but it meant I had to go back to Moscow again. Ilya was working there at the time, he knows the city well, so he helped me with everything. I thought it wouldn't be such a bad thing to have someone like him to help me on a regular basis. For life even, because I didn't have the strength to be strong any more. I had had enough of being on my own. I fell in love with him in a single day. He was on his own too, because the girl he had been living with had dropped him when she found out he was a carrier. He was very upset.

Because she dropped him, or because he was infected?

Both, I should think.

And had he infected her?

No.

In two years together? That's a miracle. The risk of infection during inter-course with a seropositive partner is much greater for a woman than for a man. I had it written down somewhere . . . Oh, here it is. For a woman it's one in

600, for a man it's one in 2000. Well, it's a real miracle that she managed to avoid it.

Maybe, but my heart was so starved, I was so keen to love someone ...He used a trick to propose to me. The TNT television channel was making a documentary film about me, so Ilya gave them the idea of getting me to marry. They loved the idea of two young, educated HIV carriers getting married, but as they're always in a hurry with television shows, the year's engagement we had planned was over in three months. First we had a civil wedding here in Kazan in front of the cameras, next day a reception in Moscow for HIV friends, and finally a church wedding in my family village. As a Tatar, Ilya was a Muslim, but I had him christened.

And how did he contract the virus?

Through sexual intercourse. The doctors said he must have contracted it during the past two years, so he made a list of the sexual partners he'd had in that period, and then they told him it must have been in the previous four years. So he tried to remember his partners from the past four years, but then the doctors changed their minds again and said they meant six years, or even eight. He managed to make a list covering the past three years.

Lots of partners?

Lots. A hundred.

In three years?! What's so funny? Aren't you even a tiny bit jealous, not to mention the fact that he may have infected all those girls? A hundred young women! Did he try to find them or call them when he found out?

He tried calling almost all of them, but it wasn't clear which one he may have caught it from.

Never mind who he caught it from. What matters is whether he infected them. They should have tests to make sure they don't pass the virus on.

Not one of them called him back. But he couldn't have infected all of them, because at the start the concentration of the virus in the blood is so small that the danger isn't great. But we were worried, because he could have been accused of deliberately infecting someone. We talked to the lawyers about it. Here in Russia there are two relevant legal articles which are mutually exclusive. Guilty or not, he could have been taken to court, and that's not much fun. Besides, with the casual partners he always used a condom. He only went without one with his steady girlfriends. And there were only about fifteen of those.

What do you mean steady? How steady is that? That's an average of two-and-a-half months for each one. And he was unfaithful to them too, because he had about eighty bits on the side in that period! And you still find it funny . . .

Because this isn't Iran. Here in Russia that's normal. People have that many partners.

And that's why they call Russia 'the second Africa'. That's why in Russia three in every hundred people are HIV-positive. And what about you, Sveta, how did you contract it?

Also through sex of course. In 2003. I know who from. I was on holiday on the Black Sea coast and I had an adventure.

Didn't you use protection?

It's not so simple in this country. The women are extremely docile, timid and submissive. If a girl insists on using a condom, it means either she's got some illness or she doesn't respect the boy and has doubts about his sexual habits. For him that's a mortal insult, a sign of lack of respect and trust. Russian men take it extremely badly.

What arrogant bastards.

A condom utterly reduces their sense of value, of virility. And sex without one is proof of love and affection. Not to mention that the girls often get pregnant as if by accident and trap men that way. Because then he has to marry her. At all my meetings I repeat ad nauseam that girls should have self-respect, and not put themselves about like that. They meet a boy at a club, and an hour later they're making love with him. The situation here is tragic – especially in the countryside. There's a dreadful slackening of morals, and common sense just can't keep up with it.

Sveta, for God's sake! A short while ago you were proudly telling me about your husband's sexual blitzkrieg, and now you're complaining that Russian girls have no self-respect.

Let them at least protect themselves! Bloody hell! You might think you're talking to a happy young woman with a beautiful child and a future. But do you know, my own mother-in-law is terribly afraid?

For you, her son and your daughter.

Hell, no. She's afraid of us! She's scared of getting infected. It's terrible! She's ashamed and afraid of her own son, before the family and the neighbours – an educated woman, a lawyer. She won't let anyone speak aloud and openly about AIDS in her presence. Every time she sees me she begs me not to give any interviews and tells us never to breathe a word to our daughter in the future.

What about your mother?

She's a village, collective-farm woman. After I took part in a talk

127

show on the television she burst into tears, hugged me and said she couldn't and didn't know how to give me much in life, but the Good God was watching over me, and thanks to this illness I have such a fine, interesting and unusual life.

Even the most cautious specialists will give a limit of no longer than ten years. Cancer will be as trifling as a cold.

Report from the Twenty-First Century, 1957.

Mikhail Timofeyevich Kalashnikov

Comrade Kalashnikov

I can't find him in the red *Book of Soviet Geniuses of Science* published in 1954, or on the list of residents at the registry office, or among the Heroes of Socialist Labour in the factory showcase. In the most recent Soviet encyclopaedia they didn't even mention which republic he lives in, nor did they include a picture of him. *Portrieta nyet* – meaning it's a secret.

In 1949 Kalashnikov is awarded the Stalin Prize. He receives it from the very hands of the Generalissimus in person. In 1971 he becomes a doctor of technical sciences and a member of the Leningrad Academy. He never graduated from any institution.

Izhevsk is an ugly city in the Urals. At the centre there is an enormous tower made of iron girders – Izhevsk's answer to the Eiffel Tower. Until 1991 it was a closed city. That is a Soviet speciality – a city in the middle of the country, but for some reason you're not allowed to go there, as if it were surrounded by a border. In Russia there are still cities like that to this day.

Izhevsk is the capital of the Russian arms industry. Of course there is no tank, gun or armoured car factory. This is another Soviet speciality. Tanks are assembled here at a binding machine factory, missiles at a car factory and ordnance at a plant that manufactures knitting machines. Similarly, in Tula guns are made at samovar factories. One of the Izhevsk arms factories is where, despite having retired, eighty-eight-year-old designer Mikhail Timofeyevich Kalashnikov still works.

THE DESIGNER'S SUIT

'How should we start, Mikhail Timofeyevich? Maybe like this – which sub-machine gun is the best in the world?'

'That's like asking a mother which child is the smartest. Naturally she'll say it's hers.'

'And what will the sub-machine gun of the twenty-first century be like?'

'I don't know. The Americans claim that until 2025 the Kalashnikov will continue to be the best one, and then we'll see. I'm still working. And do you know why my automatic is so popular? Because it is a soldier's gift to a soldier. The main thing is its simplicity, but not because I was ignorant, no. The hardest thing about a designer's work is to make something that isn't complicated. Complicated constructions are easy to design.'

'Why did you adapt your rifle to 5.45 calibre ammunition in 1974?'

'Because the Americans had started using that kind in Vietnam.'

'But at the time there were protests against it all over the USSR. You said yourselves it was a barbarian, inhumane weapon. Its bullets explode inside the victim's body and cause terrible mutilation . . .'

'Oh, you see now why I don't like talking to journalists? Because you all write nonsense.'

Kalashnikov was getting upset. It's true that he very rarely talks to journalists. He made a recent exception for the Russian features magazine *Ogonyok*, and now for the Polish newspaper *Gazeta Wyborcza*.

'When I went to America they wrote that I do my own cleaning at home. Is it a bad thing that I don't have servants? Or that I don't have a decent suit. He's a great hero, he's won so many awards, but he hasn't got a suit. And why on earth write about that? Did you buy a new suit on your way to see me? I can see you didn't, and you were right not to.'

THE DESIGNER'S LOOK

'What sort of conditions did you work in years ago?'

'Don't think I had an easy ride. I travelled a thorny road. Just imagine. A competition to design a sub-machine gun is announced and a fellow called Degtaryov enters it – a general – and Simonov, also a general, and Shpagin, a famous designer, and some humble little sergeant gets in the way of this august company.'

'Did you plan the work yourself?'

'Yes. I had no assistants, I made lots of prototypes myself, including the AK-47. I always regarded my work as work for the nation', says Kalashnikov solemnly.

The fatherland, the nation, work – these are sacred words for him. As he pronounces them he has a sort of proletarian look in his eyes. Although he's small, in slippers and squeezed into a corner by the piano, he proudly shakes his upswept grey hair and gives me a rather superior look.

'How did you feel in the Stalin era? Like a free man?'

'The Stalin Prize was a great distinction. Anyone who won it mattered.'

'Could you express your opinions in those days?'

'Understand that only someone who knew how to infect the entire collective with his idea could be the chief designer. I succeeded in doing that.'

'For God's sake, Mikhail Timofeyevich, I'm talking about the fact that in those days the *politruki*, the political instructors, the commissars were in charge. That must have been the case in your office too.'

'The Party took a guiding role in every field. I don't see anything wrong with our Party's guiding role. We believed in it. That's how we were brought up, and I am still a communist to this day.'

'I can see you worked in different conditions than the aeroplane designers during the Great Patriotic War.'

'Well, you can't compare me with aeroplane designers.'

Kalashnikov has very bad hearing – a professional ailment. He went deaf from the constant shooting. We're sitting at a table facing each other, but we're shouting as if we were in different rooms. Often when he doesn't understand something, or doesn't want to understand, he pretends he can't hear.

'They worked in prison camps', I press further. 'Exclusive ones, but they were camps. In golden cages. Haven't you heard about that?'

'I was never at their workplace', he cuts me short.

So Mikhail Timofeyevich and I sit there and drink tea. But what a lot of bending over backwards I had to do to get to see him. For he is a secretive man. In the 1990s no-one in the city knew Kalashnikov lived in Izhevsk, and his family only found out what he did when the weapon started bearing his name.

I spend two days besieging the machinery plant where Kalashnikov works – hours and hours outside the gate, in corridors, in rooms, offices and at admission desks. For four hours I loiter by the phone waiting for Viktor Nikolayevich, the chief engineer. Now and then I call and am told: 'He's just gone to find you, Comrade correspondent'.

I don't waste the time. I make observations to see what sort of people there are here. That one, for instance – the size of a mountain, a tight suit packed with meat. Dark face, stiff shock of hair, broken nose, bushy eyebrows – the fellow's from the Caucasus. It's immediately obvious he borrowed the suit from a friend, and usually wears army camouflage. He trudges from room to room, getting his business done. I go up and accost him. He has a large bag full of grey bits of paper.

'What have you got there?' I ask.

'Money', he replies innocently and smiles, showing his teeth. Oh my God! They're all gold. And I thought he was a man of iron.

They tell me: 'Izhevsk is a mafia city'. Why? Because they make weapons here. And what about the spruced-up pretty boy in leather who drove up in a Ford not long ago and is now traipsing down the same route my gold-toothed Azeri just took? I accost him too. He's from Odessa. He has come here from Tajikistan and is on his way to

Moscow. He's been to Poland before and even knows a few words of Polish. What does he do?

'I'm in business.'

They're highly familiar with this sort of businessman in Russia. There's a joke doing the rounds in Moscow that goes: 'What's the most dangerous animal in the world? A businessman in a BMW.'

THE DESIGNER'S INCOME

'In this picture', I say, pointing, 'you're standing next to a real American millionaire.'

Kalashnikov has been to the USA several times.

'That's Stoner, designer of the M16. He invited me. Lots of people think I'm a millionaire too. Of course I am, but I don't have those millions in my bank account, but in the Warsaw Pact. My millions are all the individual Kalashnikovs with which the entire Pact is armed, and for which I didn't receive a single kopeck.'

'You once said that if for every Kalashnikov produced they had given you just one rouble, you'd be a millionaire.'

'It's easy to calculate that it would be at least fifty-five million. But how much do I have? Nothing! When I was in America I felt like a beggar – I couldn't even afford an ice cream. The factory management said it was a private trip and didn't give me anything. Stoner has his own plane, but I can't afford a plane ticket from Izhevsk to Moscow. I go by train – it takes twenty hours.'

'How much do you earn?'

'It's hard to say. It varies by the month, but recently I've been getting a retirement pension of about 40,000 roubles [£800] per month.'

'The average pay in your factory', I start to calculate aloud, 'is about 20,000, in which case you must earn about 40,000, on top of which there's your pension, and we've already got 80,000, which is about 3200 dollars a month. Who has money like that in Russia? Even in America for that money you could buy yourself a barrowful of ice cream, and here you could fly to Moscow and back five times. Oh, and at one time you had a deputy's per diem too. There are worse-off people in Russia than you.'

'Don't think I'm complaining. My country hasn't forgotten about me. I've been awarded lots of medals. I've twice been a Hero of Socialist Labour, and I must tell you, they only give these decorations for exceptional merit. Apart from that, for six years I was a deputy to the Supreme Soviet of the Union of Soviet Socialist Republics, so I think I've been suitably rewarded, by our standards.'

'You joined the Supreme Soviet when Stalin was still alive.'

'Yes. Then I had a break, and then a few more terms in office. But don't make the mistake of thinking that was the typical order in our country, that our designers — and not just I, but all creators of Soviet technology think this way — insisted on enjoying privileges in exchange for their passion, their commitment or ideas.'

THE DESIGNER'S TEARS

'What's your dream, Mikhail Timofeyevich?'

'My heart aches when I watch the television and see how my

137

weapon has changed into an argument in debate. I dream of an end to violence in our Russia, and I think that is the dream of our entire working Russian nation.'

The designer's voice is faltering. I let him get a grip on himself.

'The nations of the Soviet Union fight against each other using your gun.'

'What is to be done? But perhaps we cannot say that if my gun didn't exist, there would be none of those wars. Right? After all, I made the gun to defend the borders of our fatherland, and now former brothers are shooting at each other.'

'But you're still working and working and working and thinking up new, ever more perfect kinds of gun.'

'I don't know how to make junk.'

'I'm sure you regard yourself as a patriot, right? Of what, if I may ask?'

'I understand what you mean. All my life I have worked for the Soviet Union, more than that, for the Warsaw Pact, and so I'm not indifferent to the collapse of our state. I'm not happy about it either. I am a patriot of my fatherland, and I see my fatherland as vast . . .'

'Meaning?' I ask in a whisper.

'The Union of Soviet Socialist Republics.'

There's a pause. A very long one.

'The politicians have destroyed it all.'

'Other nations are pleased about it – the Lithuanians, Ukrainians, Georgians . . .'

'Let me tell you. I have travelled right round the borders of the

Soviet Union twice, to all the military districts on the frontier. I wanted to be in touch with the soldiers. I was in the trenches. I embraced Kazakhs, Georgians, Chechens and all our children. And I had tears of joy in my eyes to find that we were together like that. Now when I see the same boys are shooting at each other, I'm weeping too.'

Mikhail Timofeyevich sobs.

'Now judge for yourself if I'm a patriot or not.'

THE DESIGNER'S LONELINESS

Mikhail Timofeyevich prompts ambivalent feelings. Sometimes it's dislike, anger or even aggression, and at others sheer pity. He's old, alone, surrounded by a pack of greedy, avaricious, grasping people, such as Viktor Nikolayevich S., chief engineer at the factory, who tried to feed off Kalashnikov by exploiting his merits to swindle me out of several hundred dollars for the interview.

The old designer lives alone. His wife died thirty-two years ago, and about fifteen years ago his beloved daughter Natasha was killed in a car crash. He has two other daughters and a son. In his way he is certainly an honest, proud and honourable man. He uses a very limited vocabulary. He doesn't understand a lot of words that aren't in daily use, despite his various honorary doctorates. In conversation he occasionally deviates, or else forces it onto technical ground. He only wants to talk about his gun, about the modernizations, the variants, the blowback system, the trigger force and the diversion of gunpowder gases into a tube above the barrel. He speaks about current affairs in a cowardly way, and certainly wouldn't dare to pass judgement on a bigwig, to say what he thinks about the changes introduced by Mikhail Gorbachev or the politics of Vladimir Putin.

In the 1980s Kalashnikov received a letter from America, from a military historian who was writing a book about guns and who was asking him for some information. Mikhail Timofeyevich took the letter to the factory management. A year later the Ministry of Foreign Affairs called.

'They asked if I had had a letter from the USA. And whether we had written back. (As if they didn't know.) We didn't have permission, I replied. So write back, they said, and I did.'

THE DESIGNER'S LUSTRATION

Kalashnikov's most dramatic year was 1956, when Stalin was condemned at the Twentieth Party Congress.

'It turned out there might be various claims against me. Against a man who never made any career in the name of Joseph Stalin. Out of the blue, at a meeting of the factory's Party organization, where we were discussing the personality cult, I was turned into a punch bag – anyone who wanted kicked me.'

To this day he has kept the issue of the factory news-sheet from that meeting:

Comrade designer Drodonov cited a number of examples of how some individuals ascribe all the merits due to our collective to themselves alone. In particular he spoke of Comrade Kalashnikov's high opinion of himself, who did not take a position on the previous speaker's charges and ignored his conclusions.

'The management didn't like my creative independence and the fact that I got in touch with the ministry and people placing orders over their heads. And so under the pretext of the struggle against the remnants of the personality cult they started to attack me. Wherever I appeared, I was treated like a mangy dog. So I put all my work on hold and said I wouldn't start working again until some sort of Party committee specified what exactly I had ascribed to myself. After all, I had come to Izhevsk with a ready-made automatic, which I constructed entirely on my own. So who was I meant to share the credit with? They thought I was finished, but I won the competition for the universal machine gun again, which in 1961 the Council of Ministers put into production. And again they started saying I was unbearable.'

'Maybe you qualified for de-Stalinization?'

'You're joking! I was just a designer.'

'Not just. Six terms of office, in other words twenty-four years on the Supreme Soviet. You survived all the secretary generals.'

'And what of it?' He's upset and glances at his watch.

'What about the fact that the nation was unable to elect you, because you were classified? No-one knew you; no-one was allowed to mention your name. How many meetings did you hold with the voters, Mikhail Timofeyevich? Let's not delude ourselves. You weren't chosen by the people, but the authorities.'

But Kalashnikov won't take up the debate – in such circumstances he prefers to take offence and make it plain he finds the conversation tiring.

THE DESIGNER'S SOUVENIRS

Kalashnikov lives in a nice, three-room, seventy-square-metre apartment on the second floor of a small block. It isn't just any old block made of Leningrad prefab, but a solid house made of bricks. The apartment has a piano and a fake fireplace, and is furnished with a solid suite bought with the proceeds of the Stalin Prize. The kitchen is large, and I count the refrigerators – two. And another one in the hall. A lot for a country where the citizens have trouble filling just one. So I check – two of them are switched off.

His study is a shock. It's a real museum to communism, a mausoleum of Marxism-Leninism, a repository of proletarian internationalism. On the walls are diplomas, Lenin out hunting, and the flag of the Soviet border guards. There are also Kirov, Che Guevara, an Indian headdress given him by the Americans and a tasteful clock from the Chinese, bordered in a machine-gun ribbon. I count up twenty-three heads, busts and entire figures of Lenin, as well as a dozen Dzerzhinskys, picture frames containing photos of the designer in the company of famous people, little models of tanks, battleships and planes, souvenir medals, a vast collection of metal badges marking particular occasions pinned to a piece of black cloth, an ornamental dagger, an officer's dirk and dozens of knick-knacks with an AK-47 motif: on a piece of rock, on a little stand, in a glass ball or in a green crystal.

'Let's talk about the war, Mikhail Timofeyevich', I say, trying to steer the conversation onto a pleasant theme . . . Pleasant for an old soldier, that is.

'The war? To hell with war! Come on then.'

'You were called up in 1938. You were in a tank regiment. On which front? Were you in Poland in 1939?'

'Where? In Poland . . . ?' He's gone deaf again.

'Your army invaded Poland!!!' I scream.

'Just a moment . . . There's a city in Poland called . . . What's its name? Stryj!'

'There was before the war. Now it's in Ukraine.'

'I served there.'

'Did you fight against the Poles?'

'I don't know who was there. I was just a simple, young soldier. I was twenty years old, I do remember that the girls were pretty, but they wouldn't let us out of the barracks.'

'And did the slogan "For the fatherland, for Stalin" have real meaning for you? Did you believe in it, understand it?'

'I was a child of the revolution. In those years I thought it was a grand, wonderful slogan. Look at the old documentary films, see how many people marched to that slogan. As they marched they wiped away their tears, and not just soldier boys like us, but the great men of this world.'

Kalashnikov doesn't want to show me his medals, because they aren't pinned to a suit. Finally he gives in. He fetches a bundle out of his study. He removes a rubber band and unwraps the cloth.

'Three Orders of Lenin, the Order of the October Revolution, two Orders of Socialist Labour, the Order of Friendship of Peoples, this is the Red Star First Class . . .' His voice is faltering, but he gets a grip on himself. 'Don't think they just handed them out for nothing. For this you had to work hard and make a major effort.'

He forbids me to photograph the medals. He is indignant, saying this is not for show, this is not something you trade.

'But you do sell yourself a bit', I press him mercilessly. 'You went to the weapons fair in Abu Dhabi with all your medals, like promotional key chains. You personally handed out Kalashnikov machine guns to Arab sheiks.'

It's probably emotion that prevents him from speaking. He solemnly wraps the decorations in the cloth and takes them back to his museum-room.

THE DESIGNER'S LIFE STORY

Mikhail Timofeyevich was born in Altai Krai into a large peasant family. He completed ten years at school. He was nineteen when in 1938 he was taken into the army.

'My entire earlier design experience', he says, 'was designing a control mechanism for a tank jack, which won me a competition for regimental rationalizers.'

He was in charge of a T-34 tank when the Land of the Soviets attacked Germany. He saw how much the infantry suffered, armed only with out-of-date, five-shooter rifles. Badly wounded, he ended up in a field hospital, where there was just one topic of conversation: if only they had a gun like the Nazis had. So Mikhail Timofeyevich bought a book about weapons construction and a square-ruled exercise book. On leaving hospital he didn't go home to convalesce, but to the railway depot where he had worked before the war. There his colleagues made the first automatic pistol according to his drawings.

With this prototype and a recommendation from the deputy head of the Turkestan–Siberian Railway in charge of the Komsomol he went to Alma-Ata, to see the Kazakhstan Communist Party Central Committee. He was given a warm reception and sent to the Inventions Department at the People's Commissariat for Defence in Moscow.

He was given a work permit, a room in a hotel, provisions and a salary. However, Kalashnikov's automatic pistol was rejected, and the famous *pepesha* (PPSh-41) went into the Red Army weaponry instead.

His next design was an automatic rifle adapted to fire a medium-sized cartridge. The gun was entered for a competition, where the soon-to-be-world-famous AK-47 beat the designs of the great Soviet arms makers Degtaryov, Shpagin and Simonov.

Kalashnikov was twenty-eight at the time.

GOODNIGHT, DESIGNER

'So maybe to finish it'd be worth talking about Stalin, Mikhail Timofeyevich. Did you know about his crimes?'

'I didn't know a thing.'

'Everyone says nowadays that they had never heard of the camps.'

'I'll tell you what – it's hard to get your head around it. All that happened somewhere way off, high up, and we were far away from it.'

'In an interview for *Ogonyok* you said it is hard for you to just wave goodbye to seventy years of the history of the Soviet Union.'

'Of course . . .'

'You asked if anyone could prove to you that people made a mistake. I can prove it. The communists are responsible for the deaths of tens of millions of USSR citizens. One-and-a-half million of my compatriots lost their lives in your fatherland.'

'I was far away from those things.'

I'm not entirely brutal – I didn't tell him that in Germany too, everyone said afterwards that they had no idea what the Nazis were doing at the concentration camps. A week later I was in Crimea, and I saw some communists marching with their red flags through Simferopol for a demonstration. Don't start thinking the communists have died out in Russia or flown off to Mars. Far from it – they're still there.

'Did you know, Mikhail Timofeyevich, that your automatic is known as the terrorists' gun?'

But Mikhail Timofeyevich is no longer listening. He's standing in the middle of the room, making it plain that our conversation is over. He switches on the television, which shows some Abkhazian peasants, with their hands folded on their heads. Behind them are some Georgian peasants, holding Kalashnikovs.

Or maybe it was the other way around.

An AK rifle of 7.62mm calibre can shoot through:

- seven-millimetre armour plating from a distance of up to 300 metres;
- any NATO helmet from a distance of up to 900 metres;
- any bullet-proof vest from a distance of up to 600 metres;
- a twenty-five-centimetre wooden beam from a distance of up to 500 metres; and
- a fifteen-centimetre brick wall from a distance of up to 100 metres.

One can build a dam across the Bering Strait and the Straits of Gibraltar, direct the Kuroshio current into the cold Sea of Okhotsk and create a vast, freshwater sea in the Sahara. One can direct the great Siberian rivers to the south, sending their water to irrigate the deserts of Central Asia. What is the need for putting these great projects into action? Above all peace, friendship and mutual understanding between all nations, whose common home is the planet Earth.

Report from the Twenty-First Century, 1957.

Children at the orphanage in Ayaguz

The study aids store

To tell how strange the new place was,
I say we reached a barren plain
that lets no plant set root into its soil.

Dante Alighieri, *The Divine Comedy*,
Inferno, Canto XIV, vv. 7–9
(trans. Robert and Jean Hollander)

Arzamas-16, 400 kilometres east of Moscow. Before leaving this city, even five-year-olds were instructed by the NKVD (forerunner to the KGB) that they could not let anyone know how long their plane journey lasted, because otherwise their parents would suffer a terrible misfortune. Until 1950 this place was not on any Soviet map.

It was not an ordinary city, but a 'military closed town'. It was impossible to enter or leave the place without permission.

From 1947, Soviet nuclear bombs were designed and manufactured here. The city was built for the needs of the Atomic Energy Institute of the USSR Academy of Sciences, in other words the institute responsible for making Soviet nuclear weapons. Like all the major construction projects of those days, this one too was dumped on the shoulders of prisoners. It was explained to the local population that within this vast area surrounded by barbed wire, and in the city built by the 'zeks' (prisoners), trial communism was going to be established. In terror, all the locals gave the place a wide berth. In 1949 a major armed rebellion erupted at the prison camps in this promised paradise (later described by Solzhenitsyn in *The Gulag Archipelago*). The prisoners murdered almost all the guards, got hold of weapons, occupied the zone and escaped into the steppes. Three NKVD divisions were alerted and surrounded the fugitives with a ring of steel, and using artillery, tanks and planes, wiped out thousands of people.

After this lesson the composition of prisoner labour forces was changed. The prisoners on long, serious sentences, who had nothing to lose, were replaced with *dekretovtsy*, people sentenced to short terms by decree of the Presidium of the Supreme Soviet. They were serving a few years for hooliganism, voluntarily abandoning the work place, stopping a train, or for 'spikes', meaning picking up ears of corn left behind after the harvest in collective-farm fields.

But what was to be done with the prisoners once they had completed their sentences? They might betray the location of the newly built city to the enemy. So after serving their entire stretch, all former prisoners were sent for life to remote Magadan, where they couldn't betray anything to anyone.

The plutonium-239 for the Soviet bombs was produced in a similar town near Chelyabinsk. The place is called Chelyabinsk-40.

And so the bombs were made at Arzamas-16, the charges at Chelyabinsk-40, and the whole thing was tested even further off, in Polygon (testing ground) 52-605 near Semipalatinsk in Kazakhstan.

To serve the needs of the nuclear industry a city was built here, called Semipalatinsk-22.

In 1953 the entire nuclear complex was incorporated into the Ministry for the Construction of Medium-Sized Machinery.

THE VESTIBULE OF HELL — THE CANCER HOSPITAL

Altysh is eighteen . . . I mean was, because she died before I left Semipalatinsk. She was a Kazakh. She spoke Russian very badly. She was lying in the District Oncology Clinic.

'I'm a shepherd', she told me, 'like my parents and brothers. I live in the village of Kaynar. One day I fell off my horse and hit my stomach. It didn't hurt, but a couple of weeks later my stomach started to swell like a pumpkin. I was terrified, but I didn't tell anyone. I was dreadfully ashamed. I put on loose clothing so it wouldn't show, but eventually I was so fat I couldn't get on my horse, and then it all started . . .'

The family suspected her of being pregnant, and tried forcing her to name the father. Her brothers lashed her with ropes used for tying up horses.

'When they brought her to us, she still had marks from the beating', says Dr Alexander Ivanovich Erayzer.

'What on earth could I tell them?' The girl burst into tears. 'When I didn't know myself what was wrong. Finally my father said they'd give me away to the worst old man in the village, and they did. He's an old Kazakh, a widower, who could be my grandfather. He's sixty, and he beat me so badly and did such vile things to me . . . It was hell.' Altysh covers her head with a pillow.

'He said he'd taken in the worst whore in the village, so he could do what he liked to her.'

After a year the girl's husband realized that something was wrong, and took her to hospital in the city.

'I immediately operated', says Dr Erayzer. 'She had a huge fibroid in her uterus. It had already become cancerous. Round here cancer is lightning quick. There's metastasis to everything. You know what? To this day she is still a virgin.'

'What about the husband?'

'Some sort of pervert. We don't let him into the hospital, and she'll never leave here now.'

The oncology clinic in Semipalatinsk opened in 1948, a year before the Polygon. Lots of young doctors came here from Russia on compulsory employment. They got down to the job so energetically that in the first year they came second in the district in a socialist labour competition. They found forty-five malignant tumours, mainly of the oesophagus, stomach and uterus. I read all this in the clinic's records book.

After that, until the collapse of the Soviet Union, all the cancer statistics were classified. For ten years the book was not kept up, and then it became top secret. In 1958 the clinic had 574 cases of cancer, and in 1963 it had 861. At present the cancers usually attack the lungs, stomach, breast, thyroid, skin and female reproductive organs.

'In 1999 we examined all the women in the Abay region, which is on the border of the Polygon', says Dr Erayzer. 'Out of 4054 women, eighty-two had already had mastectomies, and 156 had had their ovaries removed. In twelve more we found cancer, and in 1182 precancerous cells, and we only examined the breasts, ovaries and fallopian tubes. One in nine of the women there has cervical erosion, on top of which there is terrible anaemia, gastric diseases, tooth loss, infertility and developmental anomalies I'd never dreamed of. I'd been a gynae-cologist for twenty years before I came to Semipalatinsk, and I only knew from literature that this sort of thing was possible. Here from one village alone five women came to see me who each had two wombs. Several others had two cervices.'

'Impossible.'

'All of us at this hospital are constantly shocked by the fact that these tumours of ours don't stick to any rules. They're always surprising us. At college they taught us that Kazakh women almost never get breast cancer. That's their nature. But here they have ten children each, they all breastfeed, until suddenly they start producing milk with blood in it. We know from the literature that children can have leukaemia, lymph or bone cancer, but definitely not thyroid, uterus or bowel cancer ... Now we know nothing is impossible. Fifteen-year-old girls die of breast or ovarian cancer. Sometimes the cancer attacks two organs at once, and it's not metastasis, but two entirely unrelated tumours with totally different structures, which we should combat using different treatments. For me as a doctor the worst thing is that very often I have no way of treating these people. Chemotherapy works badly on them, because they have awful blood morphology. The worst problem is the lack of white cells. You only have to live here for a bit and the number of leucocytes drops. We've all got it. I bet yours have done it by now too.'

There are areas within the Semipalatinsk district where 85 per cent of the population have severe anaemia. Out of 412,000 inhabitants in the entire district, 175,000 suffer from it.

From 1949 to 1989, 469 nuclear explosions were carried out in the Semipalatinsk nuclear Polygon. Seventy-three were on the ground and eighty-seven in the atmosphere, the rest underground.

'Now there's no doubt at all that the authorities were treating the local population like laboratory rats', says Professor Murat Urazalin, deputy vice-chancellor of the Medical Academy. 'Unfortunately doctors took part in these experiments too. They researched the results of the explosions, the effect of radiation on the human organism. 1.2 million people were exposed to radiation in the Semipalatinsk and Karaganda districts in Kazakhstan, between which the Polygon was located, and also hundreds of kilometres from here, in the Altai Krai in Russia. After one of the big explosions there was tremendous radioactive fallout there.'

However, the population of the Semipalatinsk district were the most badly harmed, suffering from diseases of the cardiovascular system, blood, blood-producing organs, nervous system, endocrine, sensory organs, lowered immunity and cancer.

In eleven out of fourteen regions in the district, 70 per cent of people were proved to have chromosomal aberrations. In women of the second generation to be exposed to radiation, there were twice as many incidents of gynaecological, pregnancy and birth abnormalities. The mortality rate for infants in the district is three times higher than in the rest of the country – 64.6 for every 1000 births (in Poland it is 13.6). One child in fifty is born mentally handicapped.

One person in ten in the district has received a one-off dose of radiation exceeding 100 roentgens – which is the admissible norm, but for an entire lifetime.

In 1993 a law was passed in Kazakhstan concerning those injured in the course of nuclear research. These people were supposed to receive compensation, but there wasn't enough money. The victims were going to be given a pension, but the authorities backtracked, and it ended with some minor tax concessions for cancer sufferers. However, they still had to prove that the tumour was not 'natural' but a result of the Polygon.

Professor Urazalin is one of those injured himself, because he was living in the city during the experiments.

'From 1959 to 1963 I was a student at the local medical academy. In that period they were doing the final nuclear tests here in the atmosphere. I was doing practical studies at a clinic in the city centre. Before the explosions we were warned to take the patients outside into the courtyard, and everyone came out of their houses too. This was just in case the buildings collapsed on their heads. They told us that apart from causing a slight earthquake the tests were completely safe. Some of the experiments were done fifty kilometres from the city.'

THE FIRST CIRCLE – THE STUDY AIDS STORE

Professor Urazalin leads me down some long corridors to the study aids store.

'Do you know how happy we were about the bomb?' he says on the way. 'We needed it. America was threatening the Soviet Union, but even we medics didn't realize what the effects of the experiments were, because the research and statistics were all inaccessible.'

We're there. He opens a door, lets me in and goes back to his consulting room. He says he doesn't like this place, and that here I'll find those 'effects'.

They're standing in a corner by the window in several dozen large jars filled with formalin. They're labelled anencephaly, exencephaly, hydrocephaly, osteochondrodisplasia, sirenomelia . . .

Exencephaly is lying on its stomach. On the back of its head there's a huge growth, like a second torso, but more in the shape of a brain.

Anancephaly has huge eyes like a frog's. It has no neck at all. It looks as if it is shrugging in surprise.

The only bit of osteochodrondisplasia that looks vaguely human is its head. Otherwise it's like a large walrus abdomen ending in a human foot.

Sirenomelia has its eyes shut. It looks as if it has no bones at all. It is suspended in the jar by tapes.

Iniencephaly is just a lump that doesn't look like anything.

'As a student I wanted to specialize in obstetrics', recalls Professor Urazalin, when I go back to him, 'but when in my practical studies I came across births of this kind, I quickly dropped the idea. But I still had to complete the practical studies. Even though I was a committed communist, at every birth I prayed for it to be a normal human being. I'm a doctor, dammit, and it upsets me to this day. So I became a dermatologist.'

The professor shows me a map of radioactive contamination in the district. One of the mightiest clouds came out of the Polygon on 12

156

August 1953 after the first thermonuclear explosion conducted by the Russians. The explosion had a force of 400 kilotons (twenty times more than the one at Hiroshima).

THE SECOND CIRCLE — KEEPERS OF THE PEACE

'We lay on the ground, facing the epicentre of the explosion, which was thirty-five kilometres away', wrote Academician Andrei Sakharov in his memoirs, creator of the Soviet thermonuclear bomb, in those days known as the hydrogen bomb. 'Then the agonizing wait began. A loudspeaker next to us gave the countdown: ten minutes left. Five minutes. Two minutes.'

We put on our protective goggles. Sixty seconds, fifty, forty, ten, nine, eight, seven, six, five, four, three, two, one. At that moment something flashed on the horizon.

Then a violently growing white sphere appeared — its brightness engulfed the entire line of the horizon.

I took off my goggles, and though dazzled by the change from dark to light, I managed to see the expanding, vast cloud . . . After a few minutes the cloud went black-and-blue, ominously filling half the horizon. I could see that the mountain wind was gradually carrying it south towards the mountains, steppes and Kazakh settlements. Half an hour later the cloud had disappeared from view.

Out of the shelter came Vyacheslav Alexandrovich Malyshev, deputy to Chairman of the USSR Council of Ministers Malenkov, who observed the explosion and in the name of the Soviet government hugged and kissed Sakharov 'for his huge contribution to preserving peace'.

Then they changed into protective overalls and went to look at the effects of the explosion.

'Suddenly the cars braked abruptly', recalls Sakharov. 'There was an eagle lying on the ground with burned wings. It was trying to take off, but it couldn't. It was staring with cloudy, blinded eyes. One of the officers got out of the car and finished off the unfortunate bird with a powerful kick.'

It was 1953. The Americans called the test Joe-4, after Stalin, who had died five months earlier, and because it was the fourth Soviet nuclear test in a row.

Sakharov wrote his memoirs a good thirty years later, and he did it from memory, because the KGB had stolen his notes. But he made a serious mistake. The cloud did not go south. In this part of Kazakhstan, for twenty-seven days a month on average the wind blows from west to east. The cloud went straight towards Semipalatinsk, then a city of a 250,000 people.

There was a big problem with the cloud in general. Quite simply, no-one had thought about it earlier. Only two days before the test did someone finally slap their forehead and say out loud that a radioactive mark would appear on the earth's surface at the site of the explosion. It was clear that with the anticipated explosion (400 kilotons, which is equivalent to 400 million kilograms of TNT), the contamination would go far beyond the borders of the Polygon, which was half the size of Belgium.

The scientists who had gone there for the test gathered at their hotel and conferred. Marshal Vasilevsky, deputy to Minister of Defence Zhukov and military commander for the experiment, was furious.

'What are you making such a fuss about, comrade scientists?' he shouted. 'All military manoeuvres involve a few victims.'

As Sakharov noted in his memoirs:

We assumed that a dose of 100 roentgens sometimes leads to serious paralysis in children and weak persons, while 600 causes the death of half of all healthy adults (that was the belief at the time). So we regarded a dose of 200 roentgens as the limit. A decision was taken to evacuate people from the leeward side of the sector, which would get a dose exceeding 200 roentgens.

Nowadays we know that a dose of either 100 or 200 roentgens means radiation sickness for adults, and for children 200 can mean death. The genetic effects are unequivocal.

1955 came. Thanks to the efforts of the NKVD and its agents, the Soviet Union had caught up with the United States in nuclear weapons production. Regular military manoeuvres were being held using nuclear warheads, which foreign correspondents were invited to attend.

On 22 November 1955 Andrei Sakharov was once again at the testing site at the Semipalatinsk nuclear Polygon. The first Soviet tri-phase warhead was going to be tested. The anticipated force of the explosion was 1.6 megatons.

The experiment was a complete success. The glass blew out of the windows up to 100 kilometres from the explosion site. At a meat processing plant in Semipalatinsk the windowpanes shattered into some sausage meat. Ten tons of sausages went to hell.

That evening the entire scientific, military and political cream who had come for the experiment gathered for a banquet at Marshal Mitrofan Nedelin's invitation.

The marshal was the commander-in-chief of missile forces. He asked Sakharov, as the designer of the bomb and guest of honour at the reception, to raise the first toast.

'I propose a toast', said the academician, raising his glass of neat vodka, 'to the wish that our products will always explode with the same result, but only over testing grounds, never over cities.'

All round the table a deathly silence fell. Everyone froze on the spot.

'That's not your concern', said Marshal Nedelin and raised his glass.

'I drank my vodka', recalls Sakharov, 'and kept my mouth shut for the rest of the evening. Many years passed, and to this day I still feel as if I'd been lashed with a whip. The marshal had decided to defy my unacceptable pacifism. We scientists had constructed the most terrible weapon in the history of mankind, but its use would remain out of our control. They would make the decisions.'

Yet the academician was awarded another medal, his third Gold Star of the Hero of Socialist Labour, so by law he was due a bronze statue in the capital as a gift from the Soviet authorities. He got another Lenin Prize (the previous one was a Stalin Prize), worth half a million roubles (a fairytale fortune equal to his similarly fairytale, twenty-year earnings). He was also given a house outside Moscow, a personal bodyguard consisting of two KGB colonels and frequent invitations to sessions of the Politburo. He was a Soviet god. The Soviets had just invaded Budapest.

'In the 1950s I thought nuclear tests in the atmosphere were a crime against humanity', he wrote, 'no different from secretly releasing disease-carrying micro-organisms into the water pipes.'

In 1961, after the most powerful explosion on record was detonated in Novaya Zemlya, Sakharov started insisting that the authorities must stop nuclear weapons tests. A year later he proposed the idea of an international moratorium on tests on land, water and in the air. The authorities rejected this plan and Sakharov fell into disfavour, though in 1963 the superpowers did sign an agreement to this effect.

At the Polygon near Semipalatinsk the era of underground explosions began. There were 309 of them.

THE THIRD CIRCLE — GOLD FEVER

Daniar Zaskalykov lives on the edge of the Polygon in the village of Sarzhal, which in Kazakh means Yellow Mane. Like everyone there, he was originally given a home by the collective farm. He was a shepherd. In its final years the collective farm hardly paid any money, yet the meat, milk, flour and coal paid in lieu of wages were enough to keep the family going somehow, and whenever guests came, Daniar butchered the first sheep to hand, and told the foreman wolves had taken it.

The tragedy began when the collective farm was closed down. The management divided it up in a criminal way. Each worker got sixty-three hectares of land (there is plenty of that around here) and something else as well. Daniar was given sixty sheep, but they made deductions for fuel used while mowing his field. So instead of sixty he got ten, but he sold them when his son went to business school in Semipalatinsk. A year's study there costs 300 dollars. Then one of their cows died, they ate the other one, and finally gave away the land because they had nothing to pay the land tax. They aren't yet eating boiled grass like their neighbours, but they're going hungry.

'When they first established the collective farms we were starving, and now they've closed them we're dying of hunger too', says Daniar.

In 1932 the Bolsheviks took away all the nomads' animals and told them to cultivate the land. Of course no-one knew how to do that, so most of the people died of starvation.

Now Daniar's family is eating up the remains of what they have managed to rip out of the mountain.

The mountain is called Degelen. It isn't all that large, 1085 metres above sea level, but it rises suddenly from the dead flat steppe, so you can see it from anywhere in the village, even though it's fifty kilometres away. Degelen is at the centre of the Polygon, and is the place where, starting from 1961, 209 nuclear explosions of a force of up to 140 kilotons were detonated.

In 1989, when the military carried out the final test, peace and quiet reigned, until all of a sudden, five years later, someone found treasure hidden in the mountain. Great seams of . . . copper wire. Everyone living in the neighbouring villages immediately set off for Degelen. There was real gold fever in the air, as people left their homes, families and flocks to go and dig copper wire out of the mountain. The dealers would pay a dollar for one kilo of copper – big money. The locals had to compete with people from Semipalatinsk, and the individual copper hunters soon lost out to organizations. Once organized groups, companies and mafiosi had appeared and driven them out, the shepherds got together and formed brigades, just as they used to at the collective farm.

Like most of the men from his village, Daniar went to get wire too. In a group of five, they had earned almost 6000 dollars. Today he's coming with me to show me the tunnels cut into the mountainside, where the nuclear tests were carried out. It was from these tunnels that they pulled the wire.

Our driver is called Kulanysh Makashov. He is a man who did extremely well for himself in the Soviet era, and who now belongs to the village aristocracy. Naturally, he drives a Volga. He was the book-keeper, in other words Number Three at the local collective farm.

First we go to get fuel. Of course there isn't any, so we go to the little office at the petrol station, pay a bribe and are handed a canister. Then we drive to the shop for vodka. We buy one-and-a-half litres of pure wheat vodka.

'That's against the malady', says Daniar.

'Against radiation?' I ask.

'Yes. We're used to this.'

'So do you have to drink it before or after?'

'After coming out. And you have to wash your hands. We all did that. We lugged whole caseloads of vodka to the mountain. Otherwise it'd be bad for us.'

However, we haven't gone ten kilometres before they open the first bottle. We have to drink to our friendship. First Kulanysh, then Daniar, and finally me.

'Careful', warns Daniar, 'my lip's cracked.'

There's a trace of blood on the glass. We're all drinking out of the same one. I wipe it on my trousers and take a swig.

I'm familiar with this Soviet faith in vodka – that it cures everything, any infection at all, even radiation sickness. Here half the alcoholics drink 'for health reasons', and the other half 'for spiritual pain'.

'People go into the tunnels and they die', says Daniar, wiping his bleeding mouth on his sleeve. 'Every few days someone disappears. Recently four people went in and never came back. Some others went after them to rescue them, but three of those men died in the tunnel and a fourth one has something wrong with his head, so they sent him to the madhouse, and two weeks ago the fifth one cut his own throat, though they were only in that passage for an hour. Hell knows what was in there: gas, or maybe exhaust fumes, because they were clearing water out of the corridor with a combustion pump. But I think it was the malady, because the one who killed himself had all his hair fall out, his eyebrows, eyelashes, and even the hair on his privates, because when I dressed him for the coffin I saw it.'

'So you drink this vodka out of fear, not for your health?'

'How can you fail to drink it, when they say anyone who's seen the Polygon won't die a natural death?' says the collective-farm worker.

'Everyone in Sarzhal has seen the Polygon, because it starts right outside the village', I say.

'Yes, and who dies a normal death in our place? The usual thing for us is to suffer from cancer.'

We drink up. Daniar leaves a bloody stain on the edge of the glass again.

From the steppe we drive down into a mountain valley. At close quarters it turns out that Degelen is not just a single hill, but a small chain of mountains, about thirty-five kilometres long, similar to Poland's Western Tatras, but without any forest cover. Once all the valleys were inhabited, but when the experiments began, the people were resettled. Yet this place is a Kazakh spiritual Mecca. Somewhere round here Abay, the national bard, was born and lived. He must have died somewhere near here too, but it's is hard to point out the exact place, because like all Kazakhs he was a nomad. However, this valley is where he bedded down for the winter with his flock, because there's good grass here and water in the valley. Nowadays people don't bring their flocks here because it's too far, but they still come to mow the hay.

It's clouding over and getting gloomy. Powdery snow starts to fall. Around us are heaps of fine, granite stone – they must be output from the tunnels. There are some pieces of old railway tracks, some fallen power poles and ruined houses overgrown with osier. There are lots of bits of metal lying about all over the place, but so bent and torn apart that it's hard to tell what they were once part of.

We have trouble finding the tunnel. The entrances to all the paths Daniar knows have been blocked. For some years Americans in silver overalls have been roaming about the mountains. They look like spacemen. At the expense of an American ecological foundation they are stopping up the entrances to all the corridors. The Americans aren't exaggerating with this precaution. My Geiger counter shows that in the valley there is radiation of 50 micro-roentgens an hour – two-and-a-half times higher than the norm, in other words the natural background radiation that's present everywhere.

In one of the side valleys we come across a lorry carrying a large pipe. They're treasure seekers from Semipalatinsk, looting anything that can be used for building. They have black faces like miners. They won't let me take their photo, but they say that prisoners do the work to block the tunnels. They show us how to get into one passage that's not yet closed.

Outside the tunnel entrance there's a snowdrift. Easy access to the path is obstructed by some rotten wooden beams which are blocking the entrance, though there's room to squeeze through. But I'm disappointed – Daniar says he's not going in. To fetch wire he would, but they took it all out of here long ago, so he's not going to take the risk just for sport. I offer to pay him, but we can't agree on a price – he's asking for too much. Kulanysh has never been in here, and he's not going in now either.

I squeeze past the pile of beams and stand in the corridor. I measure the radiation – it's 160 micro-roentgens per hour. A lot. Somewhere at the end of the corridor, about two or three thousand metres away, the bomb went off. But what kind? An ordinary nuclear one, which causes massive contamination, or a 'more ecological' thermonuclear warhead? How big was it? One, twenty, one hundred, or maybe one hundred and forty kilotons? And another question – when did it happen? Ten, twenty or thirty years ago? That's significant. But the main thing is whether it caused an eruption of radioactive gases.

The tunnel is cut out of solid granite rock, but just like in a mine, the walls are supported by wooden props. Lots of them are cracked, probably during the explosion, under the weight of the rocks that have showered down and created heaps of tiny stones underfoot. Here and there I can see the buried tracks of a mine railway. Naturally it never occurred to the Soviet managers that before setting off the charge they could have dismantled the rails. After all, there are several kilometres of track and thousands of wooden sleepers that could have been used in the next tunnel.

I count my steps. After going about 300 metres I stop by a wall made of reinforced concrete. There's a steel pipe about thirty centimetres in diameter sticking out of the middle. That's where the wires came through for the bomb's fuse and for dozens of research instruments positioned the entire length of the tunnel. Next to the pipe the copper hunters have carved out a narrow passage in the concrete.

I check the radiation again. 320 micro-roentgens. Not good. I scramble through the passage.

The partition is ten metres thick. To carve through something like that, the copper hunters must have worked away for about five months with hammer and chisel. They did it all by hand, without any machinery, taking turns to hack every half hour.

In the next chamber the corridor turns right at a ninety-degree angle. There's lots of equipment smashed by the coloured metal hunters and by big rocks that have fallen from the ceiling.

There's another 300 metres, another wall with a passage hacked through it and another right-angle bend, but this time to the left.

The radiation is 1170 micro-roentgens an hour.

Time to run!

I go back to the surface. Such high radiation relatively close to the tunnel entrance testifies to the fact that the force of the explosion must have destroyed a number of thick partitions closest to the epicentre. That very often happened here.

In the atomic silo shut inside the mountain the explosion melts, fries and vaporizes hundreds of tons of rock. Pressure measuring millions of atmospheres can tear through all the barriers and shoot a geyser of radioactive gases out of the tunnel. On Degelen there were even incidences when the barriers held out but the mountain didn't. The explosion blew its insides out, and not just in the vicinity of the tunnel, but in completely different places too. That is what happened on 17 February 1989 during the final nuclear test in Kazakhstan. A vast radioactive cloud escaped into the atmosphere, where the wind drove it onto the city of Chagan, halfway to Semipalatinsk.

No-one would have worried about it, but for the fact that Chagan was a closed military town with a large airfield. There were some Soviet strategic air force squadrons stationed there, which transported nuclear detonators on board bombers. Panic erupted in the city. The women and children fled, and the pilots, the elite of the Soviet armed forces, raised a rebellion.

It was 1989, and perestroika was in full swing, so instead of sending some KGB divisions, as they usually did in such cases, the authorities announced a moratorium on nuclear testing in the Polygon near Semipalatinsk.

Until late 1996 there was still a medium-sized atom bomb lying in the mountain. As treasure hunters pillaged the entire area, there it lay. It should have been detonated seven years earlier, but just then the authorities had announced the end of the experiments. Panic erupted when the DIY enthusiasts from Sarzhal started tinkering with the warhead. They reckoned just about anything could come in handy on the farm – screws, hinges, cogs . . . Finally some experts came from Russia, removed the uranium, and blew up the rest of the bomb with TNT.

At the tunnel entrance my Kazakhs greet me with a glass of vodka. I've been gone for more than an hour. They were starting to worry.

'Now drink', says Daniar. 'And another one . . . Bloody lip. It's still bleeding.'

We go back to the village.

Eighteen kilometres outside Sarzhal a huge mound of fresh earth rises from the steppe, just as if a giant mole had dug it up yesterday. Daniar and Kulanysh say it appeared in 1959. Then why isn't it overgrown with grass, like the entire steppe around it? I scramble up to the top of it and then I know – not even grass will grow in a crater left by a nuclear bomb. In the middle there's a big hole full of water.

The bomb was very small, with a force of 1.2 kilotons (more or less the same as 1200 of the biggest air bombs used during the Second World War combined). The small lake is sixty metres long and thirty wide. It's called Tel'kem-1, and it is the most badly radioactively contaminated place on earth, apart from a few spots on Degelen and in the so-called research field (fifty kilometres west of here, where most of the overground and underground tests were done). Here the radiation is 400 times above the norm – it's 8000 micro-roentgens.

169

At one point there's a narrow passage dug through the top of the crater. The herders drive their animals here to drink, including mares that they milk, and then give the milk to their children to drink.

In 1959 the prisoners were released from the Gulag, so in someone's sick mind the idea was born of digging canals using nuclear warheads – one bomb blast after another, and your canal's ready. They also seriously considered mining deposits of natural resources with the help of nuclear warheads. In January 1965, in other words two years after the USSR signed the treaty banning overground tests, thirty kilometres north of Sarzhal, near the village of Znamienko, a thermonuclear explosion with a force of 140 kilotons created a large reservoir 400 metres in diameter and 100 metres deep. The Soviet scientists planned to irrigate all the deserts in the country in this way. A few years later fish began to appear in the reservoir near Znamienko – but they had no eyes.

In all, my walk along the tunnel and by the lake cost me the same number of roentgens as two big X-rays, of the spine or the rib cage for example.

THE FOURTH CIRCLE – THE SUICIDES

I've seen various messes in my life, including more than one collective farm, but what I saw at Sarzhal passed all imagination. They say the nomad doesn't respect his place, because no place is really his – tomorrow he'll be leaving it and moving on. The Bolsheviks forced the Kazakhs to lead a settled life, but in more than ninety years they've never managed to get used to it. Even the very solid farmsteads that the Kazakhs bought from the Russian Germans when they left for the West (Stalin exiled them here in 1941), after three or four years were reduced to ruins. The gardens shrivel up, the paint peels, the fences and outhouses rot and fall over . . .

I spend the night at Daniar's home. In the morning his cracked lip is still bleeding. We have breakfast – buckwheat with sour mare's milk, known as *rymchik*, and we say farewell.

Here, although it's a village, life begins somewhere around ten. They get up, do the milking and water the animals, if they have any . . . They move slowly, as if every day were Sunday. The men spend all day doing nothing, except changing the site of their confab – now on a metal bar sticking out of the ground for no reason, now on a fallen concrete pillar, a beam, or a heap of rubble . . .

The houses in the village are set out in several straight rows a good hundred metres apart – unusually broad for village streets. The idea was to chuck out the sewage from each private outhouse onto these very streets. Every few days a collective-farm bulldozer came along and in a single go cleared the entire street's 'output' away from the buildings. But the collective farm has gone, and the broken bulldozer has been given away for scrap – though not all of it, because there was no way to lift it. Everything that could be unscrewed from it has gone for scrap. The rest stands in the middle of the street, buried in manure. It's a veteran bulldozer, an exemplary worker bulldozer, a Hero bulldozer. It fell on the field of labour.

And so among the houses mighty slag heaps of sewage are rising, and even though we are on the icy, desert steppe, the entire village is covered in appalling, stinking mounds of frozen shit. Some people burn the tops of the mounds that have dried in the sun, but that doesn't improve the situation at all, apart from making it harder to breathe.

Amid the piles of shit there are wrecked cars, pieces of concrete structures, piles of solidified cement in sacks, and rickety outhouses with wide open jaws, which every few days are shifted to perch above a different hole. There are lots of stray dogs everywhere, or rather dog skeletons coated in scabby skin. The cows and goats are let loose in the street to compete with them for refuse, children black with filth rummage with sticks in the rubbish heaps, while the men sit and stare. They hate the Russkies, their president, civil servants – everyone. They even hate Kazakhstan, because what sort of a fatherland is it that can't even remove the sewage? They hate everything that isn't the Soviet Union. I'll have you know the Soviet Union even left them that wire when it went, so they'd have something to live on for a few more years.

Kulanysh Makashov, the man who drove me to the Polygon in his Volga, never went to Degelen. While everyone else in the village was extracting wire from the mountain, he was busy hollowing out the collective farm, from which he extracted 323 hectares of land, 400 sheep, a herd of horses, some cows, two tractors, a combine and three lorries. He had his gold mine right here, and a better one than any other. As the bookkeeper at the collective farm, he was responsible for closing it down and dividing up the property.

'Only fools went to fetch wire', he says, 'shepherds, tractor drivers and loaders. Haven't we got enough misfortune? They're still keen to go there. In the past three years sixty-nine people have tried to take their own lives here. Young and old, normal people, not drunks at all. They left children . . .'

'Maybe out of poverty?'

'No way. Rich people did it too. In the evening they're still laughing, meeting for a drink, saying what they'll do tomorrow, and next morning they're hanging in the attic. Children here hang themselves, the mullah – he was a really religious guy, but he killed himself, though he only lived here for three years.'

'Maybe out of fear?'

'Maybe. People are afraid to live to forty, because most of them contract cancer, but the children do themselves in too, and the women. You don't live to fifty here. But why do the children cut their own throats?'

There is a rule known from Hiroshima that cancer usually attacks between the tenth and thirtieth year after the radiation. Research conducted in Nevada and on islands in the South Pacific, where the Americans did their atomic tests, has confirmed this, and it has also been observed near Chelyabinsk, where there was massive contamination in the 1960s following an accident at a plutonium factory. It's the same here. Cancer has been devastating villages in the area since the 1960s. The suicides began after the Polygon was closed, that is from 1991. With each year there are more of them, lately about three a month.

Professor Murat Urazalin of the Medical Academy in Semipalatinsk told me that some Canadian research has proved a link between radiation higher than the acceptable norm and disturbances in certain centres within the cerebral cortex.

Garin Kadbenlo has an excellent memory of various images from childhood.

'How could I fail to remember when I spent all day in the car. Even when they went to collect a patient they had to take me with them.'

Garin's father was a doctor in Sarzhal. Half the house was a small hospital, and the doctor's family lived in the other half. Outside stood an ambulance.

'I was four. It was August. It was hot and I was in that car. Finally I ran to my mother and complained that the window was so dirty that I couldn't see anything. So she wiped it clean, and ten minutes later I couldn't see anything again, and so on, all day long. It was a sort of slightly pinkish dust. People aren't quite so dumb – they knew at once it was from the bomb that had exploded the day before. The earth here is red.'

The day before, troops had arrived at the village. They told people to turn off the cooker, not to switch on the lights, to stay indoors and not to approach the windows.

'My mother hadn't switched off the cooker because she was cooking for the hospital', recalls Garin, 'so when it went off, the stove lids and the flames in the cooker shot up to the ceiling. The window-panes rattled, the door slammed, the cupboard came away from the wall, and some of the wallpaper tore. Then an immense mushroom cloud arose. My mother was pregnant at the time. She had just gone outside, so it blew all over her, and my sister was born with epilepsy.'

Garin is 49. He sounds hoarse, as if trying to speak in a loud whisper. He had a tumour in his larynx, but they cut it out.

'Two years later, in November 1955, they took everyone forty kilometres away from here, to the city of Abay. We were one hundred kilometres from the biggest explosion there ever was here. They made everyone go outside. They told us to lie down on our stomachs and wouldn't let us look, and the mothers were supposed to cover the children's eyes, but as they'd said that, people were all the more curious to see what it was like. The kids were the most inquisitive of all. To this day I can still see it vividly: everyone's lying down, but they're craning their necks to get a better view.'

They weren't allowed to return to Sarzhal for six months.

Garin is a *metysh*, which is what the Kazakhs call people of mixed race. The only Europeans to have lived here were Russians and Germans, but Garin's mother, Wanda Kamieniecka, was a Pole, though she wasn't a deportee, like all the Poles in the neighbouring district of Karaganda. Garin's father was an army doctor. They fell in love in 1945 when he was on his way back from Berlin, so she went off to Kazakhstan with him.

Garin is the richest man in the village, far richer than even Kulanysh Makashov who plundered the collective farm.

'I got myself a licence to trade in metals and sold the wire to China. I helped our people to clean up the Polygon', he says, bursting with laughter. 'When there wasn't enough copper, I sold them scrap metal and anything that wasn't nailed down. They knew perfectly well where I got it from, but that's business, you have to make a living. They sold it on somewhere too, apparently to Japan. One time a Japanese guy set a Geiger counter to the scrap and there was a big fuss, because it was radioactive. So now the Chinese sell it to someone else. The worst thing is that those of our people who used to go and fetch the wire fall sick, die or hang themselves even more than others. All because they're such a terribly ignorant mass. They don't use Geiger counters, they're clueless, yet there are places there where it's a thousand or more micro-roentgens per hour, and they bring it all in to me. I've never been inside any of those tunnels, but to this day I never go anywhere without my Geiger counter.'

'Why is that?'

'Because I have children. I can't risk exposing them or myself. It's quite enough that one of my children has died. I work with metal every day, and if something's harmful, I keep well away from it.'

'Do you throw it away?'

'What do you mean? I don't touch it. I don't even go near it. The people do it all themselves.'

Garin paid the treasure hunters a dollar per kilogram of copper. Depending on the current price on the London exchange, the Chinese paid him 1.1–1.3 dollars. He said he exported more than 2000 tons of it, so he must have made almost half a million.

Garin built a mosque in Sarzhal at his own expense, and brought in a mullah, but the fellow hanged himself, so he brought in another one.

In 1959 two small atomic blasts of 1.2 kilotons each were detonated within the Polygon, eighteen kilometres from Sarzhal. The result were the lakes, Tel'kem-1 and Tel'kem-2. Garin was ten years old at the time. It was during the summer holidays, so he spent all day out on the steppe with the work brigades, who were busy harvesting the hay.

'One day some army people came and told us to stay at home tomorrow, because there were going to be some tests. What, and leave the hay unharvested? That's a good one – what foreman would let that happen? When it went off, I was no more than two kilometres from the site of the explosion. Some people were barely a kilometre away. Everyone who was closer than that was driven away. It was terrible. Our hayricks fell apart, and the people who were nearest to it were blinded. We piled onto the lorries and went back to the village.'

Right behind them the army drove in with medical teams. They gathered all the people who had been close to the explosions. They lined them up in the street, told them to undress and very carefully examined each one, looking them over, taking measurements and blood for analysis, making notes and taking photos.

'They weren't quick enough to examine everyone – some people died in the queue for the doctor.'

Then the doctors made a list, with 275 names on it, men and women, old, young and children. These people were always falling ill. Every so often they had to go and be examined at the oncology clinic in Semipalatinsk.

'They kept us there for ten to fifteen days and examined us again, did X-rays, took blood and photos. By then we knew it was a death list, and that all the people on the list were bound to die, and die they did. First of all from radiation, then from cancer, if they hadn't hanged themselves or cut their own throats earlier. Only eleven people from that list are still alive. I'm the eleventh.'

The military and scientists who conducted the tests worried most about the wind. The main thing was that it shouldn't blow north, because there, on the border of the Polygon, was the city of Semipalatinsk-22, where they lived. In 1960, following the death of Igor Vasilyevich Kurchatov, the man who built the atom bomb for the Soviet Union, the city acquired his name.

At one time 30,000 people lived here, nothing but scientists and military. You could say they were the Soviet elite. Almost all of them were Communist Party members, and almost all of them were Russians. There were no academic institutions training nuclear energy specialists in Kazakhstan.

In Kurchatov there are four scientific institutes concerned with nuclear physics. There are three atomic reactors in operation here. Dimitr Zelensky is director of the Institute of Atomic Energy. He has been living here for thirty-seven years. He is a citizen of Russia in the service of Kazakhstan.

'Why are you asking about the winds?' He's not happy that I've started with this. 'After all, there were just some isolated incidents when radioactive gases were released from the tunnels. And as soon as the eruption took place, it was all dispersed in the sky, spread and blown around.'

'Except that the oncology hospital . . .'

'Oh! You're still on about that hospital. People contracted cancer here in the days of Ghengis Khan as well, and there weren't any explosions then. People fall ill because of tough living conditions, and

178

because of dirt, especially in the villages, where there's no hygiene or decent food. Poverty is a hundred times worse for cancer than radiation.'

'Then why do more than thirty people commit suicide each year in Sarzhal?'

'While the nuclear tests were being conducted here, the Soviet Union pumped loads of money into developing the region around the Polygon. When the Land of Soviets collapsed, the Soviet money came to an end, and these people were left with no source of income. They have nothing to feed their children. After the Russian army left, out of 30,000 people living in Kurchatov only 10,000 remained. The place emptied.'

The flats are unoccupied. Windows look eerie with their frames torn out. The Irtysh restaurant and the Rossiya department store have closed down. Once my hotel was full of scholarly guests, but now I am the only customer. I'm the only person in the city to have hot water on tap. Even the house of Lavrenty Pavlovich Beria, head of the NKVD, who as chairman of the USSR's special commission on armaments, built this city, has been converted into a church.

'Our city used to be awash with flowers and full of children', says Larissa Yakovlevna Bogushova. 'You could leave your baby outside and go and gossip in a shop for hours. No-one would do him any harm. There was no fear of the pram being stolen. The women used to hang their washing out to dry in the yard and it never disappeared, even if you left it there for a week, but now we've been invaded by collective-farm workers from the greater area, and they're a completely different sort. You never hang your washing out nowadays.'

Larissa Yakovlevna is a clerk at the city administration. Her husband was a colonel, military commander for all the nuclear tests in the final decade of the Polygon's active life. They're waiting to leave for Russia, but there's no apartment for them there. The fatherland no longer needs a physically and mentally ill officer suffering from lapses of memory.

'It's all because of the work he did, but here we never used to make a fuss. An army man's an army man. The Party told him what to do and that was that. If I knew life was going to be the same as it used to be here, we'd never leave. But they're always bringing in new people. There used to be nothing but Russians on our staircase, but two Kazakh families have moved in now. I've got nothing against them, but they're different, so unpleasant, the place is so full of them, they spit on the stairs, but it wasn't built for them. We're at home, but it doesn't feel like our home. It's impossible to live here.' Tears drip onto her knees, but suddenly her eyes light up. 'Down this street, which runs from the administration building, there were always parades on 9 May. The army used to march past at a ceremonial pace. So very neat, so extremely elegant, so smart! Officers and young men, the soldier boys. Our husbands came at the head, and we women would be there in our light clothes, short coats, with the children, waiting for them. There was laughter, joy, balloons, red carnations . . . and suddenly it's all gone, and that was my whole life. I'd give anything to have it back.'

'Your husband is seriously ill because he served within the Polygon.'

'We were proud of this posting.'

'Proud?'

'Of course. He did exceptional things. The Party let him in on the Soviet Union's top secrets. He was chosen for it. He did important, useful and necessary things.'

'Necessary to whom, Larissa Yakovlevna?'

'To you as well.'

'Me?'

'Yes indeed. You. The entire socialist camp. It was necessary for the balance of power in the world, for peace.'

Larissa Yakovlevna's parents come from Armenia, although they are Russians. She was born in Batumi on the Black Sea, where her father served in the army. Then they lived in Brest on the Polish border, and when she married she came to Kazakhstan.

'So where is my fatherland?' she wonders. 'Maybe it's like in the song: "My address is not a city, a house or a street. My address is the Soviet Union." When a person lived in communism, he saw a light ahead of him, he had hope for the future, but once that hope is gone, he doesn't feel like living.'

Tears drip onto her knees again.

'I haven't seen my parents for seven years now. I'd like to go, but whenever a person visits their old father and mother, he should take something, help them somehow, but I haven't the means. And I don't know if it would be better to go to them with my pockets empty, or send them a little money, though of course they could die at any moment.'

THE SEVENTH CIRCLE — THE STUDY AIDS STORE

In a corridor at the Institute for Radiation Safety and Ecology in Kurchatov there are some exhibits in jars full of formalin.

The rabbit is ideal for researching ocular damage. So in the jar we have a whole, black rabbit with burned-out eyes. There's also a sheep with no wool, some lacerated camel lungs, burst dog hearts, brains with haemorrhages visible to the naked eye, and an entire piglet that looks roasted, as if it were fresh off the grill. There's also a cow's head and a dog with its fur burned off, stark naked. It must be a mongrel, or a Pomeranian, but it's hard to tell without the shaggy coat. Or maybe it's a Laika, like the dog abandoned in space to die of starvation or suffocation. Instead of a collar there's a piece of steel wire embedded in its flesh because of the heat. It had to be tied up somehow so it wouldn't scarper from its zone. Even so it was lucky – the one from the 1250-metre zone didn't croak until the next day.

THE EIGHTH CIRCLE — CHILDREN OF THE POLYGON

Father Fyodor from the Semipalatinsk church tells me about her.

She was a Russian. Her name was Sveta. She lived in Semipalatinsk. She was a student in Moscow, at the Patrice Lumumba Peoples' Friendship University, in the highly prestigious department for diplomacy and international relations. That was in the Soviet era, when the Land of Soviets used to educate thousands of left-leaning students from Third World countries. Perestroika was soon to begin.

The girl married a black student from the same department, broke off her studies and went with him to Sudan. Once there, her husband turned out to have three wives already, and several mistresses, whom he kept in a harem. He was a communist, as well as being very rich and a devout Muslim. In Africa that is entirely possible.

So a girl from the fatherland of Valentina Tereshkova, first woman in space, ended up in a harem. And she fought. A hundred times she tried to escape. Once she was even hidden on the yacht of a French journalist who tried to steal her away, but somehow they always caught her. Not even the Soviet consul's intervention was of any help.

Finally the girl gave birth to a son. He was very badly handicapped. The husband threw Sveta out, so she took the child and went home to her parents in Semipalatinsk.

'What a life she had', says Father Fyodor out of pity. 'It was painful to look at them when they arrived here. The child – not just black as the devil, but sick too.'

He was ten years old when he died.

Even the smallest dose of radiation can cause damage to the hereditary mechanism, in other words the DNA molecules, and consequently lead to the genetic disorder, handicap or death of the irradiated person's offspring.

There is no threshold, no minimum dose below which no damage will ever occur. Genetic defects are probabilistic in nature, which means that the probability, i.e. the frequency of disorders, rather than their nature, depends on the dose of radiation.

The greatest number of disorders are found in Ayaguz, 300 kilometres south of Semipalatinsk.

There were two cities in the Soviet Union – Odessa, and small Ayaguz, a city of 50,000 – two cities deserving the worst reputation as the most dangerous, bandit-infested places. Odessa had the sea and a port, while here there is nothing but the steppe and some prison camps – dozens of them. So it has remained to this day. Most of the bandits eventually come out of prison, but as they have no money for a ticket home, they stay here and do their robbing in Ayaguz.

The children's home, or *dyetdom* as the Russians call it for short, was founded here in 1942 for war orphans evacuated from Russia. By 1956 the orphans had grown up, but meanwhile a large number of mentally handicapped children had suddenly appeared in the area. The home changed its profile.

A gate. On the fence, high up, there are tangles of barbed wire. A courtyard. A group of boys have come out for a walk – but they're not allowed to. Now and then an old bag in a white coat screams 'Sit!!', and the boys sit down on a bench.

'Sit!!' This time it's a trusty who screams it. It's easy to recognize him by his better clothing. The trusties are cleverer than the others, they're able to talk, so they are the chosen few, they're set apart and are more important. They do loyal service and they know no mercy. Sylvia, for example, is so good that they let her stay on at the *dyetdom* even though she reached the age of seventeen twelve years ago. She's very smart. She got an Adidas tracksuit from the principal, because she really is good.

The art of it depends on keeping the kids in a single bunch. The old bag in white sits and keeps an eye on it all from a distance like a shepherd. The trusties are like sheep dogs – if a kid wanders off, he smacks him on the ear. The children are sitting squeezed onto the bench, on the rim of a small sandpit and in a metal cage suspended above the ground. This is the place they like best, so about six of them are crowded in there. Once upon a time there was a slide here too, but it broke.

For twenty-seven years Sabr Ramazanov taught PE, and now he's principal of the orphanage. His face is almost purple, with burst blood vessels in his eyes.

It's fitting to drink to our acquaintance. He gets a bottle of 'Old Russian' vodka out of the cupboard.

'We've got twenty morons, 120 imbeciles and eight idiots here, and I have to feed them', he says. 'Let's do it this way. You send me, that is the children's home, humanitarian aid, I'll write you out all the necessary receipts, so you won't pay any customs tax, and we'll split the profit.'

The kitchen manageress brings a snack and the chief accountant the relevant document. It's already filled in, all that has to be added is what, where from, and the dispatch date.

'I did some business here in the Soviet era', says the principal. 'I fired bricks. In a single season I used to deliver a million of them to the state farm. I wasn't even in the Party, because a Party member couldn't get away with doing business.'

During the day the children aren't allowed to sit in the bedrooms or in the dayrooms. Each group has its own tiny room, with the charm of a prison cell. They're not allowed to leave it, or Sylvia will give them a slap. There's nothing here apart from benches fixed to all the walls. The children are on sedatives. All day they sit and rock. They have no occupation, no toys, and in the entire house I only found one board game. When I stretch out a hand to stroke their faces, many of the children flinch as if dodging a blow.

I go round all the groups, but at the end I go back to the little ones again, where I started. The ragged clothes they were dressed in when I looked in on them the first time are their 'Sunday best'. They were changed again while the principal was treating me to Old Russian. Now I'm seeing the kids in their everyday tatters, miserably torn and dirty. They're barefoot and almost naked.

THE NINTH CIRCLE — THE ROOM UPSTAIRS

The ninth circle, inmost hell, is in a room upstairs. This is the room for children who cannot control their bodily functions, but they are not entirely disabled and are not lying in bed. They've devised a very sophisticated instrument of torture for them – all day long they suffer in the stocks.

You know the sort of church furniture that stands against the walls in the chancels of old cathedrals? They're choir stalls, long carved benches with armrests. The children in this group are stuck in something similar, but smaller, with a hole instead of a seat. Their little arms and legs are tied to the bench. The seats have been cut out of their clothes, I mean their rags, so their bare behinds hang above the holes, with full potties underneath them.

All day long they writhe, bend, flex and tense in their bonds. But they want to run, fly, or scratch their ears . . .

For the time being we are designing our apparatus on the supposition that there are no sentient beings either on Mars or Venus. But what if they are discovered there? Then we shall try our best to construct equipment enabling us to make wireless and television contact with them. Only then shall we set about man's flight to those planets.

Report from the Twenty-First Century, 1957.

The town. The men are moving a piano.

A small corner of heaven

The first time, Christ rode on a donkey, drank wine and lived in chastity. Now he prefers a Yamaha snow scooter, he's a vegetarian and teetotaller, and his wife is pregnant again. His second wife. He divorced the first one, so she went off to the city and started studying clinical psychology.

Three of the world's six living Christs are in Russia. One of them has not yet manifested himself, but he already has followers and his own Church. The second is called Grigory Grabovoy and he's in prison, because he took money for their resurrection from the parents of children murdered by the terrorists at Beslan. The third is Sergei Anatolievich Torop, a former militiaman and self-taught painter whose followers call him Vissarion, which means 'Life Giving'. However, their usual name for him is the Teacher.

But this Christ doesn't shout himself hoarse by a lake, in a town square or up a hill. He is happiest using the Internet, where his *Last Testament* is being published on a running basis, a vast, currently eight-volume tome in which an ex-rock musician called Vadim Retkin, who is now Vissarion's court evangelist, records his deeds and words. This book provides very strict regulations for the life of his followers, who claim to number almost 100,000 worldwide.

The Teacher instructs them on how to satisfy a man in bed, as well as how to keep him happy at the table, how many children to have and how to bring them up, what to eat, how to boil the water to make tea, for whom to vote in elections and where to piss – meaning where not to.

In the Soviet era the Russian got used to prohibitions, so the Teacher has been able to serve them up as many as sixty-one commandments. Here we find a creative development and elaboration of the ten that mankind received from God on Mount Sinai, such as the ban on taking offence, for example, on gossiping, or on eating meat, which is obligatory even for animals – it definitely falls within Moses' 'Thou shalt not kill.'

But that is not the only reason why the Vissarionites do not eat meat. Fear is encoded into every cell of a slaughtered animal – so says the Teacher. So when a person eats it, he takes in negative energy and is filled with terror, panic and death.

Believe it or not, even their dogs are vegetarian! And they're as meek as kittens. This is the only place in Russia (including the capital) where I can calmly walk down the street without constantly looking round to see if some beast is about to attack me from behind.

This is the only place in Russia where I meet happy people – cheerful, jolly, calm people who actually greet a stranger in the street, talk to him, smile and ask how they can help, and where the doors of the houses have no locks. Even the children are on first-name terms with everyone. Apparently 60 per cent of the adults have higher education. They talk slowly and quietly, they are never in a hurry, they don't swear, they don't drink and they don't smoke. They have the highest birth rate in Russia, they never hit their children and they are almost never ill. The men have beards and long hair and don't watch television. They are completely uninterested in politics, and their outhouses are very clean and comfortable as they are the sit-down, not the squatting variety like everywhere else in Russia. This is the happiest place I came across in the course of my four-month car journey from Moscow to Vladivostok.

The authors of the *Report from the Twenty-First Century* never once used the words 'God', 'prayer' or 'religion' in their book, because those things weren't supposed to exist any more. Vladimir Lenin, creator of the Land of Soviets, repeated after Karl Marx that religion was the opium of the people, a form of spiritual moonshine, and thus it was bound to disappear. But it was the Soviet Union that vanished, and in the place where it used to be, apart from all the major world religions, there are more than eighty large sects in operation, with about 800,000 followers.

There is no omnipotent General Secretary of the Communist Party any more, but there are no fewer than three incarnations of Jesus Christ.

I THOU SHALT HAVE NO OTHER GODS BEFORE ME

'It was like a flash, like a bolt of lightning', says Galina Oshchepkova, a specialist in natural medicine from Mazyr in Belarus. 'I knew it was him as soon as I saw him in a video. My heart was pounding. My chest went tight, joy and tears all at once. I hadn't even seen his face yet, just his feet, but I was already certain. Back on Earth again! He was walking across the grass, taking firm steps, but he seemed to be floating in the air. I wondered if it was a montage, or a camera trick, but it wasn't, because I watched his feet and they didn't even crush a single blade of grass. Although he walked across it, the grass looked as if no-one had come that way at all. A miracle. So it was him! Him, him, him! Christ. The Messiah. The Saviour. The man sent by God.'

Lieutenant-Colonel Vladimir Fyodorovich, head of the economic crime unit for the Republic of Khakassia, became a believer at a meeting of a club for those interested in paranormal phenomena, of which he was a member.

Grisha Gulyaev was converted at a penal colony for recidivists and dangerous criminals near Angarsk. It was at the start of his third sentence, this time ten years, which he got for grievous bodily harm.

'It was the Lord who sent me Slava', says Grisha. 'They put him on the bunk above me. He got eight years for drugs, and when the militia came to take him away from home, his wife threw a book into his bag. It was the *Last Testament*. I read it out of boredom. Then I read it three more times and became a believer. In there the biggest problem is getting enough to eat, getting a smoke and wangling some tea, but my one and only interest was talking about God. I fell into a strange state of non-stop prayer, I fasted, gave up smoking and drinking tea. They treated me as if I were mad. Or the enemy, even, and it was a top-security penal colony, two thousand lads, dangerous thugs. Never a month went by without someone being murdered there, and I was the biggest weirdo of all.'

At the very last moment the Lord sent a neighbour to Igor from

Alma Ata. The man gave him an audio cassette and told him it was Vissarion, the second incarnation of Christ.

'I listened for half an hour and knew I had to go to him. That very day I stopped taking my daily heroin fix. My fear and drug craving vanished, and I stopped eating meat immediately. All in a single day, though only the night before I had been considering suicide, because I had tried every treatment method, I'd been through detox at least ten times, suffered clinical death and been to prison. Even my parents had given up on me.'

Igor went to work, and once he had paid off all his debts he headed for Siberia, where the other followers were living.

Misha Orlov is from Podolsk near Moscow. Misha was the leader of one of the mafia gangs. He was twenty-five when in December 1996 he went to collect the monthly protection money from the owner of a publishing firm specializing in religious literature. On the publisher's desk lay a photo of an angelically smiling, bearded man with blue eyes and shoulder-length hair. Misha asked who he was, and heard that this was the tsar of all tsars.

'It hit me so hard', says Misha, 'that I didn't take the money, just the photo, and next day I was on the plane to Siberia. I met the Teacher. We spent two hours talking about art, about life in harmony with nature, and why people are happier without money ... I went home and told my wife I was leaving Moscow to live beside Christ. I gave away everything I had.'

'What did the gangster's wife say to that?'

'She decided to come with me. On a trial basis. We've had three children born here, and after ten years I think she has come to terms with living in the middle of the taiga. We live modestly, quietly, peacefully and very happily. My children don't know what arguing, fighting or aggression are . . .'

'Nor do they know who Ivan the Terrible was, or Napoleon or Stalin. They've never heard of the October Revolution or the Second World War, because you don't teach that in your schools.'

'But they know a lot about Raphael, Rembrandt, Cervantes, Rimsky-Korsakov . . . And our older son, though he's only nine, can already handle an axe and is helping me to build our house, because we're still living in a provisional one.'

Among the Vissarionites I also met Sergei Chevalkov, a former Strategic Rocket Forces colonel, who is now one of two priests for the community, Captain Oleg Patulov, a veteran of the Afghan war, and Captain Sergei Kozlovsky, who fought in Chechnya. The former captain has become a sort of local theologian, while the other is headman at the biggest settlement for followers. Sergei Morozov used to be a research worker at a secret military institute, a fanatical communist and Party secretary. Following the fall of the USSR he madly sought something he could use to fill the void. He started with the Orthodox Church, then he was with the Hare Krishnas, the Buddhists, and even took up shamanism.

A large number of the men at the community are former soldiers, militiamen, prosecution service employees, intelligence services officers and also artists whose names are not famous. Vissarion, and thus the founder and head of the Church of the Last Testament, which is the name of their community, still paints in pastels to this day. I talked to several dozen of his followers, and everyone, without a single exception, had formerly been an atheist, often to a militant degree, and a very large number had been Party members, ideological or even fanatical communists.

It took me eight days to drive there from Moscow. At Krasnoyarsk, in the middle of Siberia, you have to turn south, and 400 kilometres later, at Abakan, you go east. Two hundred kilometres further on, at the heart of the taiga, is their promised land.

II THOU SHALT NOT TAKE THE NAME
OF THE LORD THY GOD IN VAIN

'The Teacher knows the answer to all questions?'

'Of course!' says Galina Oshchepkova from Mazyr. 'He is Christ, the living Word of God.'

'Can he drive a car?'

'He doesn't drive . . .'

'So can he ride a bike?' I go on.

'Yes! And he rides a horse. And when he does, he's like a great tsar. When the governor of our province came and they walked up the Mountain, the whole entourage, governor and all, gave up the ghost halfway there, but he flew like a bird. He's so fit and strong. And in such perfect harmony. He's never ill.'

'Don't talk rubbish. He had a hernia. He had to have an operation.'

'That's the first I've heard of it. He sometimes gets tired, but that's the result of intensive creativity and deep thinking about our fate. It's not easy to know everything. I myself once asked him if I could use a microwave, because I'd heard dishes cooked in them aren't healthy. He said that by blessing our food before our meal, we remove all the harmful energy that's in everything, even in a bottle of the best quality oil, because it was made for money. Not to mention the bad thoughts of the people through whose hands the bottle has passed before it reaches us.'

'And why can't you bring water for tea to a boil?' I ask.

'Because the Teacher said that boiling it renders it lifeless.'

He was brought up by his granny. She was a cleaning lady. He blundered his way through his military service in the worker battalions, which in the USSR was where the biggest weeds and wimps ended up. To this day he reckons there is no sillier place or people in the world – the army is a dreadful cultural desert, full of primitive violence, boorish behaviour and vulgarity. He survived by painting portraits for the commanders.

After the army he tried to set up a business, but without success, so he became a militiaman.

His first contact with religion was an order from the Orthodox church in Abakan for an icon of the Virgin Mary. They paid him well, but when he finished, the clerics were outraged because the Mother of God had hands as large as a collective-farm worker's. They said she never worked. The artist insisted it was a very faithful portrait, and refused to make any changes. He had to give back the money.

The revelation came to him in late 1991 in his home city of Minusinsk, to the south of Krasnoyarsk in Siberia. He was on the trolleybus, when he realized why he was so sure he knew how to paint Mary – because she had been his first mother.

Just then the Soviet Union collapsed. Torop was thirty years old. He gave up his job with the militia and started teaching, first of all at a social welfare home where he found his first follower. He said he hadn't come back to Earth again in order to judge the living and the dead, as the Evangelists wrote, but to save mankind from mass destruction. The Evangelists had made lots of mistakes, because they wrote their books from memory, more than ten years after Jesus's death. The entire truth is only contained in the *Last Testament*, because it comes from him, from Christ himself.

The destruction awaiting us will not be a divine punishment – instead man will bring it on himself, through religious wars, economic collapse and ecological disaster. Only a handful of people will survive, gathered around him in Siberia. So far there are 4500 of them – not many, but Noah's family was even smaller. Afterwards the survivors will rise from the Earth, which is going to be annihilated.

They have come from the furthest corners of Russia and the former Soviet republics. Not just Russians, but Kirgiz, Yakuts, Latvians, citizens of Dagestan . . . Russian-speaking Germans, Americans and Jews from Israel, a large group of Bulgarians, a Belgian who teaches chess, and even a Cuban, but he's from Sweden. They live in about a dozen villages, not all of which have electricity.

The biggest is called Petropavlovka. It consists of about 250 wooden cottages, and the followers live in 200 of them. Each family has produced three, four or five children. If the parents cannot cope with bringing up their offspring, they take in a follower who is single, male or female, to perform the role of a grandparent, aunt or uncle for their children.

Vissarion lived in Petropavlovka for several years, but in 1997 he announced that the centre of the world was a few dozen kilometres east, on a hill, among the marshes in the depths of the taiga. They decided to build their capital there. They started from scratch by cutting out a road, which is only passable for vehicles in winter, when the marshland freezes over, and then only for snow scooters and horses. In summer you have to go on foot by a roundabout route through the mountains. Then on the mountain that they named the Altar of Earth they erected a temple and a Heavenly Abode for the Teacher. They usually call this place the Mountain, and the Abode of Dawn, the town they built at the foot of it, is known for short as 'Gorod', meaning the Town. The Vissarionites' symbol is the sun with fourteen rays shooting out of it, and that is how their capital is built too: it has a central square for prayer with fourteen streets radiating out from it. For now there are only fifty cottages and about two hundred citizens – the religious vanguard of the Vissarionites.

III REMEMBER THE SABBATH DAY, TO KEEP IT HOLY

They have three holy days. The 18th of August is the Feast of Good Produce in memory of Vissarion's first sermon. In April there is the Feast of Spring, and on 14 January the Birth of God – Vissarion's birthday.

Every Sunday, whatever the weather, the followers from the Town go up the Mountain en masse. The culmination of the rituals is a carefully rehearsed meeting with the Teacher, ludicrously modelled on Christ. He sits among the rocks on an armchair under a large red tasselled umbrella, dressed all in white. He wears a long robe known as a chiton, trousers, woollen mittens and headgear of the kind worn by men in the Near East. He holds a microphone and has a pair of large, rather comical sunglasses balanced on his nose.

There's no physical contact. At a safe distance the followers fall to their knees and remain in this position throughout the entire meeting.

First, in total silence, for several minutes they join hands, meditate, and merge spiritually into a single whole, into one harmoniously functioning organism. You can almost see the frost nailing down all the thoughts and sounds in the air with a large hammer. Several women lose consciousness and slump silently to the snow. The local doctor comes to their assistance with his army first-aid kit.

Afterwards there is time for questions. Vissarion's followers are full of neophyte enthusiasm. They could hold forth about their Teacher ad infinitum, breaking down theological complexities into atom-sized pieces, but at the Sunday gatherings they are only allowed to ask about specific matters – bringing up children, sex, cultivating the garden, selling or building a house, work . . . Someone asks whether they can enter their own candidate for the local elections in town.

'Absolutely not!' the Teacher erupts. 'Keep away from politics, don't aim for power. You should go and vote, but never stand for office.'

They always have a 100 per cent turnout. I was there during the last parliamentary elections. In Petropavlovka the polling station was closed several hours before the end of voting because everyone had already cast their vote, and anyone who held back was urged to go and do it by phone. In all the villages the followers have their own, internal phone lines.

The Vissarionites always vote for the party that is in power. They say openly that if things were different, the authorities would long since have sent troops armed with sub-machine guns into the taiga and scattered them to the four winds.

IV HONOUR THY FATHER AND THY MOTHER

A few years ago a desperate man from Murmansk came to see Vissarion, and accused the Siberian prophet of having taken away his wife and broken up his family. Vissarion gave no reply and calmly took several mighty punches in the face. This event is described in the *Last Testament*.

'I couldn't live with him', says Lyubov Derbina from Petropavlovka, the assailant's ex-wife. 'My husband doesn't believe in our Teacher. I left him, my mother, father, job and flat and I came here, where I don't live just for myself, but I can do a lot of good for the community, while also perfecting myself spiritually. I only took my son with me.'

'You took the man's child away from him?'

'But then he took the child from me. To tell the truth, my son went of his own accord. He wanted to spend some time with his father. He said he'd be back when he finishes school.'

Let's establish the facts. This is Lyuba's only child. The boy was nine years old when she took him away from his father, and eleven when he went back to him. He is fourteen now.

'You haven't seen your son for three years', I say. 'Isn't that hard?'

'Yes, it is.'

'So why didn't you go with him?'

'Because there are no brothers there. People who are like me, who live as I do; in a community. Back there everyone is separate, entirely alone, but I can't develop my soul on my own. I can only live here.'

'It's so strong that you can even leave your child behind?'

'Yes. To be with the Teacher and the brothers.'

Lyubov used to be an English language teacher, but now for the needs of the community she runs the 'Pole of the Earth' tourist agency, so called because the Vissarionites believe that the North Pole is not in the Arctic Ocean, but on the spot where the Teacher's house stands. The agency takes care of followers who come to look around before settling here permanently.

When Lyubov's son left, his mother got married for the second time. Her new partner had divorced shortly before, because his wife was not a believer either, although she did live with him in Petropavlovka for several years. She came here for his sake, and so that their two daughters would have a father. After the divorce she and the girls stayed put, as she had nowhere to go back to; they had sold their flat in Smolensk in order to set up home here.

'We have a great many divorces', says Lyubov. 'We do not exclude anyone, but anyone who doesn't fit in, or lives a different way from us, isn't going to feel all right among us, is bound to keep coming into conflict, will start to sicken and finally die. But please don't think I am a heartless mother – before letting my child go, at one of the Sunday gatherings I asked the Teacher if I could, seeing as his father is a non-believer. He said yes, and I immediately felt better. He knows everything, he sees everything . . .'

'How does he do that? How can an educated person allow

a stranger to make decisions about his marriage and his children?'

'That is faith. I spent a very long time searching for it. I went on a meditation course, a bio-energy course, to a bible group, I even practised yoga, but no-one could give me the answers to all my questions. But the Teacher knows everything.'

V THOU SHALT NOT KILL

Vissarion's followers do not drink alcohol or smoke. You have to remember that in Russia, especially in the provinces, for a man that is a patent symptom of a lack of virility. Worse even – you might have doubts about the sexual preferences of a guy like that.

Even in the shops run by the followers there are no products that involve killing, including fish and meat. Dairy produce is not prohibited, but only children eat it, and in very small quantities. It doesn't come from the shop but from the followers' own goats, which aren't killed, but allowed to live out their old age and die a natural death. When they drop dead, they are eaten by dogs belonging to the non-believer neighbours. Their cats eat the mice that the followers catch alive in their houses.

Oleg Patulov stopped eating meat from one day to the next.

'I simply felt like throwing up at the very sight of a tin of spam,' he says.

That day, he had taken a bayonet, stuck it in the lid, and thick fat heated to the consistency of broth in the Afghan sun had splashed onto his uniform, but everything had kept rising to his throat, so he couldn't even drink vodka to settle his stomach.

That was a few days after fifteen tanks in the company he commanded had run over an Afghan village. There was a gang of armed people hiding there, and he had received an order over the radio to capture and hold the buildings until reinforcements arrived.

He did it without firing a single shot.

'Maybe there weren't any civilians in the houses', I console him.

'What do you mean? I saw them trying to hide as we ploughed through them. Remember the Kurosawa film, *Seven Samurai*? We raced about that village like madmen in a similar way, but in thirty-seven-ton tanks. When I drove into a clay hut it didn't even feel as if I'd stepped on something. That's why I can't look at meat. Especially mince.'

Ten months later, in February 1989, Captain Patulov led his company out of Afghanistan and was discharged from the army – Gorbachev was reducing the military.

Oleg was thirty-four years old and already retired. He enrolled in a philosophy course at the Pedagogical Institute in his home city of Oryol. In 1993 he met Vissarion at a Philosophical Congress in Moscow. Now he is his chief theologian. He conducts optional world outlook classes in the mornings for women and in the evenings for men. Once a week there are compulsory classes for teachers.

For the first six years the Vissarionites teach girls and boys in separate schools. The point is for the girls not to see the boys' inevitable moments of weakness, which in the future could obstruct them in understanding the fundamental truth of the Siberian Christ's teaching, that man belongs to the world of the spirit and woman to the world of nature, which serves the spirit. That is why each woman washes her man's feet every few days.

All the schools are run according to original teaching programmes approved by the Russian Ministry of Education.

I attend a two-hour world outlook class for twelve female teachers from the school for girls, about how the financial system works in the modern world.

However, Oleg starts with the information that as a result of yesterday's parliamentary elections four parties have entered the Duma. He doesn't say which ones, but no-one asks.

All the teachers have done their homework and have read the set chapter of the *Last Testament*, in which it says that the financial system was created by the Jews. There are a vast number of civilizations in the universe, and each one rules its own world, but the more powerful ones try to dominate the smaller, younger ones, including ours.

'Who's trying to dominate us?' I ask timidly and perhaps stupidly, because all the ladies stop crocheting and glance at me over their specs for the long-sighted.

'The civilization of Lu-ci-fer', they chant in chorus.

'Who chose the Jewish nation to implement his programme', adds Oleg. 'And through the worldwide banking system he controls the fate of mankind. The Jews programme monetary crashes, make financial disasters happen, and even cause wars and revolutions, which always have vastly expensive arms programmes behind them, and . . . Well, what now, Jacek?'

'Oh yes, the Yids, sure . . .' I mumble.

'All right. So there's money. And world financial circles control it.'

'Christ was a Jew', I mention, 'which means your Teacher is one too.'

'The Heavenly Father sent his son specially to the Jewish people in order to at least partly temper that nation's hideous plan. Now He has sent him once again, because mankind is standing on the precipice. Thanks to him we are building a wonderful, ecological community full of harmony and love, for which the most valuable thing are the children. Whatever we can, we do for ourselves. Imagine a worldwide cataclysm: fuel runs out, there's no energy . . . We will survive. We will have something to eat and a way to keep warm. In some of the villages we even have our own electricity from solar panels. We are still dependent on money to a small degree, but we are moving away from it.'

The community pays Oleg 2000 roubles a month for giving his lectures (£40) – as much as the doctor. By local standards that is quite a lot, considering the state electricity only costs a penny a kilowatt here, and so many people use electricity to heat their flats, because it's not worth chopping firewood. On this money the theologian keeps a wife and five children, but like everyone here, they produce most of their food on their own plot. Oleg's oldest son is now in the army, as is the Teacher's son, but they are serving in the worker battalions, so that they won't take hold of anything that is used for killing.

Oleg belongs to the community's small circle of *budzhetniki* – paid people – as do the teachers and the priests. For this and other purposes all the followers duly pay a 30 per cent tax (independent of the state tax, which in Russia stands at 13 per cent) on every kopeck they earn, even from state allowances and retirement pensions.

All Vissarion's followers swear they have read the entire *Last Testament* many times over (which I am prepared to believe), so perhaps

Oleg's knowledge isn't quite so valuable? The catch is that the *Testament* is a set of dreadfully chaotic, convoluted tomes written in incomprehensible, artificially archaic, often incorrect language. People like me who aren't followers are incapable of wading through as much as the first few pages.

The Last Hope, the main book of the *Testament*, hand-written by Vissarion himself, begins (in the official English translation) with these words: 'Humankind! Children of the Unique Living God. The next stage of the developing Event being predestined on Mother-Earth has come, and now I am going to tell you many things plainly. You have encountered great difficulties, but these difficulties were not caused by someone else. They are the result of your efforts giving rise to lies, envy and hatred over a long period of time. For centuries you strove to raise your name up to the Heavens, but you only plunged your face in liquid manure.'

VI THOU SHALT NOT COMMIT ADULTERY

Igor, a thirty-seven-year-old former drug addict from Alma Ata in Kazakhstan, lives alone in a tiny house in the Town. 'House' is definitely an overstatement. It is a shack made of planks and plywood insulated with sawdust, which, to make it warmer, Igor has built inside a plastic tunnel. The hut has one window, but the view from it is lousy because the sheet of plastic behind it isn't transparent. There's one tiny room, a little stove, a small bed, a physical map of Krasnoyarsk Krai which takes up an entire wall, and a photo of a child in a baby nest. That's Ilya, his son.

Eighteen months ago Igor went to see his friend Danil and his wife Tsveta to build a clay oven. A month later the woman divorced and married Igor. They had nowhere to live, so they moved in with her parents in the village of Cheremshanka.

'Is premarital sex allowed?' I ask.

'If people are engaged, then yes', says Igor. 'It used to be out of the question, but there were such an awful lot of divorces that the Teacher changed the rules. You can even have two wives, because that's probably better than secret affairs, but it doesn't happen often. My marriage to Tsveta fizzled out six months after our son was born. We agreed to go on being together, but that if one of us found someone and fell in love, the other one would leave. Tsveta did it first, so I went back to the Town.'

'Didn't your friend Danil smash your face in?'

'No way – we don't have any fighting here. And we're still close friends. He was happy the woman he loved had found love and had a good time with me. He had a spiritual obligation to make our life together possible. Whenever we went to the Town we stayed with him at his place, and whenever he came down the hill he stayed with us. You have to rise above your own egoism and thrive on the happiness of others. For us that's standard. Among the young people brought up according to these rules there are dozens of stories like ours.'

'So the only mistake was getting her pregnant.'

'What mistake? Women should have as many children as possible! Do you know what a huge queue there is in Heaven for reincarnation? They're just waiting for us to make new bodies for them on Earth.'

Lyuba bore Vissarion five children, and after twenty-five years of marriage she left him. Earlier on, to help with the offspring she had brought the exquisite Sonia into her home, the eighteen-year-old daughter of their friends, followers from Petropavlovka.

'She offered her up to the Teacher herself and waited for affection to develop', says Galina Oshchepkova, who also made friends with his wife. 'Then they lived as a threesome, and when Sonia fell pregnant, Lyuba left her husband, house and children and went away. A very brave, courageous woman. She had not been blessed with faith, she didn't accept him as Christ.'

'He was able to attract thousands of people to follow him, but not his own wife?'

'They were already a married couple when she found out she was living with Christ.'

'And she was also sleeping with him, washing his underpants and socks, removing sand from his eye, cutting his nails and trimming his nose hair . . .'

'She couldn't stand it', says her friend. 'Now she lives in Krasnoyarsk. She rented a small flat and she's studying clinical psychology.'

The story of Vissarion's new love put Galina in a mood to pour warm water into a bowl, fetch the soap and kneel before her husband.

'The Teacher said oncological diseases in women come from a bad attitude to men', she says, scraping bits of dry skin from between her husband's toes, 'from silly women taking offence, sulking and being disobedient. And from feminism. I was like that too. I was forty-four, and I was still living alone, just for myself, selfishly. I spent nineteen years without a man! I lived in the community, but only in the world of women. I had the choir, massage lessons, and a dance course, but I despised blokes. Certainly it was because of the fear I inherited from life with my ex-husband. Five years ago I got a final warning.'

The doctors at the oncology clinic in Krasnoyarsk found that she had a large tumour in her uterus. They said the situation was hopeless, but for peace of mind they could operate. Galina's friends called the Teacher, and he recommended instantly removing her from hospital. He said she wouldn't survive the operation, but that she would live. She voluntarily discharged herself.

'I'd have done anything he said', says Galina.

She came back to the community but didn't have the strength to walk, or even raise her head from the pillow. She grew as thin as a skeleton and suffered terribly. For two months she prayed non-stop and listened to her friends as they read her the *Last Testament* all round the clock.

When Vladimir Pietukh, the doctor for followers from the Town, reckoned she had two weeks left to live, the priest from Petropavlovka came to prepare her for death.

'The Teacher was standing in my room as if for real', Galina tells me, 'and in front of him I could see my organ, my uterus with a large tumour. It was huge, bloody and dirty, but all of a sudden the tumour dissolved before my eyes, and my uterus blossomed like a flower.'

A few minutes after this vision her temperature dropped, and for the first time in two months the pain ceased.

'Was it a miracle?' I ask Dr Pietukh.

'No. She was cured by the power of her faith, because she believes heroically. The crucial thing is that she had decided to change her inappropriate attitude to men. By that token, in the eyes of the Father and the Teacher she deserved to get life back again. Because her tumour was huge, as big as ...'

He looks around his consulting room.

'As your camera bag. She looked dreadful, like a pregnant skeleton. I was at her place five days after the priest's visit, and she was on her feet. I did a gynaecological examination and there was no trace of the cancer. I sent her to the hospital for tests. They did an ultrasound. Nothing there! They couldn't believe it. They did it again ... She was fine. But that's not so unusual. Here that's normal. I've seen dozens of similar cases. It's the same with the drug addicts. We've got hundreds of them, but not one of them has gone back to his habit. You see? Not a single one! Often without any medication.'

'Where does this strength come from?'

'A person who opens his heart to God is in a euphoric state like the one induced by drugs, as if he's downed a glass of morphine. We live without fear, anxiety or stress, because what is there to be afraid of here among brothers? Illnesses develop when a person goes against himself, lives in a hurry, with a sense of guilt, in sin and not in accordance with nature, when his spirit is suffering.'

'Everyone keeps telling me no-one gets sick here.'

'I spent several years living in a tent, in winter too, and I didn't even catch a cold', says the doctor. 'I wasn't much needed. I worked as a woodcutter, but our numbers kept increasing, and they were mainly educated people, from the city, intelligentsia, and now and then someone cut himself with an axe, so I stitched them up, put on plaster casts, performed minor operations and went round the houses delivering babies.'

Three years ago Galina married Kolya, who after twenty-five years of marriage had left his wife for her and for the Teacher.

VII THOU SHALT NOT STEAL

In the Town, where only followers live, none of the houses have locks on the doors. Even at night they aren't locked from the inside. The citizens leave skis, sledges, and children in pushchairs outside their houses unguarded, even axes stuck in the chopping block – in the taiga, where for a real man that is the most valuable object.

To go and live there, you have to have an invitation from a council of elders and the Teacher himself, and to enter the Town you need an invitation from the headman. You have to sign your name in the register at the gate and only move about with an appointed minder. When I break away from him and wilfully head up the Mountain, where the Teacher lives, they want to drive the poor man and his entire family out of the Town. I only just manage to appease them and explain that it's my fault. Then they discover that I have pissed in the forest, and another scandal erupts. 'It is a place for shaping the spirit', they say. 'Among us, even if a horse leaves something behind the cart driver has a duty to clean it up.'

The community's money consists of income from taxes and also from the businesses they run. They chop down the taiga and have their own sawmills and carpentry shops. They build wonderful residences and churches out of wood all over Russia. They live at the heart of the taiga, 200 kilometres from the nearest city, but they have never felled any trees or put a single stick in their stoves for which they haven't paid the foresters.

VIII THOU SHALT NOT BEAR FALSE WITNESS
AGAINST THY NEIGHBOUR

Tania Denisova was a big star as a folk singer and in the Komsomol, as well as being the Central Committee's secretary for cultural affairs. In the 1970s she twice won the main prizes at the biggest folk-music festival, and when communism collapsed she became a star in business. She knows the artistic cream of Moscow, was a friend of the famous singer Bulat Okudzhava, earned as much as Croesus, did a lot of travelling, meditated at monasteries in India, China and Nepal, and in 1999 she ended up at Petropavlovka.

She had prepared a concert for the followers, which was held at the Creativity Centre. She had chosen twenty-five of the most moving, dramatic ballads, the pearls of the classic folk repertoire, but after only a few songs she could feel something wasn't right. There was no reaction. The harder she tried, the more feeling she put into it, the more the audience sat there subdued, gloomy and sad.

'My soul's howling, my heart's leaping, and that lot show no response at all!', recalls Tania. 'There they sat on their benches and chairs, making themselves smaller and smaller, pulling their heads lower and lower ... Finally I sang Okudhava's *Three Loves*, which always has the audience on their knees, but they just applauded and went home. They didn't even want an encore. The whole country weeps at my concerts, but these people . . . I was deeply offended. I couldn't sleep all night, and in the morning my hosts' daughter asked why was I killing myself like that? Why did I sing about nothing but wars, betrayal and hopeless love? It finally got through to me. They're classics, but they have a toxic energy.'

'But they're beautiful', I protest.

'So what? The followers aren't concerned about all those far-away, made-up problems. To them it sounds false, untrue. Why have all those wars, suffering and fear when you can leave the city, settle in the taiga and build a new life, look people in the eye, enjoy the forest, be creative . . . When the Festival of Spring comes, thousands of people gather by the river. There's no beer and no drugs, no-one makes a fuss, there's no punching in the face . . . That is a true miracle in our Russia.'

Tania says she swapped her one-room flat in Moscow for seven classrooms in Petropavlovka. In 2001 she sold her flat for 37,000 dollars. For this money she built a seven-room school for girls, and still had a bit left to buy a small *banya* – a Russian bathhouse, which she converted into a cottage for herself. She got divorced, so she lives on her own. They loved each other very much, but her husband didn't want to leave Moscow.

'Nothing happens by accident here', says Tania. 'It was God's plan. Now I can see it's very wise. If my husband had come here with me, we'd have built ourselves a house and there wouldn't have been any benefit from it. But as it is, there's the school.'

The Vissarionites have very bad press in Russia. The journalists call them a sect, although in no way do they resemble those totalitarian communities isolated from reality whose leaders brainwash their followers and clean out their bank accounts. No-one takes away the money the Teacher's pupils have made from selling their flats in the cities. They use it to set themselves up in their new place. They only pay taxes on income gained within the community.

The tax is collected by Grisha Gulyaev, among others, who is the 'elder for male labour', in other words a sort of headman, in the village of Gulyaevka, which is inhabited by eighteen men. It is pure coincidence that he has the same name as his village. He is forty-five, and has spent twenty of his years in prison, mostly the top-security kind. In his spare time from management work he repairs shoes and makes workers' boots.

He's very worried about me.

'If you write badly about me, the community or the Teacher', he explains, 'nothing in our lives will change, but the evil you do will come back to you. You'll only do yourself harm, because the energy of all of us, of our entire society, will turn against you, if you tell lies or are misleading. You cast just one small stone, and thousands, millions of them will come back to you, as many as the number of people who read your article. And they'll travel at the speed of light, like bullets, like red-hot drops of molten metal, and you'll never be able to scramble out from under them. They'll bury you.'

'Grisha . . . Have mercy. I wanted to talk about women.'

'Oh, all right then.'

'You've been living in the community for six years', I say, 'and always
in homes for single men or in the families of other followers. You see
them making love, cuddling, going to bed together, but you're still
single. And before that you spent twenty years in prison. Don't tell me
you never think about women.'

'Of course I do', admits Grisha. 'But if I haven't got one, it means
I'm not entitled to one. Once I start going my own way without any
devilry, twists and tumbles, no doubt the Father will send me a
woman.'

I can't understand why he has trouble with this, because he is an
extremely handsome, well-built, masculine type, a sort of Slavonic
macho man. He used to live in the Town, but the community expelled
him for having an 'inappropriate attitude to women'.

'Bitterness built up inside me', he says, 'until I began to boil over.
I went about feeling angry, I kept arguing, provoking everyone . . .
There was one girl, but it wasn't what you think. We used to go
dancing. In pairs and in a circle. But if you have no way of dealing
with anger, you explode! You erupt! Living with it inside you is impossible! And I was working with horses. They can sense it, and they can
show their moods too, and that made me even angrier – one of them
would kick me, I'd give him a whack, and so on, round and round. I
was shattering all the horses' nerves, so no-one else could cope with
them either. I was ruining them.'

'Were you expelled because of the horses or the women?'

'It all meant I kept causing scenes, and it even came to a fight, but there, in the Town, there's a very strict regime, you aren't even allowed to raise your voice because it's a place for shaping your spirit. I just wanted a woman, that's all.'

X   NOR WHATEVER BELONGS TO THY NEIGHBOUR

In 1961, at the Twenty-Second Congress of the Soviet Communist Party Nikita Khrushchev announced that by 1980 real communism would be built in the USSR. Now we know that none of those plans came to fruition, and that 1980 was the year in which at one of the Polish shipyards the system started being dismantled.

However, Vissarion is trying to build a mini Utopia, and in the Town, his capital, he is selecting people for it, as Noah selected animals for the Ark. He is most willing to take couples, though not according to race or type, but ability, talent, artistry and profession. There is a blacksmith, a carpenter, a cooper and a tailor, each of whom has at least one woman and children, to whom he is teaching his profession. There is a doctor, an electrician, a beekeeper and a forester – an expert on the taiga, lots of artists with a wide range of special skills, and a huge diversity of human types, in terms of personality and mentality. Altogether they bring together the wisdom and life experience of all nations and generations of the former Soviet empire.

Maybe that is why the world's intelligence services are so very interested in whether this bold experiment will succeed.

Giving to each according to his needs has proved a failure. Five years ago all the followers used to be given as much food as they wanted, and when they needed money for something the community gave it to them. They didn't get any money for working at the community businesses, workshops and studios, and the same went for everything they did for their fellow followers. If they earned money by working or selling something outside the community, they threw it into the general kitty.

They call the financial system that is now in force on the Mountain 'not entirely monetary'. Each citizen, regardless of age or occupation, receives 250 roubles (£5) a month from the community. Only Vladimir, their doctor, gets 2000 (£40) rather than just 1000 (he has a wife and two children), because he has so much work to do that he cannot take care of a garden.

Of the forty-two families who started 'taming the taiga' at the site of the Town in 1997, only ten have lasted to the present. Most of the followers who now live there joined up in later years.

'What's the hardest thing about this Utopia of yours?' I ask Grisha, who lasted eight months in the Town.

'The hardest thing is to work for free. It gives rise to envy, jealousy. You build up negative energy. I simply couldn't manage. Inside I was howling with despair, shaking like a paralytic. Sheer physical pain, impotence, suffering because I hadn't been given a jar of honey, though I'd worked so terribly hard cutting wood, or because I was given something, but only the same amount as people who hadn't worked as hard as me.'

'So Grisha, what on earth are you doing in this community?'

'I'm building a better world. Because the outside one is no good for anything.'

Dead people's bodies will be preserved in special cold stores, where the blood circulation will be artificially maintained. In figurative terms, these would be 'living corpses'. At any moment, in case of need, a surgeon will be able to take from this store of human spare parts any particular organ for transplant into a live person.

Report from the Twenty-First Century, 1957.

The town. At noon the bells ring, and everyone stops work and prays.

Black Square

A CONVERSATION WITH
DEACON ANDREI KURAYEV, ORTHODOX PHILOSOPHER
AND RELIGIOUS COMMENTATOR

What has happened to the Russians? Why such an abundance of religions? Since the 1990s, every church in the world, even the most bizarre ones, have been gathering an incredible harvest here. Plus dozens of home-grown sects.

In Egypt they used to say that on the banks of the Nile you only have to stick an iron bar into the ground and in a month a tractor will grow from it, so fertile is the soil. In Russia the spiritual ground is very rich too. Even purely secular spiritual trends grow immeasurably here. Take Marxism, for instance. It became Bolshevism. In our country there are many such occurrences. That's why the Russians are so highly sensitive, susceptible to religious nonsense, hence the multiplicity of sects. It is a positive phenomenon, because it means there is a spiritual need in people's hearts forcing them to go on a quest, but naturally people get lost, they lose their way. The Soviet system of repression worked like a bulldozer, flattening anything that grew above the surface, all religious and philosophical thought, but it couldn't get down to the roots, to the most fundamental of human needs – the need for religion.

Why don't people go to the Orthodox Church, which has been present on Russian terrain for more than a thousand years?

Out of the instinctive fear that it is a reincarnation of the Communist Party, because it's such a large, centralized and secretive organization. That's what they sense. The communists taught people not to have faith or trust. It has come to a point where the more actively we, the clergy, come out to meet people in the streets or knock on their doors, the more fear and mistrust we engender. Orthodoxy in Russia has become the 'sect' of the intelligentsia. Unfortunately there aren't any working-class people at our churches. Of course there are the traditional old ladies, but apart from that there are only intellectuals and students.

Why is the Orthodox Church so weak?

Because in the Soviet era no-one supported it in the fight against communism.

Which you lost.

Right. Rome supported the Catholics in Czechoslovakia, their brothers from the West supported the Protestants in East Germany, even the Soviet Muslims received aid from the Arabian Peninsula, but the Orthodox Church was on its own, with no financial, theological, organizational or educational help. Now we are rebuilding our intellectual fabric – with extreme difficulty, because what we were taught at Orthodox seminaries in the Soviet era was on a level with the religious instruction in pre-revolutionary primary schools. Seriously. I am a professor at the Moscow Academy of Theology, but I must honestly admit that with my qualifications, before the October Revolution I couldn't even have taught the students singing.

Have you read Vissarion's Last Testament?

I have tried, but it's quite unreadable. Complete gibberish. In fact, Vissarion describes a meeting with me in there. He was in Moscow and he invited me for a chat. He makes a big effort to have episodes from the life of Christ repeated in his own biography. Jesus met and conversed with the Pharisees, so he has this meeting too. That was how I became a Pharisee. I talked to him for three hours, and there was one thing I couldn't fully fathom – whether or not he believes in what he says.

In my view it's not a question of faith at all, but a phenomenon known to the world for thousands of years, the fact that demand stimulates supply, in the spiritual sphere too. His followers are people who have suffered terrible traumas, people with dysfunctional family or emotional lives, or the sort of people who have spent decades living in a world of absurdity, in other words within the Soviet and then the Russian security forces – mainly militia and military men. I think these people found it very hard to bear the dreadful spiritual void that arose in the place of Marxism, so along came a man who filled it. They needed a prophet, so he stepped forward and they accepted him.

And each of them imports their own ideas into his incomprehensible words. Thus they satisfy their own needs. It's like Malevich's *Black Square*. Each person understands it in his own way.

Anisya Otsur the shamaness treating a patient in Kyzyl.

My guardian angel's plait

Finally she filled her mouth with as much milk as she could fit in there. She stuck the bowl in my hands so it wouldn't be in her way, gave her head a good shake, almost took a run-up and spat the whole lot straight into my face.

Instantly I felt better. And once I had wiped my eyes, I saw a very real invoice, including VAT, for 800 roubles (£16) for a 'purification ritual'.

When I made the claim for my business trip at the newspaper office, I put it down as a 'health-care expense'.

PRICE LIST

It was 500 roubles more than we had agreed. For the full service, because she not only purified me and purged the entire space around me of bad events, deeds, spirits and memories, of all the negative energy I had accumulated over the years, but also made contact with my ancestors while she was about it, asking them to protect me from evil during my onward journey.

'Consultation' would have been much cheaper. For that they take whatever you can pay, which means at least 100 roubles (£2), because that only pays for a five-minute reading from fortune-telling pebbles which will say what I am sick with and what's ahead of me in the next few days, months or years.

The ritual for purifying a passenger car at a cost of 300 roubles, or a lorry at 600, means that the vehicle will serve for many years to come without accident or breakdown. The same ritual to purify your flat costs 500 roubles. Purification of a herd of goats, sheep, horses, yaks and all manner of livestock costs up to 3000, and of a school, hospital, office, restaurant or any kind of business costs 5500. When the shamaness who spat milk at me was asked to come and purify the Republic's Ministry of Labour, she rounded the figure up to 6000.

The remaining items on the price list at the Dungur Shamans' Cooperative are blessing a spring and a tree for 1500 roubles, family rituals of feeding fire or water for 2500, and funeral rites at home or at the cemetery on the seventh and forty-ninth day after burial and a year after the death for 2000. For each item, the price is a thousand roubles higher if it requires a trip out of town. For 'suppressing hysteria', 'saving from fear', 'guaranteeing success in business, love, study and family life' and for 'help in choice of profession and also of life partner' no price is given. It depends how complicated the case is. The same goes for healing sicknesses of the soul, protection from witchcraft and removal of curses.

HOSPITAL

I met her at the Children's Hospital in the city of Kyzyl, in the Tuva Republic. On my car journey from Moscow to Vladivostok,

I had to make a detour of almost a thousand kilometres south to get there.

In a white tiled ward, among the traction hoists for broken legs and the IV stands, there's a wailing woman buzzing about in an Indian headdress and a dirty, full-length smock, from which hang hundreds of coloured bits of string, wings, fangs, paws and bones of various animals. This is shamaness Anisya Otsur. From a sheep's tibia made into a wind instrument she extracts the most appalling noise in the world. It's also because of this awful blare that Kyzyl's Orthodox believers and Jehovah's Witnesses call the shamans servants of Satan.

The woman waves a smoking conifer branch to fumigate the area around the bed of a terrified nine-year-old boy with an oxygen mask on his face. She uses a raven's wing to sweep the smoke onto the white bedclothes, the weeping parents, nurses and doctor, who are all standing by the patient's bed. The smoke from this high-mountain shrub, called *autysh*, purifies and soothes, and also drives away evil forces. The boy's mother is holding an *eren*, a hideous doll very like the shamaness, with a black face. With the help of a *dungur*, which is a shaman's drum made of goatskin, the old woman casts a spirit into it, which is meant to save the boy, who is dying from stomach cancer.

So she bangs away as if possessed and sings in a drawling, trance-like way, and all the children in the ward start to cry in despair. Finally, she cleans the boy with the stick she has been using to beat the drum, as if now it were a clothes brush, and splashes the walls, windows and floors with vodka and milk out of a plastic teat.

Tuva is the most godforsaken corner of the world, certainly of the

Asian continent, the geographic centre of which is on the banks of the Yenisei River, only about fifteen minutes' walk from the children's hospital. There are no roads here. The one you take to get here also ends here. Tuva has no railway, and hasn't even got any neighbours. It is surrounded by overgrown taiga and uninhabited mountains. On one side there is the Sayan range, on the other the Altai, and to the south are the wild Mongolian steppes. The first Christians reached Tuva in the nineteenth century, and the first house was not built here until the following century. And there is absolutely nothing here – no ancient sites, grand buildings or industry; 90 per cent of the Republic's budget consists of grants from Moscow. It is such a hole that not even an international burger chain has set up a diner here.

The Tuvans are the only nation in Siberia to be the national majority within their administrative region. And by a long chalk, because of the 314,000 inhabitants, only about 30,000 are Russian.

A LONG TIME AGO

The first time they locked up Kuular Khandyzhap Medi-Kyzy was in 1929. People called her Ulu-Kham, which means Great Shamaness. She was forty-four at the time. The previous Great Shaman was shot by the Bolsheviks immediately after the October Revolution.

It was the secret police's first campaign against the shamans. They drove people into the squares and burned all the drums, *eren* dolls and ritual costumes on bonfires. Any kind of shamanic practice was made illegal. Ulu-Kham and her entire family were expelled from their village and deported for ten years hundreds of kilometres south, to the

Mongolian border. For a Tuvan, being uprooted from your homeland is a terrible punishment.

A few years later she was arrested again and sentenced to five years in prison for being the mother of a counter-revolutionary. Her son was a Tuvan state official. During the great purges of the Stalin era he was taken to be a Japanese spy, an enemy of the people, and was shot.

She served the entire sentence, and then in 1947 she was arrested a third time. In defiance of the ban, she had gone on treating children in her native village. This was regarded as an assault on Soviet medicine, and she was given twenty-five years in a labour camp. She was sixty-two years old.

MONGUSH

You can find him daily at the Tuva National Museum, which on sunny days is open from ten o'clock until six, and on cloudy ones from eleven to seven.

His study door is blocked by a large stake, and there is a sign on it saying: 'The Honourable Mongush Borakhovich Kenin-Lopsan, doctor of historical studies, chief expert ethnographer, living treasure-house of shamanism, Tuva Republic Man of the Century, national writer, founder and honorary president of the Tuvan Dungur Shamans' Cooperative.'

Underneath there is another, even bigger sign: 'Fee for entry to see the president . . . [all the titles are repeated in reverse order] ten roubles.'

That's a zloty (20p). And the stake is at least a metre long, thick as an arm, gnarled, crooked, and painted in pale colours. It is leaning against the door, though I was told the Honourable Mongush Borakhovich was in . . . *Weeell*, maybe I'll take a peek, I think to myself and stretch out a hand.

'Stop!' cries an old man with long white hair. 'That is a sacred stake!'

Later on I discovered that it comes from the shamans' cult tree, and that Mongush Borakhovich has been using it for fifty-five years instead of a key to his study. It is a sentry that no Tuvan thief would dare to touch.

For starters I had to say when I was born. It turned out I was born in the year of the rooster. Mr Mongush took out his fortune-telling pebbles, arranged them in small piles, nodded his head and said: 'You have to know when a man, horse, calf, or camel was born to know what he's worth. I was born on 10 April 1925. It was the year of the cow.'

He is the nephew of the Great Shamaness Ulu-Kham, the only descendant of a powerful shaman family, because the communists murdered every single one of Ulu-Kham's children.

He refused to let me ask a single question. Every time I tried, he shouted at me, saying my questions were like those of a first-former, that I hadn't read his books, that I had tried to take his business card with my left hand and that I don't understand the East, and to make matters worse I talk too loud, while he is a man who 'works with his senses', and on top of that a man who is on his way out.

But he handed me a small comb, told me to tidy my hair and take my own photo, then I had to enter my name in his visitor's book. He said I was to praise him and thank him nicely for everything. When I had finished writing, he was asleep with his head on the desk.

CLINIC

The Dungur Shamans' Cooperative has its headquarters in a tiny wooden cottage at 255 Rabocha Street in Kyzyl. They run the shamanic clinic with a price list, invoices, twenty-four-hour shifts and home visits. The association has a secretary and an accountant, and pays taxes, pension contributions and health insurance for the shamans.

The head of the clinic is Nadyezhda Sam, a fifty-four-year-old retired geography teacher. She employs ten of the 300 Tuvan shamans who operate officially (meaning those who have a certificate from one of three associations). Sometimes they come to work in the capital from very remote mountain villages, because only here can they earn a decent wage.

Nadyezhda splits her sides laughing when I tell her how the Honourable Mongush Borakhovich received me. In all Tuva no-one ever mentions him without the epithet.

'You should have had a present for him', she says. 'Best of all a huge box of chocolates.'

'Why do the doctors let you into the hospitals?'

'Because we have miracles happen, and they don't. No-one is as able to stop a haemorrhage as I am. And when someone is bleeding because of haemophilia, the doctors call me themselves.'

'How do you do it?'

'I talk it round. I pray it away.'

Nadyezhda blows into her clenched fist, whispers something to it, mutters, swings her arm and claps it against a spot on my thigh where there's a make-believe wound.

'Shamanism is a belief in the power of nature and the spirits of the ancestors', she says. 'It's not me that does the healing, but an unknown force that I ask for help. And if the haemorrhage doesn't stop, I do a ritual to bless water, but the live kind, in the river, beside which I light a fire. I throw various things to eat and drink onto it, and like that, through smoke, I feed the spirit of the river. And the whole time I pray, using words and the drum. Then I scoop up some water and carry it to the hospital. It is no longer ordinary water, but prayer-filled. The patient drinks it and washes with it. Like this a harmonious, steady, united rhythm of water, fire and man is created. The perfect rhythm.'

'Why are you so similar to the North American Indian shamans?' I ask Nadyezhda. 'The same feather headdresses, drums, rhythms, tunes and ways of singing. And similar rituals.'

'It is they who are like us. After all, they come from here. Twelve thousand years ago they set off from central Siberia, crossed the Bering Strait and populated both Americas.'

TRIP

Shamaness Anisya Otsur, the one I met at the children's hospital, doesn't want to tell my fortune. She has a very poor command of Russian. She says that for divination you need lots of 'unsimple' words, and in this language there aren't any.

I'm really sorry, because Anisya can tell fortunes from a sheep's shoulder blade, which she thrusts into the fire, and then watches how it burns. She is a very humble village woman of over seventy, who smells of smoke and animals, and whose face is suntanned even in winter. Anisya rattles like a skeleton, because her ritual costume is festooned in lily-white goat and sheep bones. She comes from the village of Iskra, known in Tuvan as Tsubon-Sazhenalak, where to this day the Iskra herder's state farm is still in operation. For more than half a century, ever since she discovered her own shamanic power, successive communist state-farm managers facing animal pestilence, natural calamities, and even financial collapse or lack of fuel for the machines, have ordered her to perform the relevant rituals in secret.

The woman lights a sprig of *autysh*, purifies and warms her hands in the fire, then blows on the flame, so the plant starts to smoulder profusely, like a smoke bomb. She fumigates me very thoroughly, including my feet, crotch and armpits. She fumigates a stool, part of the ceiling and the floor, on which she places the seat. She tells me to sit down.

She performs lots of bizarre acts. She pours milk and vodka into various small containers, strokes a dry snake that is hanging on some deer antlers, rattles her black magic jewellery and keeps bashing me with a strange wooden sceptre with a big tangle of shamanic debris attached to it: bones, fangs, claws, feathers, ribbons, rags, bits of metal and wood. This is the *aberyok*, Anisya's extremely powerful personal bodyguard, something like a shaman's vitamin complex, a mixture of talismans, each of which protects against something different.

'Does your heart ache?' she asks.

'No.'

'But it will start to. You should not drink. Remember. You have immense willpower. And imagination. And a long road ahead of you. But it is open. Watch out for a large metal object. It is very dangerous for you.'

'I came here by car. And I have to go beyond Baikal. To Vladivostok.'

'You must go to the tyre centre and check. Wheels. I can see wheels. I call on the spirit of the place where I was born to make sure your head doesn't spin.'

She tells me to drink the milk and vodka out of several containers. I have to close my eyes, so I switch on the Dictaphone to record what she is doing by sound at least. The air becomes thick with smoke, and she starts banging a drum, harder, faster and more steadily with every beat, as if wanting to drive someone away or defeat them with this music. Or kill them. And she wails wistfully, more and more wildly, narcotically, throatily. Only some Tuvans are capable of making their vocal cords shudder in this unearthly way, producing several sounds of various pitch simultaneously, and triggering vibrations that change the rhythm of your heart.

After three or four minutes she falls silent and spits the milk at me.

When I listened to the tape a week ago, it turned out it wasn't three or four minutes. The tape was wound onto the end, so at least an hour had gone by, while she never stopped drumming and singing. And where had I tripped off to? Had I fallen asleep as I sat there? Had I died a little?

I bought the biggest box of chocolates I could find in Kyzyl, and went to see the Honourable Mongush Borakhovich again.

The last time he saw his aunt, the Great Shamaness Ulu-Kham, was in 1947 before leaving for college in Leningrad. She told his fortune and said under no circumstances should he return to his homeland until six years had gone by. Soon after, she was arrested for the third time.

At the headquarters of the Kyzyl NKVD on Komsomolskaya Street they cut off her hair and took a photograph of her. In it, Ulu-Kham is still in her coat, reaching below the knees, which the Tuvans call a *del*, but she would soon exchange it for a prisoner's donkey jacket. She was given a twenty-five-year sentence and transported from Tuva to the Far North, to the Charnogorka women's camp in Krasnoyarsk Krai.

Six years were up in 1953, after the death of Stalin, so Mongush Borakhovich went home. At the railway station in Abakan a man came up to him and asked for money, saying he had none to pay for his journey home. Mongush gave it to him, and then the man said he knew who Mongush was, because he had just come out of a labour camp, where he had met the shamaness Ulu-Kham. He told Mongush that in the camp she had had a prophetic dream.

'The sun was surrounded by a black ring', the Honourable Mongush recalls the stranger's tale. 'Silver rain fell from the sky and a hurricane came. A crack appeared in the earth, out of which flowed a red river. Ulu-Kham related her dream to all the prisoners and explained that something unusual was going to happen in the country.

235

The next day, Stalin died. My aunt also told that man he would soon leave the camp.'

The shamaness told the stranger that the young man whom he would ask for help on the way, and who would give it to him, would be the last male descendant of her clan. He was to bid him farewell from her, as they would never see each other again.

The prison camps emptied. At Charnogorka, where Ulu-Kham was the last Tuvan woman left, the governor was a Russian NKVD general. His daughter was seriously ill. She had even been treated in Moscow, but there was no hope for her. She was dying, so in extreme despair the governor turned to the old shamaness for help.

Ulu-Kham cured the girl. In his gratitude, the general arranged her release and put her in his own car. Then they set off on the journey back to the shamaness's homeland.

Their last stopover was in Tuva, where they spent the night by a ford with some nomadic herders. The Great Shamaness spent a long time standing by the water, singing softly, then took off her shoes, threw them into the river and said she was not destined to return home and see her loved ones again. She calmly went to bed in the herders' yurt, and died that very night.

'On 20 June in the year of the serpent', says the Honourable Mongush Borakhovich Kenin-Lopsan gloomily.

NOT LONG AGO

'I was four years old when they found out I was going to be a shamaness', says Aychuryek.

That means it must have been 1962.

'I was a normal child, but I only ever played with whirlwinds. They're very good, very jolly. I spent the whole time with them, they shaped me. In my village the men drove out to work in the taiga, and the whirlwinds always knew where they were going, they ran around them like dogs and then told me everything. One day some people were going to drive into the forest on a tractor, but there were already some evil winds sitting on it, and I had a vision, so I ran, crying and shouting, I threw myself in front of the vehicle to stop them from going, because they'd never come back. Don't go with those evil winds! My mother came and took me away. She yelled at me that I shouldn't talk like that. So they drove into the taiga, the tractor fell over a precipice and five men were killed. I used to fly with the whirlwinds, but other people couldn't see them. They told me everything in my vision.'

'And then what happened?'

'They took me to a mental hospital. The doctors said I had epilepsy and schizophrenia.'

'You call it the shamanic illness.'

'Yes. For almost thirty years I lived alternately in hospitals or alone in the mountains, near my shamanic tree. The doctors wouldn't let me have children, because they'd be like me, with epilepsy and the shamanic illness, but I had to. I fell pregnant, but I did the right rituals, made sacrifices and prayed a lot. Now my son is at the best school in Kyzyl. Eleventh-year maths and physics. And he doesn't have our illness. And mine went away too, when I gave birth.'

'What is a shaman afraid of?' I ask.

237

'Spirits, and his own shamanic illness. Only after it will he become a strong shaman. After the illness, but the fear never goes away.'

'Fear of what?'

'Visions. Because I can see what's in store for people, and also any evil they have experienced or have in their soul. It's like watching terrifying films non-stop. It can drive you mad. And what if you're four or five years old? The soul runs away from it and they shut you up in the loony bin.'

HEAVENS

Aychuryek is the most powerful shamaness in Tuva, head of the Tos-Deer – meaning Nine Heavens – Religious Cooperative. She treats people with herbs, roots and shamanic, so-called wild massage. No-one taught it to her. She knows it all from birth. But she doesn't do internal medicine, ordinary illnesses or infections. Exceptionally difficult cases are brought to her from all over Russia – wildly aggressive madmen, paralysed people, people in comas and the mentally ill.

She takes them to powerful places, to her shamanic tree, to Urgalak cave, the Arzhan spring, and to the shores of a sacred saltwater lake.

'They need strength, because the city is a very difficult space. I tell them about the spirits and the whirlwinds, and we look for strength. Just the place itself gives it, and heals.'

'I know you fight cancers in the same way.'

'The patient has to stop taking chemicals, because that causes a loss of strength. I give him a lot of smoke, and I boil nettles and fir bark for him to drink – to make his hair grow back and to let him regain strength.'

'And I couldn't meet with you for a week because you were sick with the silly old flu.'

For my journey Aychuryek gives me an amulet with three stones in a small bundle of rags. She says the stones come from three very strong places and they are to protect me from 'big metal', curses and spells, even ones cast by evil shamans and Gypsies.

'And it won't cause interference if you have a badge of your god round your neck', she says, meaning my medallion of the Virgin Mary. 'A shamanic talisman doesn't interfere with anything.'

I was also given a small *eren*, a lovely little wooden doll with a pebble inside, which Aychuryek made herself. You have to rattle it when things are very bad.

At home we call it the 'little shamaness'. It turned out to be the only cure when my daughter Oleśka had a splitting headache. Seriously.

LATELY

'Why do you let shamans into the hospital?' I ask Dr Olaga Danovich, an anaesthesiologist from the Tuvan Children's Hospital.

'Because they treat the soul. And we only treat the body. They can pray, burn incense, play the drum and sing, but we keep watch to make sure they don't give any medicines. I know 100 per cent that if the patient's condition is serious, and a surgeon is needed for instance, no folk medicine is going to help. They can be effective for chronic, long-term illnesses, sometimes even cancers, but they're most useful in situations where a psychotherapist is needed. At our hospital I often see a huge queue of patients, and I know half of them should be sent to a psychiatrist, but we haven't got one in Tuva. Nor any psycho-therapists, so they'd be better off going to a shaman, a Buddhist lama or an old woman who does herbal cures.'

'In this city you also have a qualified cosmo-energetic therapist and a Kirgiz who heals using the Koran.'

'They would do just as well. Lots of physically healthy people have psychological problems and imaginary illnesses', says Dr Danovich. 'Then the body starts to pack up. A shaman can cure that sort of illness.'

'But the mother who brought the shamaness to your ward to see the boy with stomach cancer believed she would do what you could not.'

'Of course we both know the child will not get better. But perhaps it will make the parents feel better? A sort of Tuvan psychotherapy. And possibly if the parents feel better, the child will improve too.'

'So faith cures them, not the shaman.'

'It comes to the same thing.'

TRANCE

At the Tengeri – meaning Paradise – City Religious Organization there is a ceremony going on in connection with the New Year. About a dozen shamans and shamanesses are sitting in a group, not exactly singing, and not exactly reciting, but rather shouting in a monotonous chorus, in hoarse voices that grate on the ear. There are also several dozen believers packed into this small space in an indescribable crush. They are placing gifts on little tables in front of the shamans – cigarettes, vodka, cartons of milk, plates of biscuits, butter by the weight in little plastic bags, honey, lard and tins of condensed milk.

Suddenly they all fall silent and only one shaman can be heard, then they take up the choral singing again, though this time it's a very beautiful, yearning, ethereal and unfathomable song that has trouble staying within these walls, virtually blows the hut apart, all but raises the roof and flies away.

One of the shamans falls to the floor. The others pick him up and get him back on his feet. His face is screened by dozens of little plaits, so I can only see his twisted, foaming mouth for seconds at a time, as a copious stream of thick saliva pours down his beard. They give him some vodka. The shaman drinks and spits, starts to thrash about, throw himself around the room, shrieking, raging and fuming like a spoiled child or a senile old man. But he isn't old, although his legs and back have bent double, his hands have started to shake and his voice is going squeaky.

The shaman is in a trance, and thus he is Angun, the spirit that he has let into himself – the spirit of his ancestor, a very old shaman who died almost 200 years ago. People are falling to their knees, and in this position they are approaching Angun. Each of them asks about his own affairs, about children, money, the future, or health. The spirit knows everything.

I went up too, but with a camera, and I almost lost it, along with my teeth, because Angun took fright at me and aimed a mighty blow at me with his large cane, topped with a dragon's head. He must have thought I was pointing a gun at him, the other shamans explained. He had never seen a camera. Apparently it came very close to him seizing my soul.

I retreated, and read a short essay stuck to the wall. The most interesting bit was about the shamanic illness. It starts when the spirits let the chosen person know he is to become a shaman, and he puts up resistance. The spirits break him, by sending all sorts of misfortunes, calamities and illnesses down on him. Usually mental illnesses, including alcoholism. The person loses his property, job and family. His loved ones die, and finally so does he.

CURSE

Viktor Dorzhevich Tsydypov was thirty years old when in 1984 bandits attacked him and smashed his head in with an iron bar. He was airlifted to Moscow for an operation, but it wasn't a success and the doctors said he wouldn't survive.

'I didn't give in', he says. 'I spent fifteen years travelling across the entire former Soviet Union to find the best hospitals and doctors. They couldn't help me at all. I had the right tests, even neurological ones, and a CAT scan of my brain, but I couldn't stand up, because I kept falling over. I could only walk on all fours, but after ten metres I would pass out from pain and exhaustion.'

Then he went to see all the famous monks, lamas, folk healers, miracle workers, shamans and energy therapists, of whom there are swarms in Russia. He even went to see the popular psychic healer, Anatoly Kashpirovsky. But still he kept on conking out.

'During that time my father, my uncle, my brother Sasha and my cousin all died of cancer', says Viktor. 'My brother Lovka died of meningitis because he was bitten by a tick. How on earth did that happen? In February, when there aren't any ticks! Loshka and Mishka died in an accident, and the last one, Seryoga, was killed by a piece of metal. I had five brothers, and now only the girls, a couple of grandparents and I are left.'

'What do you mean, by a piece of metal?'

'By a bullet.'

'Bandits?' I enquire further.

'No – we were at war then. Chechnya.'

In 1999 Viktor was taken to see a very powerful Mongolian shaman. He let Angun come inside him, who said it was the shamanic illness, the curse of Viktor's ancestor. The spirit had chosen him, and wanted him to become a shaman.

'But why didn't he choose Lovka?' cries Viktor. 'He studied the humanities, he wrote books and poetry, he'd have been more suited to a life with spirits, but I'm a mechanical engineer, a down-to-earth person who had never once been in a church or a Buddhist datsan before the accident.'

'So you could say your ancestor has murdered your entire family.'

'Yes. To make me become a shaman. There are thousands of people like me in the world. Half the people who populate all the mental hospitals.'

243

The day after, at the New Year ceremony, Angun entered into Viktor's body. When he left it, as usual the shaman could not remember what had been happening to him during that time. He sits in his old armchair, extremely worn out, drinking revolting Mongolian tea with milk, salt and fat in it, and for several minutes more he still has one foot in the world of spirits. He can see more, hear more and feel more.

'Do you know', he asks me in a weak voice, 'that your guardian angel is a woman?'

'How do you know?'

'I can see her. It's very rare for a woman to look after a man. I think it's someone from your family. It must be your granny.'

'Which one?'

'How should I know? I don't know your grandmothers.'

'What does she look like?' I persist.

'She's got . . . Our women don't do that. Plaited hair.'

'A plait! Long and thick? It's Granny Irena. She died eight years before I was born. What's she doing now?'

'She's smiling. After all, she can hear us. But I think she died with a wound in her heart. I wonder why she chose you?'

'So why did she?' I ask the shaman.

'How should I know?'

With the help of radar a spacecraft will constantly monitor inner space. The moment it discovers a meteorite at a threatening distance and a collision proves inevitable, a powerful ray of energy will be fired in its direction. Under its effect the meteorite will reach such a high temperature that it will disintegrate into tiny pieces, which will evaporate from the heat.

Report from the Twenty-First Century, 1957.

Masha and Maxim in the taiga. The white fever is starting.

White fever

A voice grants the herder three wishes.

His first wish is a crate of vodka, and he gets it. His second wish is another crate of vodka, and his third is one more.

'So you're a golden fish, then?' jabbers the herder.

'No, man. I am the White Fever.'

Telling this joke is as low and tasteless as telling jokes about Jews, ovens and gas chambers.

But the Evenks tell it, and fall about laughing as they do so.

Because it's about them. And vodka is their equivalent of Cyclon B.

Except that it works more slowly.

Now watch out. In this chapter the words 'die', 'kill' and 'death' appear more than fifty times. The word 'rifle' comes up eleven times, 'vodka' twelve times, and only once does the word 'love' appear, but in an unhappy context. If that doesn't suit you, don't read on.

A LETTER TO GOD

Before their very eyes the shamaness changes into a 100-year-old woman. She develops a hunchback, her legs bow beneath her, and her voice is as creaky as a coffin lid. She tells Lena to write down every-thing she needs from the spirits.

So Lena starts like this: 'Dear Sovoki. At the start of my letter, I am writing to you with a humble request for the Russkies to vacate our land . . .'

The shamaness reads it and splits her sides laughing. 'That's how you might open a petition to the governor, not a letter to God. You have to do it in a purely human way, like writing to your brother.'

'But I don't know how', says Lena. 'All my life I've only ever written to officials. There was always "we demand", "we require", "our land", and "we, the Evenk nation".' So she dictates, and the shamaness writes it down in a human way. 'The first request is for the Russians to give back our land, then for the Evenk nation to stop drinking, and for a purpose to appear; for the young people to finish school, and for my Dima to be set free and never to drink again, and as well as him the same goes for my Yura, Svetka, Masha, Tinka, Borka, Tania, Maxim, Danka . . .'

There's a lot of it. Two pages written out in fine script on both sides.

Then the shamaness says Lena has to sing the whole text in her own language, because the old woman who enters her during the rituals doesn't know Russian, and only she can transmit the people's requests to the spirits.

'So I began to sing for the whole taiga', says Lena. 'And my nation was with us. The herders and hunters.'

The horror-struck people listen to Lena's husky wailing. 'Belekeldu! Belekeldu! Save us, good Sovoki, because we're dying out!' Shivers run down their spines, scratching like claws, and they're seized with fear, as when they meet a bear in the taiga, or the devil himself.

THE BRIGADE

Lena Kolesova is a petite person with small but very rough, coarse hands, tinted glasses and an elaborate blond perm. She was born fifty years ago in the taiga and grew up in a tent, so she never feels the cold. All winter she goes about in an autumn jacket and *unty* – high boots made of reindeer skin. The problems she has with her knees are probably the result of her being overweight, which is rare for her nation. The Evenks are very thin, small and wiry. They have dark skin and hair, chestnut-brown eyes and an oily complexion. There is something tragic about their faces. The men in particular glower gloomily. They have flat, stubble-free faces with prominent supraorbital ridges and foreheads that are wrinkled from birth, making them look severe. If you offer one of them a friendly greeting, you can be 100 per cent sure he won't snap back at you.

The women, old and young, although very slender, move heavily and awkwardly, as if carrying a great burden. They have small breasts and a straight waistline, but fortunately their slanting eyes do look as if they are just about to squint into a smile.

Lena is a widow who lives with her family in the village of Bamnak in the Amur district, eastern Siberia. She is the leader of the local Evenks.

In March 1985 Mikhail Gorbachev came to power in the Soviet

Union. Perestroika began, and Lena got a job as an animal husbandry specialist at Udarnik, the local state farm. Her brigade, Number One, included seventeen herders, two of whom were women, two were fourteen-year-old boys, and there were 3500 reindeer.

ONE — THE LUNGS

Six-and-a-half years later the Soviet Union collapsed, and in Brigade Number One Sasha Yakovlev was killed when the ice broke as they were driving the herd across a river.

Sasha graduated from flying school in the city, got married there and had a child. Then he divorced, returned to his home village and began to drink heavily. He was thirty years old.

There were sixteen herders left in the brigade.

TWO — THE THROAT

He was fifty-one. On 27 March 1993 he drank himself to death. Yuri Trifanov was foreman of the brigade and also Lena's uncle. He left a widow, Tamara. The Evenks rarely register their marriages. They come to an agreement with a woman and move with her into their own tent or house. That is what their weddings are like. They never have a celebration to mark the event.

Yuri spent his whole life in the taiga. He didn't even have a house in the village, like the other herders, but when he died Tamara moved there for good and drank non-stop until it paralysed her. She could no longer go to the shop or even raise a glass to her lips, and so she died.

She left three children, who were not Yuri's offspring, but from her first husband. Two of them died soon after. The third, young Yura, is a legendary figure.

He is a herder. One day he ran out of the tent in the middle of winter without his jacket and hat. He was entirely sober, but this was soon after a tremendous, four or five-day drinking spree. He ran blindly ahead without stopping for two days and nights. He had only a small loaf of bread with him, and at night the temperature fell to minus forty degrees. A Russian hunter came upon his footprints on his hunting territory. He was convinced it was a poacher, so he set off after him in a caterpillar-track vehicle. He drove 120 kilometres across the taiga in deep snow before he caught up with him.

Yura didn't know why he had run like that or for how long. He thought he was running towards his own campsite, but the whole time he was getting further away from it. The hunter saw Yura's huge, terrified eyes and his unnaturally dilated pupils, so he didn't ask any questions. At once he recognized the white fever.

After the foreman's death there were only fifteen herders left in the brigade.

THREE — THE HEAD

The herders' deaths weren't a problem, because after the collapse of the USSR subsidies for collective farms came to an end and the herd rapidly ebbed away. The two others had long since been killed off. The Udarnik state farm was dying.

The slaughter was always carried out at the winter encampment. In

1993 it was the same. On 29 November helicopters came to fetch the meat, and as usual they brought provisions for the herders. As usual, it was mainly vodka.

The starving herders drank themselves senseless, and in the morning they found the dead body of Sergei Safronov near his tent. The lad had got drunk, fallen over, hit his head and frozen to death. He was the youngest in the brigade. He was twenty-one. The new foreman spent three days carrying him across the taiga by sledge to the village. In Bamnak the local doctor discovered that Sergei had not frozen to death, but had died of a 'cerebral and cranial injury, including broken skull bones and damage to the brain stem', and thus he died of a blow to the head from a heavy object.

There were fourteen herders left in the brigade.

FOUR — THE CHEST

Sergei Trifanov was the new foreman. He was my Lena's older brother, as well as being the nephew of the previous foreman. Sergei Safronov's family placed the blame for the boy's death on him. Trifanov drank in despair until the New Year, then sobered up, but early in January he set off into the taiga. In the hospital records it says: 'Bilateral shotgun wound to the rib cage'. He was thirty-eight when he shot himself through the chest with his rifle.

His wife very soon remarried, but she drank heavily, so her husband used to beat her without mercy.

'Because he was a Russki', says her sister-in-law, Lena Kolesova. 'A year later she died of all that beating. It was spring, there were ice floes on the river and we couldn't take her to see a specialist in town – and so it all came to nothing.'

Lena's brother and his wife left two little daughters, who were taken in by their mother's friends.

There were thirteen left in the brigade.

FIVE – THE HEAD

The herders conducted their own inquiry, and it turned out that Volodya Yakovlev, the older brother of Sasha, who had fallen through the ice and drowned three years earlier, had killed Sergei Safronov. Volodya was an old village thug who had already served one ten-year sentence for murder. When things started to get hot for him, he hid in the taiga.

Some militiamen came from the town, but they hadn't the slightest chance of tracking a real man of the forest, a native of the taiga like his grandfather and great-grandfather before him, so they declared that anyone who saw him had the right and duty to shoot him like a rabid dog or a wolf.

The Amur district is as big as Poland. It is almost entirely covered in uninhabited taiga, and the Udarnik state farm's land covers almost a tenth of the province, some 3.8 million hectares, so the hunt for Volodya lasted an entire year. Only on 30 December 1994 did his colleagues from the brigade finally track him down and corner him. They did not even appeal to him to give himself up. He was fifty. He lived alone, with no family.

And then there were twelve.

A drunken Evenk, Buryat, Mongol, Tuvan or Chukcha is an extremely painful sight. The first thing to say is that they are knocked off their feet by a dose of alcohol after which a Russian, a Pole or even a German would have no trouble driving a car – but they end up lying on the pavement. The peoples of Northern Asia have a very low level of alcohol tolerance. But the difference is not just quantitative. The Russians say that after vodka the northerners behave 'inappropriately', which is a very apt description. They start doing things that bear no relation to reality. They get undressed in the freezing cold, jump off bridges into frozen rivers, or sit down in the middle of busy roads . . . Normally serious and introverted, they become very noisy, and laugh in a false way, as if forcing themselves to be happy. Normally abstemious, or even frigid, incapable of showing their emotions and intolerant of Slavonic affection and the way Russians are always kissing each other, after drinking vodka they become obscenely tactile, but only seconds later, without any provocation, they reach for the knives that traditionally they always carry.

Every time a drunken Evenk accosts me on the street in Bamnak, he always makes a request of lunatic idiocy – wanting me to take him with me to America, escort him to the Moscow train (there is no railway in this village), or give him 10,000 roubles (£200). Where else in the world does a drunk demand such a sum? When I try to find out where on earth he got that figure from, he cannot explain and resorts to violence.

The Russians contemptuously call all the non-Slav citizens of

Siberia *churki*, meaning 'blockheads'. They make up endless jokes about them, just as the English make jokes about the Irish and the Americans joke about the stupid Polaks. For instance, why do pilots dislike flying over Chukhotka? Because the locals like getting in and out on the move. Like most jokes, these too are derived from observation of everyday life – in this case the life of drunkards.

In Bamnak there is a tiny hospital with a small number of beds and one retired doctor – a paediatrician, who also delivers babies, pulls teeth, performs abortions, and determines the causes of all fatal accidents in the village and its neighbourhood. She records each one in the register of deaths that she has kept since 1964.

'Even when the body isn't recovered', says Dr Natalia Borisova, 'as in the case of Sasha Yakovlev, who was dragged under the ice.'

Four hundred and eighty-seven people live in the village (or at least are registered here, because many of the herders and hunters only show up for a few days a year). Two hundred and eight of them are Evenks. The number of births is declining. In 2007 there were four, and in 2008 there were five.

I leaf through the register of deaths. On average there are ten to fifteen entries each year. For example, in 1992, when the Land of Soviets had just collapsed, Dr Borisova made ten entries. Three Russians died a natural death, and seven Evenks died tragically. Two died of alcohol poisoning, one was drunk and fell out of a boat, a twenty-seven-year-old girl died because she had 'numerous breaks to the pelvis with injuries to the internal organs', but Dr Borisova cannot remember what happened to her. It sounds like a car crash, but then there aren't any roads around here. Fifty-six-year-old Lidia froze to death on a village street, forty-five-year-old Oleg hanged himself, and thirty-year-old Alexander was killed by a bullet. 'A shotgun wound to the head, dislocating the cranium.'

'They always shoot under the chin', whispers his sister Yelena sadly, a mature, well-groomed woman, beautiful in the Evenk way. 'It's the only way to do it with a rifle. My father shot himself that way. And my brother. They drive into the taiga, the vodka's finished, they sober up, but that's when the hallucinations start, the white fever.'

'Did they drink less in the old days?' I ask.

'Not at all. But there were no reasons to do themselves so much harm. Nowadays life is poorer, so there's a great deal of home brewing and they drink their own concoctions.'

'Today I came back from the taiga, where I was treated to pure spirit.'

'Which they know how to spice up to make it stronger, by adding Demerol, sedatives, for instance. There are a great many poisonings from that. They freeze to death, burn in their tents, grab their knives . . .'

'The Russians drink a lot too.'

'Sure, but they can drink a glass of vodka and then walk about normally – the Evenks fall over.'

'And there's also the hatred between the Russkies and the Evenks', adds Dr Borisova. 'Maybe it's because of poverty? Because of the lack of hope, lawlessness and unemployment? Our young people cannot even sign on for unemployment benefit, because they have to register in the city, then show up once a month, and that's a huge expedition, a two-day trip.'

'How many patients do you have at the hospital now?' I ask finally.

'One. Lenochka Kolesova, the three-year-old granddaughter of Lena, with whom you're staying. Her mother has been drinking herself unconscious for a few days now, so we took the little girl in for foster care. We always do that when the parents get sloshed. In the daytime the children are at playschool, and at night they're with us. It's a sort of village emergency shelter.'

For a while Dr Borisova was lost in thought.

'At first I only recorded people over seventy or eighty in the register of deaths. Now there aren't any. A fifty-year-old man is a patriarch, a freak of nature. The fifty-year-old women have senile dementia. Here people live to forty.'

SIX – THE CHEST

He shot himself with a rifle in the chest. That was on 21 March 1996. He was called Pavel Yakovlev. He was a widower with no children. He was not related to Volodya and Sasha, who died earlier. Almost all the local Evenks have one of five Russian surnames which were assigned to them in the 1930s.

Pavel was sixty-six and he was the oldest herder in the brigade.

A few weeks earlier he burned himself very badly with some boiling water, but didn't have it treated, so the wound became infected. He came back to the village from the taiga but didn't show up at the hospital. He lived like a beggar in huts and sheds – he had no home.

And then there were eleven herders left in Brigade Number One.

SEVEN – THE CHEST

Ten days later, at four in the morning, Sasha Markov fired a shot at himself in Bamnak. His wife ran to fetch Lena Kolesova, because in the taiga it is customary for the animal husbandry expert to treat people as well as reindeer.

Sasha had a small wound in his chest, from which no blood was flowing. He was sitting on the floor. The herders can't stand domestic appliances. On entering their homes they don't hang up their jackets, but throw them underfoot. They sleep and eat on the floor, and if they have to sit at a table, they squat on a chair with their knees close to their chins, as by the stove in a tent. Lena had the wounded Sasha taken to hospital, but Dr Borisova was not able to carry out the complicated operation he needed. Sasha died in the car on the way to town.

And so there were ten herders left in the brigade.

EIGHT – THE THROAT

Number eight was a woman, Lena Safronova, who was Sasha's wife. A month after he died, in May, she drank herself to death. They had no children in common, but she had two from before she married, twelve-year-old Masha and fourteen-year-old Tania. They went to live with an aunt, then ended up at a children's home. Both drink heavily. Last year a court placed Tania's two sons in a children's home.

'One time we came to see her', says Dr Borisova, who is a member of the village's social committee, 'and she was feeding her four-month-old baby a bottle of water left over from boiling noodles.'

Now there were nine herders left.

NINE — THE SKIN

On 19 June 1996 he burned alive in his tent. But he was terrifically drunk, because he had been celebrating his thirty-fifth birthday. He was called Gena Yakovlev, he was the stepbrother of Pavel, who shot himself three months earlier. Like him, he didn't have a wife or children, so he was celebrating his birthday with no-one but a herder friend, and after that man had gone off to his own tent, the reindeer skins on the floor were set on fire by the stove.

And so there were eight herders left in Brigade Number One.

TEN — THE THROAT

Sasha Likhachev was twenty-eight. He too lived all alone in the taiga. He died of excessive drink in his tent in the middle of the worst year in the brigade's history.

There were seven left.

AUNTIE VALYA

'She was the object of our terror', says Lena Kolesova, 'a real monster. The worst teacher at the boarding school for Evenks. We feared her as much as an evil spirit from the taiga. I was eight years old when my parents took me to Bamnak and handed me over to Auntie Valya. I didn't stop crying for two months. I didn't know a word of Russian, and we weren't allowed to talk in our own language.'

For the first few days the children went about in the clothes they'd arrived in from the taiga. They had *unty* – boots made of reindeer skin – on their feet, which shed hair copiously.

'Auntie Valya liked to grab a small child by the scruff of the neck and sweep the floor with his head. She hated Evenks. Then they took everything away from us. Our jackets from the taiga, our *unty*, toys and keepsakes, and gave us children's padded jackets, felt boots, school equipment and books. It was the same every year. When I was in the fourth class I ran away from the school in the winter and lived in my parents' house, which was empty because they were away in the taiga. The people from the boarding school came and took me back there, but I ran away again, so then they boarded up the door and windows. I escaped once again, and prised off the boards, but they came and took me away again. And so on, a hundred times over. It reached a point where Auntie Valya used to tie me to the bed at night, so then I would escape from school during the day. They Russified us by force, and now they're surprised we've lost our culture and forgotten our language.'

'You don't even know how to tan hides any more.'

'Because they forced us into the state farm and un-taught us everything, gave us everything – clothes, housing, food – they even brought firewood to our cottages all neatly chopped and cut, so all we had to do was put it in the stove.'

There are forty-five small indigenous races that inhabit Siberia, not counting the big ones, like the Buryats, Tuvans or Yakuts, of whom there are around half a million in total. In all, there are only two million indigenous Siberians, and everywhere apart from the Tuvan Republic they are an ethnic minority.

According to the 2002 census, there are 35,500 Evenks, but barely 15 per cent of them know their own language. It is one of the bigger nations, because for example there are only 237 of the Enets left, twelve Alutors, and eight Kereks; of the remaining 346 Oroks barely three can speak their own language, and none of the 276 Taz can.

Even Lena's children can only speak Russian.

'Why didn't you let the little Evenks speak in their own language?' I ask Valentina Tsaytak, also known as Auntie Valya, who following her retirement still lives in Bamnak.

'I simply didn't allow the Evenks and Russians to sit at separate tables in the canteen. I sat them so every second child was from the other group – six children per table.'

'So they couldn't chat in their own language?' I guess.

'Our children, the Russian ones, couldn't speak their language. And do you know how happy those little Evenks were when they got felt boots and could go about dressed like the other children?'

'Why do so many Evenks kill themselves?' I ask the old Soviet pedagogue.

'Vodka! And they go straight for their knives. Even the women. Among them, if a woman doesn't kill someone, she's not a proper Evenk. Best of all kill a Russian. If she drinks blood, she's one of us. An Evenk woman told me herself – my assistant at the boarding school. They knock out the windows in their houses, they smash everything, they destroy it all, then go to the state farm or the village council to get them to do the repairs for them. Or one of them has too much to drink, sits down in the middle of the road and stays there. The cars have to drive around him. One idiot got drunk and sat down just like that on the train tracks. He thought the train would drive around him too. A Bamnak lad. He spent all day driving to the main line, just to sit on the tracks.'

'What happened to him?'

'His legs were cut off', says Auntie Valya, laughing.

ELEVEN — THE CHEST

In early 1997, after serving a twenty-year sentence for murder, Sasha Romanov from Bamnak came out of prison. He drove straight into the taiga to visit his friends, and then shot them in a tent with a rifle he wanted to steal from them. He was very quickly caught. He was sentenced to death, but was not executed, because for some months a moratorium on the death sentence had been in force in Russia. One of the three people he killed was Sergei Romanov from Brigade Number One. He was twenty-six and lived alone.

The victim and the killer were not related.

And so there were six herders left in the brigade.

At this point the governor of the Amur district summoned Lena Kolesova, leader of the Bamnak Evenks.

'And he says as I'm such an Evenk patriot', Lena tells me, 'I should take on the lease of the entire agricultural complex, including two farms, a hunting district and a herd of reindeer, of which only 700 were left. I didn't really want a corpse like that and all its debts, where the managers and bookkeepers had stolen everything that could be sold, but I agreed, so that my people would not lose their jobs.'

First of all, she took on four young herders to join the decimated Brigade Number One.

Now there were ten of them again.

TWELVE — THE THROAT

But only for a few days. Because on 18 February Klim Romanov drove down to the village, a legendary figure who had once run out of his tent into the taiga in the middle of the night. He had been extremely drunk, but was already sobering up. He hadn't put on his boots, so his two teenage sons rushed after him. They couldn't find him, because Klim was hiding on an island in the middle of the river. The boys decided to come back in the daylight, but next morning there was a flood which swamped the entire island. For three days and nights they couldn't get onto it, and when the water finally receded, the sons went to look for their father's body. But Klim had survived. For three days and nights he had sat out the freezing cold in a tree; the only provisions he had was a bottle of water, and he was also holding his beloved dog in his arms.

He is a legendary figure for having no luck with women too, though generally it was he who brought them bad luck. The first was Zhenya, who brought her illegitimate son Vitya to the marriage, and then bore her husband a son called Arkady. Soon after, Klim caught his wife in bed, or to be precise on a pile of reindeer skins, with another man.

So he shot her, served a five-year sentence, and on coming out of prison married Anna, fifteen years his junior. They lived happily, but not for very long. A young vet called Andrei turned up at their camp-site in the taiga, a Russian lad from the city. A tree that he cut down fell onto the tent and killed Anna.

Klim's third wife was called Lidia. On 18 February 1997 she held a riotous fiftieth birthday party for her husband, but somehow the birthday boy couldn't stop drinking, and on 23 February, Defender of the Fatherland Day, in the local hospital's register of deaths, next to his name Dr Borisova wrote 'Alcohol poisoning'.

It is a very odd holiday, celebrated in exactly the same way as 8 March, which in Russia is Women's Day, in other words as a nation-wide vodka-drinking contest. Only for men, of course.

Not long after, Klim's third wife died.

Now there were only nine herders left in Brigade Number One.

THIRTEEN — THE NECK

But only for one day, because on 24 February, at the news of the death of his adoptive but much loved father, twenty-year-old Vitya Romanov hanged himself on a tree in the taiga.

Then there were eight.

FOURTEEN — THE HEAD

Arkady Romanov, known as Arkashka, because he was so young and small, had lost his mother, father and finally his half-brother. He and Vitya were new brigade members and lived together in the same tent.

Arkashka was eighteen years old and dreadfully alone. On 24 July 1998 he shot himself in the head with a rifle – the same one his father had used years ago to shoot his mother.

There were seven left.

HOLE IN THE HEAD

'Terrible', I say, unable to stop myself, because I can't bear to hear yet another story starring death as the main character.

'You bet it's terrible!' wails Lena Kolesova. 'It's enough to drive you mad, but we have to live here! And that's just one brigade – there were three like it! And it was the same in every single one! A few months ago a nine-year-old boy committed suicide! Because his reindeer died. And so many of the children live without their parents. In my home too. That's why I'm in despair, because the inevitable is approaching and nothing's been taken care of.'

'Lena, you're only fifty.'

'But I can feel my health starting to go. I'm afraid.'

Because Alina is only twelve, Sashka is fifteen, and what's more she's started hanging about with a Russian boy. Because Vovka and Rostik spend all day huddling by the stove, smoking cigarettes and blowing on the ash pan. Then they gawp at the television until dawn, sleep until midday, and if there isn't any firewood, they puzzle out where to get 2000 roubles from (£40), because that's what a tipper truck of wood costs, although just the other side of the fence the spring flood has

265

tossed thousands of lovely, great big tree trunks onto the riverbank. They'd only have to saw it up and chop it into firewood.

But they'd rather buy an old dog from a friend of theirs, and then they swap it with the Korean lumberjacks for wood that's ready to burn – for them dog is a delicacy. They'd only have to hire a lorry and drive fifty kilometres into the taiga. So they spent ages totting it all up, and finally worked out it wasn't worth it. It'd cost a bit less money, but they'd lose an entire day.

The boys are stepbrothers. One of them is twenty-six, and the other is twenty-four. They've been at Lena's for twenty years, and the girls for eleven. They are all the early children of Lena's three sisters, who drank, dumped their offspring and left the village in search of men. Sasha's mother is no longer alive. She got drunk and fell asleep outside in the winter. There used to be another girl in the house too, but Lena has already married her off.

'What about their fathers?' I ask.

'They don't have fathers', she says, pouting. 'Not many of the Evenks do. They don't live long. And Alina's mother was my beloved sister Lila. She was five, and I was eighteen when our mother died. I brought her up badly – I should have smacked her and kept an eye on her so she wouldn't go wandering, but I already had a job and two sons of my own. Now they've called from the hospital to ask me to take Lenochka too, my son Slava's daughter, because her mother has been boozing again. But I haven't enough time left to bring her up! I'm too old now, and Sashka is too young.'

'So what will happen to her?'

'She'll go to the children's home in the city.'

It may be that Rimma Salnikova, the hospital cleaner, will take her, Slava's first wife, who has a nine-year-old son by him, whose name is Viktor.

'You want to bring up her child?' I ask. 'She stole your husband!'

'That's nothing', whispers Rimma. 'I can't have any more children, and like this, brother and sister would be together. They had the same father. I was with Slava for three years, and then I left him. He used to drive off into the taiga, disappear for three or four months, then come back and drink non-stop. He started when he was fourteen.'

'Did he drink at home?'

'What do you mean? Of course not – he used to go off somewhere. And then go and sleep at his mother's house. He'd come back when he was sober – when the worst bit began. The white fever. It comes on later, after excessive drinking. The person starts seeing things, or hearing things . . . One time he had a dreadful headache, and something said into his ear: "Get a gun and make a hole in your head, then all the pain will fly out of it." I managed to grab hold of the gun at the very last minute. Or a voice would tell him: "Go outside and run, run, run . . ." So he'd tear off and started shooting at animals that weren't there. He could see devils. He used to see his father, who had died long before.'

'And can you talk to someone in that state?'

'Yes. He's a sober, seemingly normal person, but has strange, lifeless eyes, a mindless expression. Such huge, dilated pupils, even when he comes out into the light, onto snow. Once he woke me in the middle of the night, sat by the stove and asked me to talk to him so he couldn't hear the goblins, those evil little people who were telling him dreadful things. Afterwards, once it had passed, he laughed at that, but I know he was dying of fear. So was I.'

'And when you left with your son', I ask, 'did he come crawling after you, whimpering like a dog for you to return?'

'Oh no! He adored us, but that's not something they do. They're people of the taiga. Terribly proud. I said: "It's me or the vodka", and he chose the vodka.'

'And Sveta.'

'A girl from the children's home', she says haughtily. 'But she is an Evenk – I was never "one of us" because I'm a Russki! My son asked me, who's he going to be when he grows up, an Evenk or a Russki? And I know the only chance for him is to get out of here. There's nothing good here. But he's already dreaming of going into the taiga. Of doing some hunting. Like his father! What the hell draws them to it?'

FIFTEEN — THE HEAD

In late 2004 the Udarnik state farm finally gave up the ghost. The state leases the land left over from the collapsed farm to a Russian oligarch from the provincial capital. Since then everyone has to pay him for every elk, reindeer or sable they hunt. Lena Kolesova says that like this the Russians have stolen the Evenks' land.

At that point Lena shared out the 276 remaining state-farm reindeer among the herders in Brigade Number One. One of the last seven was her son Slava.

Shortly before the New Year began, he and Sveta set off into the taiga. They drank until New Year's Eve when their supplies ran out. She regained consciousness on 4 January. Slava was lying beside her. A bullet had ripped off his entire face. He had shot himself with a big game rifle.

For another month Sveta lay with him in the tent on a single rug made of animal hides. She didn't eat or even light the stove, because it turned out she'd been shot in the foot and couldn't move.

'I have no idea what happened', says Sveta Kirova. 'I was terribly drunk.'

'Did Slava know you were six weeks' pregnant?'

'He did and he was very pleased. He enjoyed life. He was so gentle and quiet. He never even shouted, never swore, but he did suffer terribly because of his brother, because he was such a hooligan. That very same day when Slava committed suicide, his brother shot a Russian girl in the village. Strange things happen in the taiga.'

Sveta was rescued by Slava's uncle, who came to visit.

She is a beautiful twenty-six-year-old woman, damaged by vodka. She has a sensual mouth and prominent cheek bones, and is extremely tall for an Evenk. But the most unusual thing about her are her lovely long hands, with delicate, fragile fingers. It's hard to tear your eyes away from them, because how does a herder's wife come to have hands like that?

'They want to take your daughter away from you', I say.

'I've been given one last chance again.'

'Lena says the little girl is like her father.'

'But if she ever starts to sleep around and drink vodka, I'll kill her myself.'

From former Brigade Number One there were six herders left.

They were Vladimir Romanov and his wife Lidia Timofeyeva, parents of the Sasha who shot Sergei from their brigade, for which he was sentenced to death.

In mid-2005 they came back to the village from their camp in the taiga. They stopped for a rest. They were found a year later. Their bodies had been torn apart by bears, and flies had done the rest, so it was impossible to establish the cause of death. The skeletons of their reindeer were found tied to a tree.

People suspect that Lidia and Vladimir shot each other. They were both over sixty.

There were four herders left.

EIGHTEEN — THE CHEST

The Evenk drinking den at the state-farm living quarters is different from other drinking dens around the world in that among the rags, bottles, crumbs, bits of paper and filthy dirty plates covered in cigarette butts there are fish heads lying all over the place.

It's cold, it stinks and you're too disgusted to sit down.

There are three women, pissed out of their skulls, and four-year-old Vladik in felt boots. Raisa is the cousin, Vika the sister and Tina the fiancée of Oleg Zakharov from Brigade Number One.

Some years ago, when Tina's husband was knocked down in the taiga by a tree which he himself had felled, she and her son Vladik moved into Oleg's tent. When he asked for her hand, she ran away to the village.

In late December 2005 the herder came out of the tent and shot himself in the rib cage from the left side with a *melkashka*, a small-bore rifle for hunting fur animals. Oleg was forty-two.

'But I hadn't run away from him', gabbles Tina. 'I'd just sat on the stove, burned my bum and had to go to the doctor.'

She is thirty-four, but she looks twice as old. For a year she worked at the local bakery, but whenever she went on a binge there was no bread in the village, so she was fired from her job.

There were three herders left.

SAINT VALENTINE'S DAY

A sad morning. The fourteenth of February, Saint Valentine's Day. At breakfast Lena gets news that Vanya Zatylkin is dead. He was doing teacher training in Saint Petersburg, but he hanged himself at the student hostel, apparently because of an unhappy love. He was twenty years old.

The Evenks take distant journeys away from home very badly. They are especially poor at adapting to cities. When they go away to study, most of them don't finish the course – they start to drink and come home without a diploma.

So Lena and I are sitting in the kitchen over a salad of raw fish, quietly mourning Vanya, without any tears – because here never a month goes by without this sort of news arriving.

Then Tania and Masha come by, the daughters of Lena Safronova from Brigade Number One, who drank herself to death twelve years ago. They and their family have driven down to the village for provisions and – as usual among those who live in the taiga – they all got furiously drunk and went on a bender, while Masha's children ended up in hospital. Masha is desperate to drive them back to the camp in the taiga, because the militia have come from the city with a committee to take her daughter and son away to a children's home. A year ago the same committee took away two of Tania's children.

In a few minutes Lena's Lazhik is ready to go. At the wheel is Rostik, her adoptive son, and I'm sitting next to him with five-year-old Igor and three-year-old Katya on my knees. In the back are Tania with her husband Borka, and Masha with Danka and his brother Maxim, with the carved-up face. They're all blind drunk or in a state of transition to a hangover.

'Why the hell did you come for provisions in such a big gang?' I ask Masha, as we drive onto the frozen river beyond Bamnak.

'To take a break, drink some vodka. We hadn't been to the village for eight months. But we're going home quickly, or we'll die here, because we'll never stop drinking.'

All day we keep driving along the river, but we stop once an hour, because the herders have to have a drink. They've got some pure spirit in a large plastic carboy, diluted to a strength of 30 per cent. They don't eat anything. They pour the vodka down their throats thirstily, as if afraid of sobering up or putting an end to the binge; in fact Masha and Borka, who have already stopped drinking, look the worst. They have a terrified, vacant look in their eyes, which are wild, not even blinking.

Their encampment is also a drinking den, but a nomadic, travelling one. All over the place there are big piles of dirty dishes, gnawed bones,

272

horns, hooves, dog and human turds frozen solid. The frozen eyes of slaughtered reindeer stare out of the trees. As the brain, nostrils and eyes are the greatest delicacies, the herders hang the heads on the trees by the antlers so the dogs can't reach them.

Before nightfall we're all sitting in Masha and Danka's tent. The girl is twenty-four and is already on her third husband. The previous one, Dima Yakovlev, father of Igor and Katya, was a herder in Brigade Number One. Following the collapse of the state farm he waged a private war against a powerful cartel of gold prospectors called Vostok.

'Reindeer always calve in the same place', Masha tells me. 'There's no point telling them to do it somewhere else. They'll always go back to the place where they were born and where they have always given birth. You can't train it out of them. A hundred years ago or more they chose the river Yalda as the place to calve, but now that lot have started digging for gold there.'

'And the Russki will murder anything that moves to stuff his gob with meat', puts in her husband. 'They pretend they can't tell the wild reindeer from ours, although all the domestic ones have ribbons and stakes tied round their necks so they won't wander too far.'

'So my Dima goes to see them', Masha continues, 'and explains, even asks them not to kill our mothers, because they can only give birth there, but they just laugh, and that foreman of theirs, a big, beefy, revolting Russki guy, says we can't prohibit them from doing anything they like because it's Russki land, not ours. In the second year of this war we drove the herd 150 kilometres into the mountains, but even so seven of the mothers ran off to give birth on the Yalda. They killed every single one. Dima went crazy. He grabbed his rifle and raced to their camp. He smashed the foreman in the face and then started shooting, but only to scare them.'

After this incident Dima hid in the taiga. The militia tried to catch him, and even used helicopters to hunt him down, but they had no chance of finding him because only a man of the taiga can track another one, and no-one was willing to act as their guide. The militia proclaimed that Dima was a dangerous killer. Fifteen years earlier he had shot his first wife.

NINETEEN — THE CHEST

One night at the end of 2006 Dima left his tent and shot himself in the chest.

'He said he was going to relieve himself', Masha recalls. 'He had no more strength to fight.'

He left his wife and two small children. He was thirty-six years old.

Two remaining.

TWENTY — THE THROAT

Meanwhile Vasily Yakovlev came back to his camp in the taiga from the village. He had been drinking heavily, so with the last of his strength he dragged himself there and then died. He was fifty.

One.

Towards the end of 2007 Igor Likhachev, the last living member of the herder brigade, was coming back from town across a lake. Halfway across the ice lay a dead crow. How had it got there? Had it flown and flown until it dropped? Had it died in mid-flight? 'A lake that's white, a bird that's black — a sign that shows bad times are back.' Worried by this omen, he went to see Lena Kolesova to tell her about it. He took the opportunity to borrow four canisters of petrol.

Next day he and a friend, Volodya's brother and his son Dimitri, drove off into the taiga. They were drunk. They were smoking. They didn't even have time to get the door open when just outside the village their car exploded. Some militiamen came from the town, but they were so drunk they couldn't do any investigating.

In the register of deaths Dr Borisova wrote: 'Unfortunate accident, cause not established.'

At the wake after the funeral the third of the Likhachev brothers drank himself to death.

Igor was thirty-six. He lived alone.

And so in sixteen years, of all the herders in Brigade Number One at the Udarnik state farm no-one was left alive.

DRESS REHEARSAL

It was an ice-cold night, disturbed by dogs barking because they sensed a stranger, by the children's nocturnal fears and Masha and Danka's drunken lovemaking. In the morning my host splits a reindeer head with an axe, because fried brains is the best cure for the white fever.

'How do you shoot yourself in the chest with a rifle?' I suddenly ask as we're eating. 'You've got to have terribly long arms.'

Danka puts down his spoon. Without a word he picks up a rifle and goes out of the tent. He cocks it. He grabs hold of the barrel, rests it against his chest, hooks the trigger over a larch branch and pulls . . . Click! I felt . . . I felt shivers down my spine, even though it was thirty below freezing. It wasn't loaded.

He shows no emotion, as if he practised doing it every day.

They have domesticated death like a dog or a reindeer. They live in a single tent. They drink, sleep and eat together. They even go for a shit together.

One can imagine the prosperity that will prevail if nations cease to waste their strength on the arms race, but instead devote it to creating peaceable items. For example, growth stimulants will make it possible to achieve two potato harvests in a single year, or to cultivate cabbages more than a metre in diameter or carrots a metre long.

Report from the Twenty-First Century, 1957.

Doctor Lyubov Passar in the room in her clinic where she hypnotizes her patients.

The drunks' shamaness

A CONVERSATION WITH DOCTOR LYUBOV PASSAR, UDEGE DOCTOR, NARCOLOGIST AND PSYCHIATRIST FROM EASTERN SIBERIA

What does a narcologist do?

He treats addictions. I specialize in alcoholism. I have 1757 patients. My surgery belongs to the psychiatric hospital in the city of Khabarovsk.

But it's an ordinary flat on the ground floor in a hideous, shabby block on the Nekrasovka housing estate.

It's been in the same place for twenty-two years.

Have they ever renovated it for you?

But my patients feel fine at my place! They're not ashamed to come here, as they would be at a psychiatric clinic. For sixteen years I've also run a mobile practice. I travel all over the Russian Far East, to villages inhabited by indigenous peoples, Siberian aborigines.

And what's that like?

I can see that they're dying out. It's extinction. Physical annihilation. Entire races are drinking themselves to death and disappearing from the face of the earth.

You are a native Siberian too.

Yes, an Udege.

That's a very small race. In my list of the indigenous peoples of Siberia it says that there are only 1657 Udege people left. That's the entire race! Less than the number of patients at your surgery.

There are smaller ones. And they all accept me as one of them – the Evenk, Even, Ulch, Nanai and Udege peoples. Working with them is not one of my duties. I go to them because my heart aches when I see what is happening to my people, and because they beg me for help. Of course the Russians drink very heavily too, but the indigenous people . . . It's shocking. It's a holocaust. What's more, it's the youngest group who are dying, who should be the ones with the greatest prospects, mainly men. They die in terrible ways. They drink themselves to death, or shoot or hang themselves, or lie down on the train tracks. We're dealing with a plague of suicides. And murders. They fall out of boats in winter, or get run over by a car, set themselves on fire, freeze to death or just die of drink.

So every single death involves vodka.

Yes. It's no longer a mystery that the indigenous races who live in the North have a genetic predisposition to alcoholism. It simply can't be helped. For thousands of years we've been living in lands where because of the severe conditions not much grows, so we eat meat, dairy produce and fish, and in the process of evolution we have developed a protein and fat metabolism. You, like all people of Indo-European origin, have a protein and carbohydrate type of metabolism, because for hundreds, thousands of years your ancestors lived mainly on plant foods.

And what does that have to do with vodka?

The fact that like every alcohol it is made of corn, potato or fruits. To process it through the organism you need a particular enzyme, of which there is plenty in your organism, but of which there is very little in mine, because I have a different metabolism. That's the physiology.

So what happens when you have a drink?

My organism doesn't metabolize the alcohol, like any other poison – it hardly even fights it, so the vodka does what it wants, mainly in the nervous system, in the brain. The person becomes very aggressive, emotional and expressive. But recently I had a heart-warming experience. I came back from the village of Ayamo, where I first went eight years ago. I had thirty patients. Of that group seven people still aren't drinking to this day.

That's a great result. An almost 25 per cent success rate.

The most important thing is that in this group there were several mothers with lots of children. In the meantime they have managed to bring up the children, although formerly they were roaming round the village like ownerless stray dogs, grubbing food out of dustbins. Treating such simple, collective-farm people is an extremely thankless task. There's no question of using any fancy forms of psychotherapy, not to mention group ones. Usually, I switch on the patient's most basic instinct – self-preservation. I do it with the help of a chemical called esperal. The patient knows that if he's taking it, it's impossible to drink. I create a chemical aversion to alcohol. I can also do it through hypnosis. We call it *kodirovanie*, 'coding'.

Aversion therapy. I've heard of it – the top achievement of Soviet psychiatry. You persuade the patient that if he gets drunk his testicles will fall off.

That's roughly how it works. With the collective-farm workers, herders and hunters I usually implant the chemicals for six months, or a year, and then the person doesn't drink. After that he comes back, and I implant him with esperal again. That's the life style – a cyclical one, like in nature. After winter comes spring, and after spring comes summer. They often arrange things so they'll only drink in the winter when they haven't any work to do. I have some regular clients who haven't drunk for two or three years and who are putting money aside because they know that eventually they'll go on a bender and end up at my surgery in a very serious state. They're saving up for good treatment. They're quite simply planning their drinking sprees. In Russia only drug detox is free and available to anyone on request, whereas treatment to cure alcoholism has to be paid for. All the more since I support it with bio-energetic therapy.

Do you have the power?

Yes. I can purify the patient's energy fields. Of course I wasn't taught that at medical school. It was only twenty years ago that I felt this power within me. And I'm fifty.

It fits together perfectly, because that's the same age as me and the book called Report from the Twenty-First Century, *whose trail I am following. According to the authors, in the twenty-first century all diseases are supposed to have disappeared, including cancer, mental illnesses and cardiovascular problems, just as in those days tuberculosis had been entirely eradicated.*

What liars! Neither then, much less now has tuberculosis been eradicated. The TB hospitals are bursting at the seams, the mental hospitals too. They haven't dealt with a thing. Russia is top of the world league for the number of murders and suicides. Every year 40,000 people drink themselves to death. The average citizen drinks seventeen litres of pure spirit per annum.

The average Pole drinks more than nine. But for every bottle of legal alcohol the Russian additionally drinks four bottles of home brew, which isn't accounted for in the statistics. And what are these photos? I can see that's you. What about this one?

That's me too, but as a child.

Good Lord! There's a sort of glow all around you, like a halo. Like a saint in an icon.

That's an aura – a visible, very strong energy field that comes out on traditional photographic film but not on digital pictures. It's around this man too. He's a very powerful shaman from my native village, Krasny Yar, which is in the middle of the taiga on the Pacific. It all started when I took up hypnosis. I noticed that a doctor who puts a patient into a trance also changes his own state of consciousness. Around each person I can see an aura that . . .

Wait a moment, or the paragraph will be too long. Go on.

In some people the aura is thin, and in others it is thick and dark, or coloured, usually like a greenish, shimmering, transparent light. I tried, and the very first time I lowered my father's blood pressure from 160 to 130. All I did was lay on my hands, and I cleared his kidneys of sand. I suddenly started getting wonderful responses from my patients. They'd arrive in a dreadful state, we'd have a chat, and they'd say they already felt better. No injections or pills, but the treatment was taking effect. I started exploring my ancestry. I got as far as the sixth generation back. In each one there was at least one powerful shaman.

And what's this?

It looks like a talisman. As soon as you came in I saw, that is I sensed you had round your neck a powerful ... As if you'd broken off a piece of the sun.

You could have asked.

Oh no! It's not right to do that. We don't ask about things like that. May I touch it? It's burning!

You don't say! It's some pebbles in a rag. And they're not burning at all.

You silly Christian! Because they're yours! You were given them, so they protect you. Where did you get them?

I was given them by a very powerful shamaness in the mountains in Tuva, southern Siberia. It was meant to protect me from 'big metal'. That's what she said. And two days later I had a terrible accident on the road. Some protection! I only just escaped with my life.

What a silly Christian! If you hadn't had it round your neck we wouldn't be having this conversation. Don't you believe me? Then throw it away!

No way.

You see? You're afraid to!

You awful witch. Better tell me about your shaman ancestors.

They guide me and save my life to this day. A few years ago my friend Dankan from Krasny Yar lost two children in a fire. But it's a long story ... All right, as you wish. So Dankan had suffered no physical effects, except that he started to die. He ended up in intensive care in hospital, where they kept him in a drug-induced coma to switch off his mind, but even so he was dying. His father came to see me and begged me to save him. I fetched him from the hospital and took him to our native village in the taiga. The old shaman was very unhappy that I was helping Dankan. Nevertheless, somehow I pulled him out of it. A few months later I myself started to die. They found some horrible worms in my lungs that develop and live inside large larvae filled with fluid.

How ghastly. Where had they come from?

Probably from animals. They're lethal, deadly bugs. They were planning to give me an operation, but on the CAT scan I could see those disgusting larvae were quite close to my windpipe. As soon as they got into it, I'd be able to cough them out. And that's what I did – just by thinking about it. The night before the operation I coughed up several litres of fluid which had those worms in it. Afterwards people told me it was a punishment from our shaman in Krasny Yar. They're capable of things like that. I had betrayed the spirits of our ancestors, I had gone where I shouldn't.

Lyuba, for God's sake! How can a doctor seriously tell such stories?

Just after that our old shaman died. It was my fault. I shouldn't have cured Dankan. He should have died, because it was his destiny. That's why afterwards the person who saved him was meant to die, but I defended myself. So the old shaman took Dankan's death on himself.

Do you believe that?

I know it for a fact. This world is ruled by balance. If something arrives somewhere, somewhere else something has to leave. In our world, in Krasny Yar, the man who was meant to leave didn't go, so another one went instead. Our shaman.

In Tuva I went with the shamaness to a children's hospital. A child's mother had asked her to save it, because the doctors were helpless. They let us in, on condition we wouldn't give the child any shamanic medicines. It was a white, sterile ward, with nurses, doctors, IV drips, and there was this dirty old woman in a feather headdress, festooned in coloured ribbons, bird wings, animal and snake skins. She fumigated the bed with smoke, wailed to the beat of a drum and splashed milk on everything. The children were crying with fear.

Siberian peoples cannot live without shamans. You can train to be a priest, but you have to born a shaman.

The doctors told me they regard these rituals as a form of psychotherapy, mainly for the family. But we were going to talk about vodka and drunkenness among the aborigines. They have a predisposition, we already know that, but that doesn't mean they have to drink a lot.

But they do, because they live with chronic, long-term stress. This is the case not just in Russia but also in Canada and the United States among the Eskimos and the Indians. The races that came and settled among the aborigines outnumber them and dominate them in every other respect too. We are in our own country, but it's as if we're not. It's a terrible situation. We'd like to break free, protest, rebel, raise our fists, but we don't know what exactly to fight for.

So in the meantime they say, come on, let's down a few.

That's it! And at once it's all fine. So the issue of entire races drinking themselves to death is not a medical, genetic or biological problem, but a social one. It's a social disease. What's to blame for all the drinking is the situation the aborigines have ended up in, through no fault of their own. The children who come out of the taiga, because they're forced to go to school, learn to sit on chairs, sleep in beds, walk up stairs, eat with a spoon and a fork from a plate, and along the way they also learn to read and write, what's more in a foreign language. It's dreadful torment. They can't manage, and from the very start they're inferior. But it's you who came to our land, where we lived in peace for thousands of years quite unaware of vodka. So come on, let's have a drink or two. At once you feel better, a man becomes proud, strong, wonderful, invincible.

Except that if anyone doesn't share that view you grab your knives and rifles, which they've all got, because they live in the taiga. It's strange that you only murder each other. You don't shoot at the Russkies.

Because we drink together – not with the Russkies. It's odd that our women become very aggressive too, but I admit I have no idea why that happens. Among the Russians only the guys beat each other up after drinking. Nor do I know why it is that the women don't die in the process in such large numbers as the men, although from what I have observed they drink even more than the men do. Our women also succumb to alcoholism faster and more easily than the men, but they don't kill and they rarely opt for suicide.

But for the men . . .

It's a very easy, simple and rapid decision.

In the Evenk village where I lived for some time, a nine-year-old boy committed suicide. He was grazing reindeer and one of them died.

It's a completely unresearched phenomenon, a big problem for science. We know that the further north you go, the more suicides there are among indigenous peoples, but we don't know why that is so. Maybe because there's not much light there, but the Russians have just as little. One thing's for sure – almost every single suicide has some connection with alcohol.

From the village I told you about every year they send a young Evenk to study in the city. Only one person has ever managed to complete the course.

They can't cope, so they go home or start to drink, and while I was there a twenty-year-old called Vanya hanged himself at his student hostel in Saint Petersburg. Apparently he was unhappily in love.

We simply cannot live in cities – in an enclosed space, without our parents, without the taiga, without traditional food. I know it, because I come from Krasny Yar. For thirty years I've been living in Khabarovsk, a city of half a million people, but Moscow is quite unbearable for me. From the bio-energetic point of view, each person needs a certain amount of space in order to live. It shouldn't be radically reduced, or increased. For the man of the taiga the space he needs is vast.

That doesn't make sense to me, because Russian children from the same village somehow manage to cope in the cities.

That's another mystery. I did some research on alcoholic aborigines in the Far North. My survey included an item called 'readiness to commit suicide'. Ninety per cent of those surveyed had considered this option after drinking, and while sober too. Twenty per cent of the alcoholics surveyed had made suicide attempts, of whom almost half had done so while completely sober. These attempts are a cry of despair, a call for help.

And what percentage of your Russian patients have suicidal thoughts?

I haven't done a precise count, but about 20 per cent. In Russia there is a strong, very deeply rooted culture of drinking. This misfortune began in the days of Peter the Great, who encouraged people to open inns and to drink as much as possible. He collected masses of taxes from it.

Yesterday in Russia was Defender of the Fatherland Day, i.e. Soldier's

Day, which is celebrated all over the country as Men's Day. On this day every citizen of the male sex is obliged to get drunk. Oddly enough, Women's Day is celebrated in exactly the same way — all the men get sloshed . . . Are you laughing at me?

No, at what you described. But you're right. Do you know, I've never noticed the injustice in the way those holidays are celebrated before.

If the women can't see it, that means they've got used to it. They've come to terms with it.

It's not hard to get used to, because in Russia you won't find a single family where this problem doesn't exist. My husband doesn't drink, we've brought up two daughters successfully, but I've been through a lot in life. I even chose to specialize in narcology because of it. My father drank. He was the head of a sports school, an educated, successful man whom everybody liked and respected. But in this country any sports contest involves a party. The training camps involve parties, the victories involve parties, the defeats involve parties, buffets, dinners . . .

And so he fell victim.

But in this country alcohol doesn't get in the way of a professional career. There is immense tolerance for drinkers. Alcoholism doesn't discredit a man, but in personal life someone like that is a curse. My childhood was hell. Whenever my father got drunk he was terribly aggressive. Luckily he died six years ago.

Successful people are rarely drunks. It's people with problems who drink.

But he was an Udege. That wretched genetic, racial predisposition! I can see that my younger brother has exactly the same problem. He's

289

a forensic doctor, a leading expert. He has a job, a lovely family, money, everything he needs, but he drinks. It's hard to understand it. I'm starting to believe in a genetic predisposition to drinking. Not even starting – I do believe in it deeply.

Regardless of the genetic, racial predisposition.

Yes. The one has come on top of the other. Additionally there's also the cultural, Russian ritual of drinking at any opportunity, so a person is born and hasn't got a chance. My brother and I swore that we'd sooner cut each other's throats than make our children's lives like that. Then the years go by, they put vodka in front of the lad and he drinks like his father. So it all starts over again. It makes me want to cry when I look at his children. Will they start drinking too? How can we break the endless cycle of drinking from generation to generation?

To my mind there is hope. When I arrived here a couple of days ago, feeling terribly depressed after seeing my Evenks' drunken village, and asked you for something to give me hope that your people are not dying out, you sent me to see Dankan – your Nanai friend from Krasny Yar, whom you tore from the grip of death when his children died in a fire.

Right. The man's working, giving work to others, earning good money, so he's happy. Why should he drink?

He no longer lives in Krasny Yar. In the village he has moved to he employs all the other inhabitants at his companies. Not just Nanais, but Russians too.

Of course people drink there too, but they don't drink themselves to death. There's no holocaust going on there, because he's a proper, wonderful leader who has built up his empire purely to make sure his people have an occupation. He has created the conditions for them to live like human beings.

He told me that if a man hasn't got work or money, but gets hold of it somehow, steals, begs or borrows a hundred roubles, then naturally he buys himself a bottle of vodka. But if after a month of hard, honest work he gets twenty or thirty thousand (£400–£600) – and in Siberia that's a huge amount – he isn't going to drink it all away. He'll have a beer, and then he'll build a life for himself.

But there are races who don't manage to achieve that. They haven't got a leader like that, and they've passed the numerical threshold, beyond which there's simply no biological chance of regenerating the human fabric.

How many is that?

About 250 people.

Then from my list of Russia's small, indigenous peoples, of which there are forty-five, it appears that those with less than 250 representatives are the Alutors, twelve of whom are left, the Kereks, only eight, and the Enets people, of whom there are 237. The Taz are on the border of extinction, because there are only 276 of them. In all, including the large nations such as the Yakuts, Buryats, Khakass and Tuvans, there are two million aborigines living in Siberia, and everywhere except in the Tuvan Republic they are an ethnic minority.

A few years ago some foreign doctors came to see me. I travelled around all those places with them. Everywhere they told people about Alcoholics Anonymous associations. These days we know that method doesn't work in Russia, because if in Khabarovsk, a city of half a million, it took great difficulty to found a single group, which has thirty members, that means this approach doesn't suit our mentality. It's a method for people with an at least slightly open mind, people inclined towards self-analysis.

Could you say that once again, but in human terms.

The sort of people who are aware that they are sick, that they are alcoholics with no control over their drinking and who need help. So there has to be a certain number of people who are more or less intellectually able. You can't make reindeer herders, tractor drivers, lumberjacks and gold prospectors go to meetings and group therapies ... Neither Russkies nor aborigines. You can cure an alcoholic if he wants to be cured, if he's going to work on himself, but treating them in a group, in a community doesn't work. They'd rather drink themselves to death than tell others about their hallucinations, worms, bugs, devils, maggots and goblins ...

Finally! You're talking about the white fever.

The technical term is *delirium tremens*, one of the most common alcohol-induced psychoses. It appears two or three days after the end of a drinking spree. It starts with insomnia and anxiety, and then come hallucinations. In some people they're visual, in others auditory. They see strange, very active figures, creatures and animals. They hear voices that insult them, threaten them, call them names, accuse them or tell them to do something, for instance to commit suicide or take an axe and chop off their own hand.

My Evenks told me about voices that told them to make holes in their heads so the terrible pain that comes with the hallucinations could fly out of them. So they took a gun and shot themselves in the head. It seems to me those voices are their own sense of guilt, because they always tell them how bad they are, how hopeless, stupid, ugly and worthless. And then the person who, let us remember, is entirely sober by now, says to himself: 'If I'm such scum I'll hang myself.'

And very often the phantoms that appear keep haunting the person for years – they're always the same ones, personal, familiar, and awaited in terror after every drinking bout. Quite often they are long-dead people, whom the alcoholic wronged in some way, and now they've returned to torment him and get their own back. Or an angry God appears. Generally, in a white fever you see whatever you fear and loathe most, everything that disgusts you.

The brain sends to the surface the blackest things in your soul and mind. And all that can happen after a few days on a bender?

Yes. And it can last from a few hours to a whole month. But first you would have to become an alcoholic. It can happen in three years. I know fourteen-year-old boys who are addicted. A great deal depends on the quality of the alcohol.

With the reindeer herders I drank diluted spirit.

Well, that's a lethal drink. So is home brew, but they usually drink the mash, which means they ingest the toxic substances that are produced in the fermentation process and that should be eliminated during distillation.

Does every alcoholic reach a state of white fever?

No. It depends on the level of cerebral trauma, potential illnesses and psychological damage. It's known for example that if an alcoholic has kidney or liver disease, the white fever is far, far more likely to appear. Not to mention that if someone regularly drinks home brew, mash, or other concoctions, the fever is almost sure to affect him.

In my Evenks' village almost all the adults drink and the white fever affects most of them.

Impossible. Of my 1757 patients, only seventy-eight have alcohol-induced psychoses. Almost 4.5 per cent. And that concurs with the scientific data.

Maybe among the Evenks, the aborigines, it's different?

There is no such statistic.

And when an alcoholic commits suicide, does he do it in a white fever?

Most often yes. But he can also have a short, extremely brutal and violent attack of aggression, after which he immediately falls into a deep sleep. Afterwards he can't remember anything at all.

Sveta, an Evenk girl, told me that a few days after a major New Year's Eve binge which she and her husband Slava held in their tent in the taiga, she woke up and found him lying next to her with a bullet hole in his head. She wasn't drunk, but she can't remember a thing. And she must have slept for ages, because her husband was completely cold.

He could have committed suicide.

He could, because he had tried once before, but why didn't the shot wake her up?

I don't know. At a certain stage of the white fever terror can appear. Immense, panic-stricken, irrational terror. Inconceivable terror. The alcoholic doesn't know what he's afraid of. Maybe death, but where would it be coming from? He doesn't know. The terror grows and changes into panic, in which the person entirely loses control of himself, and if he has a gun, he starts shooting blindly in all directions, most often at where the evil voices are coming from. The sufferer hides, runs away or attacks anyone they come across, seeing their perse-cutors in them.

They told me about Yuri, who in winter, at forty degrees below, went running across the taiga for two days and nights without any clothes on. He ran 120 kilometres.

He wasn't running, he was fleeing. I'm sure he didn't know from what or where to. I once had a patient who didn't leave the outhouse for two days and nights. He said he had a snake in his belly, and absolutely had to get rid of it. He kept obsessively pummelling his stomach with his fists and twisting his fingers into his navel. Another man came to see me because he thought his mouth was full of maggots. He kept pulling them out, flicking them out onto the desk with his fingers, spitting on the floor and stamping, but there were more and more of them, pouring out in a stream . . .

Thanks, Lyuba, I think that's enough.

I'm tired too. So now what? Come and have supper.

I don't know if I'm hungry. But shall we have a drink? I've got some excellent Dagestani brandy.

And I've got some Armenian. Twenty years old!

Beneath the wings of the aeroplane thousands of hectares of ripe wheat sail by. In the middle there's a multicoloured carpet. It's a state farm drowning in the greenery of orchards. But how did this beautiful oasis come to be here, in this semi-desert area? Where do the fields of wheat, the apple trees and oak woods get their sustenance – growing in this barren land, where nothing but sparse sticks of camel thorn used to grow?

Report from the Twenty-First Century, 1957.

A roadside stall near Amur in eastern Siberia.

296 hours

For an hour and a half, covered in blood, I battle the cold, the snow and the blizzard by the roadside. No-one stops.

Only the guy with the van, who saw my car somersault along the road. I went into a skid as I started to overtake him on a steep slope. I've come to a stop with the wheels in deep snow about fifteen metres from the road. A few minutes later I scramble out of the Lazhik by the back door.

'Are you alive?' he shouts from afar.

'Yes!'

'Then take care!'

'Hey!' I scream in horror. 'Wait! Help me to get out of here!'

'Coming! I'll just switch off the engine', he says, jumps into the cab and drives off.

So why did he stop? Just to check I'm alive? What the hell for? If I weren't alive, I wouldn't need his help.

I'm stuck waist deep in snow. I fetch out a spade and sweep enough of it aside to get the door open. I get dressed, switch off the lights and staunch the blood with snow. I've only got a cut lip, but I'm gushing as if I'd stepped on a mine. It was probably the large block of wood I'm carrying in the cabin, because it was lying on my knees after over-turning.

I dig out the car and excavate a passage to the road. I can't shut the door on the driver's side, so I use a hammer to straighten the roof a bit, which has bent inwards. I work away in the dark for an hour and a half. Now and then I'm caught in the headlights of a passing car, but no-one stops. Before I left Moscow my Russian friends warned me that at night, even if I scattered diamonds along the road, no-one would stop. Out of fear of the *rekiet*, they said, meaning highway robbers.

The authors of the *Report from the Twenty-First Century* wrote that the highway of the future will guarantee absolute safety for traffic. It will never be slippery, it will clear itself of snow and dry itself. There was nothing about the white tarmac – compacted snow, as hard and slick as ice, which in winter is the greatest nightmare for Russian drivers, especially in Siberia. It was on that surface that I turned somersaults just outside Kansk.

The twenty-first century road was supposed to drive the vehicle itself, or even power it with energy, because we were meant to be driving nothing but electric cars made of artificial materials, not huge metal ones made by UAZ that in these conditions guzzle more than 80 litres of petrol per 100 kilometres. There were meant to be cables installed above the road carrying a high-frequency current. Antennae fixed to the chassis of the car of the future were meant to catch energy from the magnetic field produced around the cables, and then convert it into a current powering the engine.

Of the 13,000 kilometres that I drove from Moscow to Vladivostok, 3000 didn't have any surface at all. And I don't believe in fear of bad people on the road. It's a symptom of a completely different social disease that affects the Russians – indifference. Dreadful, cold indifference, which in its acute form becomes deep, irrational and spontaneous contempt.

Each evening on my solitary journey I wrote up my travel log.

SUNDAY, 25 NOVEMBER 2007

On the road between Chelyabinsk and Kurgan.

On the road from Ufa – the Urals, the border of Asia, and all of a sudden a radical change of weather. The temperature drops by more than ten degrees. Odometer: morning – 31,648 kilometres, evening – 32,337. I've driven 689 kilometres, average speed for the day 49 kmph.

I set the alarm for 7 a.m., but didn't change it to local time, so I woke up at 9 a.m. An awful waste of time. How humiliating. In Russia they won't let you leave the hotel until they've inspected the room where you slept. You stand about in the reception like an idiot while they check to see if you've stolen the sink.

I drive from 10.30 until half-past midnight. On the way a quick meal and forty minutes for chat and photos at the gateway to Asia. In the middle of the night I get a flat. First time. The tyre's a write-off. I must have driven a long way with it deflated, but the road is so appallingly crappy that I didn't feel a thing. I'll have to buy two new tyres, and as soon as I reach the city I have to get the clutch bearing fixed, because that hasn't escaped my notice – it's already wailing like the devil and I'm afraid I'll get stuck in the middle of nowhere.

I fetch out the jack, place it under the back axle, turn it and . . . it doesn't

299

reach! It's not the right jack for this car. I can't elevate it! What am I going to do? No-one will stop here, no-one will help. I'll have to spend the night on the road, but it's minus twenty. I knew sooner or later I'd have to, but I'm not ready yet. The nearest people are in Kurgan, eighty kilometres east of here – I'll never get there on a flat tyre. Bloody jack! It reminds me of the story about the Russian sailors whose ship sank in the Arctic Ocean. The crew escaped in a lifeboat. They had a good supply of water and tinned food, but they all died of starvation because earlier on someone had nicked the tin opener out of the lifeboat. They had nothing to open the tough Soviet tins with.

And I haven't got a stupid jack.

KOLA

I gave lifts in the car to everyone I happened to meet on the way, but in exchange they had to tell me their story and let me take their photo.

I pick up Kola Nikolayevich Pefimenko of 8 Naberezhnaya Street on the Budagovo estate – that's how he introduced himself – on the road somewhere between Krasnoyarsk and Irkutsk. His mother had thrown him out because he'd asked her for 200 roubles (£4), for school textbooks. He's in the fifth year at primary school. At the start of the school year the teacher gave him some books on condition he brought the money by December. He didn't, so she took them away.

Kola's mother drinks. She's forty-seven and doesn't work. Until now they have always lived together. Two hundred roubles is seven half-litre bottles of the cheapest shop-bought hooch. The boy doesn't know who his father is. He wants to get to the Bulushko estate, where his granny lives, but first we're going to his school. I said I'd pay for the books, but although it's only one o'clock, apart from the janitor there's no-one there. Kola says we can't leave the money with him because he drinks. The teacher doesn't live in their village, they have no church, and thus no priest, the man who runs the village council is also a drinker, and Kola's mother has run up a large debt at the local shop, so it would be risky to leave the money for the textbooks there.

As we drive to the boy's grandmother's house, he points out some people picking Indian hemp from under the snow in a roadside ditch and gives me a lecture on how to make hashish. He says that at school all his friends smoke marijuana.

We part ways at a bar called *U Druzyey* ('Friends'), where he is to wait until his granny finishes work. The woman is a porter at a mill. Kola and I have only known each other for a few hours and already he's calling me 'Uncle'. His huge round eyes are staring at me from across his plate as I vanish out of the door of the bar.

TUESDAY, 18 DECEMBER 2007

Petr's Motel. Somewhere in the taiga near the city of Alzamai, west of Irkutsk.

I drove out of Kansk at 1 p.m. and kept going until 8 p.m., but there was another time change, so in fact I've only been on the road for six hours. I've come 234 kilometres. Average speed 39 kmph. The proper road and surface has ended. The whole time it's white tarmac on top of frozen mud across the taiga. Every few kilometres there's a car in the ditch. I have switched on four-wheel drive for good, so I've got a rumble in the Lazhik as if I were flying a jet.

After yesterday's spill I wasted the whole afternoon at a car repair shop in Kansk. The car was vibrating dreadfully whenever I got to 50 kmph. It was impossible to drive. They realigned the wheels for me, but that didn't help, so they removed and checked them. The front left wheel rim was bent. A write-off. I spent a few hours searching the city for a new one, but it's not a standard size. If it fits the tyre, it doesn't fit the wheel, and vice versa. A very comical Azeri helped me, who was at the same repair place with his nineteen-year-old Zhiguli. In our search for the rim we followed a strangely devious route around town, but as it turned out, mainly to avoid bumping into any militiamen. My helper is an illegal taxi-driver – he bought a roof light saying 'taxi' at a motoring shop, and what's more he hasn't had a driving licence for the past year because they took it off him for drink-driving. He refuses to accept any money from me. He's the only nice cabbie I've met so far. Russian taxi drivers are bloody rapacious and aren't even willing to tell you the way – they just instantly tell you to hire them and drive after them.

We couldn't find the wheel rim, so the only thing I could do was to transfer the bent one to the back wheel. It helped. The Lazhik only starts vibrating when that wheel falls into a hole, and only at a speed of 60 kmph. So I put away in the boot all the heavy objects I'm carrying in the cab. First of all the wooden block that smashed me in the teeth. I found it on the road and took it because I can only raise up the car by placing my too small jack on top of it.

FROST

Nansen said you can never get used to the frost; you can only survive it, endure it.

I'm not sure that's true. At Sludianka on Lake Baikal I visited Nadia and Boris, friends from years back. They had just had a baby. When I drove up it was above minus twenty, so they hadn't lit the stove –

because it was so warm, and Nadia had put the baby outside in his pram to get some fresh air. In Poland, in this sort of weather the schools are closed (in Yakutia that only happens when it's minus fifty), so that means my Siberian pals have in fact got used to the cold.

The first time I had to spend the night in the open air outside Kurgan, I thought it was time to die. I was terribly cold, although for a month before leaving for Siberia I'd slept every night with the window open and the heating off. That's how polar explorers get used to the cold.

That night the frost was like morphine; at times it sent me into a pleasant state of bliss. I realized to my horror that I was on the edge of hypothermia, and that this is the state in which drivers set fire to their own cars, when they break down on the road at night in the Siberian wastes. So I forced myself out of the bedding, heated up the engine and ran around the car. Three months later, in March, when I reached Vladivostok, I walked about bare-headed, in an open jacket, with no gloves, and wondered why the snow wasn't melting. I checked the temperature – it was about fifteen degrees below zero. It turns out that someone coming from Europe can also adapt to an extremely cold environment, and despite widely held opinion, resistance to the cold is not passed on in the genes of people who live in the North.

But the cold can be so bad that you start to have doubts about global warming, an inhuman, beastly cold, in which the hairs in your nose go hard and stab you like pins. Metal objects freeze to your hand if you incautiously touch them without gloves on, and your eyelashes freeze, so you can't open your eyes without the help of a finger. It's easier when the hairs freeze to your chin because you can unstick them with your tongue. From my observations it looks as if the border of life is minus forty degrees. That's when the girls stop walking along the streets arm in arm, the boys no longer stand outside the shop with a beer, the athletes suspend their training, and the cars stop moving.

The shock absorbers freeze, the suspension goes stiff as in a rack wagon, and all the electrical wires become as fragile as dry twigs. Better not touch them. The biggest problem is with the brakes. The pedals harden and won't go into the floor, because the fluid in the cables has taken on the consistency of toothpaste. The car stops braking, and if you try to force the pedal down, the brakes lock like pincers and won't let go. The only help for this is to get the car well warmed up before setting off, and then drive as slowly as possible, because the faster you go, the more you cool the vehicle. And use the brakes as little as possible. In Siberia it's possible to do that because the roads are awful, there's very little traffic and no intersections. I drove 300 kilometres to Shimanovsk without using the brakes at all (a day's drive before Khabarovsk). The brake cable in my Lazhik had snapped, maybe from violently pressing the pedal in severe cold.

The drivers of cars with diesel engines have enormous problems. In winter in Siberia they sell diesel oil with a guarantee up to minus sixty degrees, but you can't give a farthing for such promises. On the road near Tynda I helped to put out the fire destroying a wonderful Land Rover Defender of a type adapted to arctic conditions. The maker had even thought of double glazing, but it never occurred to him that a Russian would buy the car, and that in his homeland diesel fuel freezes. To heat the fuel cables and the tank, the owner had lit a small bonfire underneath the vehicle, but the tank turned out to be made of an artificial material and the car had burst into flames.

THURSDAY, 7 FEBRUARY 2008

The Hotel 'Turist' in Chita.

Another wasted day. This time at the former state taxi garage. This is the only place where they can fix a Lazhik. The gearbox has fallen apart. Yesterday I drove the last 200 kilometres from Ulan Ude in third gear, because it wouldn't go into fourth.

At this workshop they've found an innovative solution to the eternal problem of tools being stolen. They simply haven't got any at their work stations. Each mechanic starts the day by exchanging his ID badge for a box of spanners, despite which after an hour's work Zhenya, who is working on my car, makes a fuss saying someone has pinched the number fourteen and the eighteen from his set. A big search ensues. It turns out he left both spanners in the pit himself.

After removing the gearbox we can see that the synchronizer has split into tiny chips of metal which have scraped off the ratchets. In the process Zhenya discovers there's oil leaking out of the engine and both axles, and the clutch disk is very thin, worn out. I'm furious, because this is now the fifth workshop where I've had my Lazhik repaired, and not long ago in Kurgan they fixed the clutch bearing. They only had to say and I'd have taken the opportunity to get the disk changed too.

That's what upsets me most about the Russians – their reluctance to do anything in advance, except what's absolutely necessary, their languid way of waiting for disaster to happen before getting on with anything. That was how

305

in the 1980s they lost 'Komsomolets', the most expensive, best ever submarine in the world. The little device for measuring oxygen content broke – costing fifty roubles – but no-one could be bothered to check the gas level by hand, so a fire broke out in which almost the entire crew was killed.

Zhenya fixes the gearbox and seals the axles. He takes 5000 roubles for the repairs. He and his assistant have been working on it all day. Including the replaced part, the entire repair cost me 10,000 roubles. That's 1000 zlotys (£200). Nowhere in Poland could I have had a gearbox replaced so cheaply and so quickly.

Ahead of me is the hardest stretch of my route. More than 2000 kilometres to Khabarovsk.

IGOR

All my passengers, the men, the women and even the children I picked up on the road, brought into the car the bitter Siberian cold, which after a few minutes in the warm lost the freshness and briskness of the taiga, the unusual charm of the continental climate, as it changed into a very commonplace, sweet-and-sour, stifling odour of poverty. The stench of unwashed armpits, pissed-in pants, gastric juices, revolting food and hands wiped on coats. A stench of being abandoned, forgotten, rejected by all – quite simply the smell of misfortune, and for many the first symptom of homelessness. It's exactly the same everywhere, in Barcelona, Warsaw, Moscow, Beijing . . . You do your best not to touch them and to take as shallow breaths as possible, like in a really disgusting toilet, so your alveoli will take in as little as possible of the air they have used.

In Igor's case I only have myself to blame. As soon as he got in, I was surprised how lightly he was dressed, so he undid his sheepskin coat to show me that underneath he had nothing but a singlet and a track suit. And to think he had acquired that smell in barely a week.

A week ago he buried his mother. His name is Igor Smirnov. He's twenty-two. His face is red, almost livid and puffy with cold, his eyes are bloodshot from sun and wind, and his lips are parched.

Straight after the funeral his stepfather, at whose flat he had been living along with his mother and eighteen-year-old brother Alexei, slammed the door in the boys' faces, so they couldn't even get a change of clothes. Just as they were, they set off on the road. To their father, and thus away from Chita, where they buried their mother, a distance of more than 1500 kilometres east, across the cruellest, ice-cold, wild taiga.

I feel uneasy about driving this way by car, but these guys set off on foot, with no food or money, because they spent all their savings – 6000 roubles (£30) – on the funeral. Two days ago they managed to stop a lorry that's going to take Alexei to their father's place. There was only room for one.

I picked Igor up fifty kilometres before Skovorodino, when he still had more than a thousand kilometres to go. He eats whatever the drivers who pick him up give him, or at roadside bars, where he can get a bowl of soup for doing some job. He sleeps in tyre workshops, and if he can't find a place to stay, he spends the whole night walking to avoid dying of cold or freezing his legs off.

'At night I stop waving at the cars', he says, 'because I know they won't stop.'

'What if there were a blizzard?' I ask.

'I'd run into the taiga.'

'It's impossible to keep walking in the forest. And last night it was minus thirty-four degrees.'

'I'd manage somehow', he says without conviction.

He wouldn't manage. For two days, since parting with his brother, he hasn't eaten and he hasn't slept, because he was walking through an extremely deserted area.

'Who gives you lifts?' I ask.

'Simple people. From villages or collective farms. Ordinary Russian cars and lorries. And they take me from one village to the next. Short stretches.'

'And your father won't turn you away?'

'No. He's expecting us. We called. He's got a cottage, a job in the forest and a wife but no children. I'll get a driving licence and transport wood', says Igor and falls asleep.

Finally I reached Skorovodino, where I was turning north towards Tynda, and he had to keep going east. I stopped the car in the sun and let the boy sleep in the warm for another hour. In his sleep he finally withdrew his hands from his pockets. They were large, red and chapped. He hadn't any gloves.

MONDAY, 18 FEBRUARY 2008

A hotel in Shimanovsk.

I left Tynda at 11 a.m. and drove until midnight. I've done 553 kilometres, at an average speed of 42.5 kmph. I'm dying of exhaustion, because today there wasn't a centimetre of tarmac on the road, and I drove at least half the way without brakes – the pedal has sunk into the floor. I'm going crazy – tomorrow I'll have to look for another workshop.

I set off late today, because this morning I came back from my beloved Evenks in the taiga. They gave me provisions for the journey – two enormous pieces of roasted reindeer loin. It's delicious, like tender beef. I've become terribly carnivorous thanks to the week I spent with them. In their village it's easier to get meat than bread.

The car spent nine days in a parking lot in Tynda. The minimum thermometer shows that at night it was 42.5 degrees below zero. The battery was in the caretaker's hut, but even so the Lazhik refuses to start. I warm the sump with a petrol burner. I can hear the oil boiling inside, then I see flames bursting out from under the bonnet. The engine and all the insides are hellishly covered in oil, so naturally they've caught fire. I grab the extinguisher, but not a drop comes out of it. It's frozen! I use a spade to toss snow inside and put out the fire. If I've burned through the electrical wires I'll have to hitchhike. With my heart in my mouth I turn the key. It starts. Yet another lesson learned – as well as the battery, put the extinguisher in a warm place overnight too.

From Tynda I take a shortcut, not by road, but along an ice crossing. That's what they call roads that run along frozen rivers in winter. I drive south down the river Tynda for about fifteen kilometres. In the city the transport services have marked out two traffic lanes with poles and put up signs setting a speed limit of 30 kmph and a vehicle weight limit of twenty-five tons.

My hotel in Shimanovsk is a horrible shack with two dorms run by Chinamen, where foreigners – with the exception of the Chinese – pay double. The bog's outside, and it's thirty below, so at night I pee into an empty Cola bottle. The hotel is located in one quarter of a small building. Another quarter houses a pharmacy, and in the third and fourth there's a small hospital. Above my sack of a bed there's a sign saying: 'In our hotel it is forbidden to throw ash into the flowers, open the windows, lie on the bedspreads, be in possession of explosive materials, use electrical stoves or drink spirits.'

LYUBOV

Lyubov Vladimirovna Chegrina from the village of Ilinka is terribly fat. She's fifty-seven, but she looks twenty years older. I only drive her ten kilometres to Nekrasovka, but her smell lingers in the car for another two days.

Lyuba is going to town to fetch her twenty-one-year-old daughter Olya. Several times a week the girl goes to church by herself, to pray and get something to eat.

'And I come to fetch her, because sometimes she feels ill and she could have a fall', says Olya's mother. 'She walks very badly and can't do anything with her left hand. A car hit her when she was nine. They operated on her head, but since then she hasn't grown. And she stopped developing, though she can read. And she can sign her name. She's due to have another operation to get her left side moving.'

'I can see you've had a little bit to drink, Lyuba', I say in surprise, as it's only 10 a.m.

'I just had a tiny drop with my husband today, for Defender of the Fatherland Day.'

'That was yesterday.'

'We didn't have any money yesterday, but today we managed to borrow fifty roubles (£1) to have a drink instead of for yesterday's holiday. My pension's due soon so I'll pay it back. I get group two disability, 4500 roubles (£90), just like my Olya. I've lost my health, because I worked in disinfection at a poultry plant. I used to bathe the birds in delousing fluid.'

'Isn't your daughter bothered by her parents drinking?' I ask.

'No, because she lives at her gran's. We've got bad neighbours at our place. They're noisy. At night there's music, screaming, and she very often has dreadful headaches. She and her older brother Andrei live at their gran's. One time the boy had a drink of beer outside the shop, and the janitor there attacked him, kicked him lying down, so badly my son went to hospital for an operation. They removed bone from his brain, so now he's got a hole in his head as big as a hand. They said they can put in a plate, but we'd have to pay thousands. He's terribly disabled, all the more since this year he lost three fingers to frostbite. That's why he can't work. He has no pension because he only ever worked on the black market.'

'What does he live off?'

'He collects bottles and helps clean at the grocery kiosk', says Lyuba. 'And his granny has her pension. But now her back's going.'

'And is everything all right inside your son's head?'

'Yes. But he puts away a lot of drink. More than us. We only have a little drop.'

'So are you happy, Lyuba?'

'When the sun's shining, my husband chops some wood, it's warm and the holiday's a success, I'm very happy. The holiday we moved from yesterday to today.'

Blagoveshchensk.

Today I've come 276 kilometres from Shimanovsk in five hours. Average speed 55 kmph. I only set off at 3 p.m. because the brakes went and I frittered away the whole morning at repair shops.

First at a former state garage. The workers keep arriving until eleven o'clock, including my mechanic. He starts with a beer, then unscrews the broken brake-fluid tube. He often uses his teeth, because he only has one finger on his right hand.

The head of the repair shop, a tipsy, unshaven fellow of Caucasian appearance, in cowboy boots with spurs, a Puma track suit and a leather waistcoat with a fur collar, looks at the tube in disgust, blows his nose onto the floor, crushes the snot with his heel and says they don't have that kind. They'll have to choose one from another car.

They've found one. It's half a metre too long, but they make it into a coil, like for distilling hooch, and then it fits.

They're all very nice, they've generously dropped their other work and spent two hours battling with my brakes. All for 600 roubles (£12), but a dozen kilometres out of town the car chokes and stops. I'm towed back to Shimanovsk by a dirty beer truck, on which the driver has written with his finger 'Better a belly from beer than a hunchback from work'.

Now I've ended up at a small private workshop in an old barn, run by Sasha Kropov, grandson of a Polish partisan who was sent to Siberia after the Second World War. Sasha's granddad was called Kropowski, but to make life easier he Russified his surname. The lad discovers that the air filter is blocked. Of course they hadn't changed it during the overhaul done in Irkutsk. Sasha doesn't have the right filter, so he cuts a big hole in the existing one. It's like carving a hole in a consumptive's chest to make it easier for him to breathe. Yet another Russian improvisation, but the Lazhik goes like a rocket.

PARCEL

In Khabarovsk, before the final stage of my journey, I send home a parcel full of personal items so I won't have to pay for excess luggage on the plane.

Beautifully wrapped, I take it to the post office, but the clerk tells me to open it, because it's too heavy (it can't weigh more than seventeen kilos), and in any case she has to check what's inside it.

This makes me feel very annoyed, so the scene gets longer and longer, as does the queue of people behind me. My posture alone is unbearable, because I have to bend double to talk to the clerk through a tiny window at waist height. Occasionally, to give my spine a rest, I kneel down, and then I have the window at face height.

Furiously I rip the cardboard box open and hand over the contents one item at a time so the clerk can weigh each thing separately. One by one the woman takes my shirts, sweaters, gloves, billycan, battery charger, cedar cones, large and small towels, and flip-flops, and puts each of them on the scales. I write down the weight to three decimal points on the parcel registration record, and give each item a separate value.

Then it's the turn of my ski boots and skates, stuffed into which the clerk discovers some dirty pants, socks and long johns. The people in the queue are craning their necks in curiosity, and the unpleasant smell of the men's locker room pervades the post office. I'm screaming at the woman like a lunatic as she mercilessly pulls them all out with her bare hands, shakes them to make sure they're not tangled together, and disgustedly places each item on the scales. Then she pushes the pile of dirty clothes back through the tiny window, permits me to start packing again and consults a huge book the size of a tombstone.

'It is not allowed to send used clothing to Poland', she drawls sadistically.

'It's personal clothing, not used!' I try to defend myself.

The security guard comes running, and what must be the entire post-office staff. Together with the crowd of people waiting in the queue behind me, they hold a referendum on who is right.

I'm the winner. And then disaster strikes. The monster in the little window weighs the entire parcel. Her weight doesn't match the total of the individual items as listed on the registration record, so the whole operation has to start from the beginning again. Some of the clerks actually sympathize with me, but they haven't the faintest idea why I'm screaming – I'm red in the face, sweating, confused and humiliated. The other people in the queue are also complaining about tiresome bureaucracy, but they endure it all meekly.

Finally the monster cuts a piece of cloth from a roll, deftly sews it up on a sewing machine and packs my parcel into it. She fixes several dozen wax seals to the stitches.

The parcel registration record covers thirteen pages. I must calculate the value of each item so that the total sum does not exceed 100 dollars, otherwise the costs will be six times higher and the sending procedure three times as complicated.

The cost of sending a seventeen-kilo parcel worth 2000 roubles (£40) was 1941 roubles and 70 kopecks (£38.83). It took me two hours and forty minutes.

MONDAY, 25 FEBRUARY 2008

Vladivostok. Room 1144 on the eleventh floor of the Hotel Vladivostok.

At 7 p.m. I'm at the end of Scott Peninsula. It's the bit of the Eurasian continent that extends furthest into the sea. I drive past a lighthouse and out onto the frozen edge of the Pacific Ocean. I'm at the end of my journey.

I drove the last 424 kilometres from Lesozavodzka in 7 hours and 45 minutes. Average speed for the day 54.7 kmph.

The odometer reads 42,926, so since leaving Moscow I have come 12,968 kilometres at an average speed of 43.8 kmph. It took me fifty-five days, during which I spent 296 hours at the wheel, which equals twenty-five twelve-hour driving days. In this time I used 2119 litres of mainly 92-octane petrol at a cost of 42,380 roubles (£848), got four flat tyres and had to have the car fixed eleven times at various repair shops, which cost me a total of 27,000 roubles (£540). As a result the final cost of the car rose to 228,000 roubles (£4560). My Lazhik packed up for the last time in Ussuriysk, 100 kilometres before the end of the journey. At the end of our friendly acquaintance the carburettor got clogged.

SASHA

She travels with me from Artyom to the border of Vladivostok, where there's a statue of a Soviet sailor by the road.

315

'Because I work there', says the girl. And seeing the dumb look on my face she adds: 'Sexual services. I'd be glad to do it with you too, but only when we get there, because this patch belongs to a different lot. I'm not allowed to do it here. How much? Depends what – 400 roubles (£8) for a blow job, 600 for straight sex, and 700 for the whole lot, but for you it'll be cheaper because of the lift. I've got condoms.'

'No thanks.'

'So where are you from? Moscow? All that time on the road and you haven't had the urge?'

'Well . . . I have, but . . . Call me Jacek. Have you ever been in love?'

'Once', replies Sasha. 'Two years ago, but I ran away from him because he started taking an awful lot of stuff. Marijuana grows like grass round here, and they import heroin for 1500 roubles a gram (£30) all the way from Dagestan.'

Sasha is a pretty twenty-two-year-old. She finished seventh class and a cookery course. She lives with her parents and grandparents. She's been going out on the road for a year and a half now, three times a week. She earns four or five thousand roubles a day (£80–100), as much as her mother gets in a month working in a shop. For each working day she gives the local gangsters 300 roubles.

'Because it's their road', she says. 'Everything here's theirs. They've got fifteen girls on this road alone, and I'm the first from the slip road.'

'You said that with pride. Do you like this sort of work?'

'Very much. You drink, you party, you get plenty of you-know-what, and money. But sometimes it's dangerous. Worst is with drunken militiamen. They're not afraid to drive after drinking, even in uniform. They've got an awful lot of money, especially the traffic cops. They're terribly aggressive, even when they're sober. They don't like girls like me, and they hit you the most if you don't agree to something.'

'Were they the ones who knocked out four of your front teeth?'

'What do you mean?' the girl says, laughing. 'They fell out on their own. I'm saving up for some new ones.'

'But not gold ones.'

'No, white. Nowadays if you're young and you've got gold teeth it's a sign you've been in prison. Some of the militiamen are awful perverts. I had one who wanted me to piss on him.'

'In his car?' I say in amazement.

'Yes. Or in a hotel room, the sort you rent by the hour. But I can do anything. Even with gays. Sometimes they stop and want me to give them a blow job, or have a chat, spend some time together, and they're not stingy. Sure they'd prefer to have a boy give them a blow job, but where are they going to find one? At least they don't have to be ashamed in front of me, they don't have to hide anything. I had a friend like that, just the one. He asked me to find him a young lad with a big dick. That's how we met. He said that if the boy was embarrassed he could bring a friend. He'd pay them 3000 roubles each (£60) and give me the same amount too. I found a guy who was willing. He's not gay, but round here no-one'll turn down 3000.'

'And how did you know he had a big dick?'

'Because he was my ex – the one who got into drugs. And then they killed that gay friend of mine. One day he found himself a partner on the beach, they went into the woods to make love, and there were some young people there drinking, who saw them together. My friend's partner ran away, but they caught him and they had him for fun. All of them, eight or nine. Real devils. And then they beat him until they killed him. In Russia they hate gays like poison. But in fact an awful lot of men here are . . . Well, you know. Sort of strange. Imagine a woman doing that! With a hand or a finger. And then massage that spot. Caress it. But I can do anything.'

'Are there lots of men like that?' I ask.

'Four out of every ten . . . Yes, that's it.'

'And why are you so sad, Sasha?'

'Everyone asks me that. I've got that sort of face.'

'Are you happy?'

'I don't know. But I don't feel sad.'

LAZHIK

It's Saturday, 1 March 2008. Tomorrow I'm going home to Poland, and today I'm selling the Lazhik. In this city that's not easy. Here everyone, including the militia, drives a used car from Japan, thousands of which are shipped across by Russian and Pakistani dealers. So I thought of sending my car back to Moscow by train, which costs 59,000 roubles plus 3000 for the insurance (a total of £1240) and takes well over a month. Grisha, who helped me buy the Lazhik, said he would sell it for about 160,000. I'd be 100,000 up.

But while I was still in Irkutsk I posted an ad on an Internet site for fans of off-road vehicles, saying I had a Lazhik to sell, and some buyers have come forward. They're a very strange crowd. I hate this sort of stereotype, but as they're three gloomy-looking fellows, one of whom is a Chechen, one is from Dagestan and the third claims he's an ex-militiaman, I'm being cautious. And they're always in a threesome, dressed in black, all very fluent in Russia's incredibly complicated car formalities.

Surprisingly enough they're not bothered by the fact that they won't be able to register the car in their own names because it's registered in Moscow to the man I bought it from. It was a notarial transaction without a change of number plates, but with the right to sell it on – but only in the same way, through a notary.

I'm sure this three-man gang is trying to pull a fast one. I hope it won't be anything worse than a bank raid. The militia will have no problem finding Andrei, from whom I bought the car, and he'll show them the notarial contract saying he sold the car to a foreigner, and there the trail will come to an end. We have agreed that they'll pay me 70,000 roubles (£1400). That's much less than the railway option, but I was extremely unhappy that the transport firm take not just the car but the entire sum in advance. These companies often vanish into thin air, taking the money with them, and sometimes the clients' cars as well.

The four of us go to see a notary in their car. They sit me next to the driver, two of them get in the back, and then the door shuts. Automatically. I tell them to pay me the money at my hotel – on the couch at the reception desk, but my worries are unfounded.

Of the 228,000 roubles (£4560) that my Lazhik cost me in total, now I can subtract 70,000. That leaves 158,000 roubles (£3160) – that's how much I paid for my dream of skipping across the world's biggest continent by car.

I came to love that car with the sort of affection you might feel for a disabled child. Time and again, after ten or more hours of lonely driving across wild wastelands I felt as if I were part of this machine, without which I'd have been helpless and doomed to disaster, if not death. It was an uncanny feeling, so in my thoughts I had started to humanize it, talk to it, call it names, pay it compliments, saying it had a lovely voice, for example. Because it did.

'Aren't you afraid we're cheating you?' asked Valery, with whom I signed the agreement.

'Just a little', I replied sadly.

'It's a miracle they didn't steal it off you on the road. What would you have done, you poor devil?'

'I'd have hitchhiked. Or taken the train. Or I'd have gone somewhere else, or maybe stayed there, on the spot. It's the journey that matters, not the destination.'

In the 1970s the combustion engine was ousted by the gas turbine. It competed with lightweight nuclear engines. Nowadays we travel in electric cars.

Report from the Twenty-First Century, 1957.

About the translator

ANTONIA LLOYD-JONES is a translator of Polish literature whose published translations include fiction, reportage, biography, poetry and children's books. She has translated several novels by Paweł Huelle, including *The Last Supper*, for which she won the 2008 Found in Translation prize. Her previous work for Portobello Books includes *Like Eating A Stone* by Wojciech Tochman, about the impact of the war in Bosnia on the personal lives of female survivors.